MW01287227

# a megaphone

# a megaphone:

Some Enactments, Some Numbers, and Some Essays about the Continued Usefulness of Crotchless-pants-and-a-machine-gun Feminism

Juliana Spahr & Stephanie Young, editors

Copyright © 2011 by ChainLinks.

All rights revert to authors/artists upon publication.

ISBN: 1-930068-47-6

CHAIN**LINKS**

Oakland + Philadelphia

Series Editors: Jena Osman & Juliana Spahr.

Design: Jacqueline Thaw.

Typesetting: King Tender.

Cover image: "Rosie" by Gary Sullivan.

# CONTENTS

7 Against Numbers
JULIANA SPAHR & STEPHANIE YOUNG

31 Foulipo
JULIANA SPAHR & STEPHANIE YOUNG

43 Numbers Trouble
JULIANA SPAHR & STEPHANIE YOUNG

75 A Word on Each
collected by ZSÓFIA BÁN, ANA BOŽIČEVIĆ, DUBRAVKA
DJURIĆ, SIMONE FATTAL, TATIANI G. RAPATZIKOU,
STANISLAVA CHROBÁKOVÁ REPAR, LIANA
SAKELLIOU, JENNIFER SCAPPETTONE, SIMONA
SCHNEIDER, PRAMILA VENKATESWARAN, PHILLIPPA
YAA DE VILLIERS, BRIAN WHITENER, LILA
ZEMBORAIN

249 Can We Do Together?
collected by ZSÓFIA BÁN, ANA BOŽIČEVIĆ, DUBRAVKA
DJURIĆ, SIMONE FATTAL, TATIANI G. RAPATZIKOU,
STANISLAVA CHROBÁKOVÁ REPAR, LIANA
SAKELLIOU, JENNIFER SCAPPETTONE, SIMONA
SCHNEIDER, PRAMILA VENKATESWARAN, PHILLIPPA
YAA DE VILLIERS, BRIAN WHITENER, LILA
ZEMBORAIN

275 Undoing Numbers
PAUL FOSTER JOHNSON, JULIAN T. BROLASKI, &
E. TRACY GRINNELL

289 This is What a (Pro-) Feminist (Man-Poet)
Looks Like
CHRISTIAN PEET

313 The Name & the Paradox of Its Contents
DALE SMITH

325 On "Numbers Trouble"
A. E. STALLINGS

335 On Feminsim, Women of Color, Poetics,
and Reticence: Some Considerations
BARBARA JANE REYES

345 Dear CAConrad,
JULIANA SPAHR & STEPHANIE YOUNG

361 Uneasy Riders: A (Soma)tic Poetry Exercise
CACONRAD

369 Contributors

391 Index of Names, Prizes, Presses, Journals,
Conferences, Anthologies, Blogs, and
Discussion Lists

# Against Numbers

JULIANA SPAHR & STEPHANIE YOUNG

We are calling this collection *A Megaphone,* as in distorted amplification, inappropriate amplification, shared amplification; as in pass on, pass back; as in Poetas de Megafono, which Mara Pastor talks about in an interview with Brian Whitener that we include in this collection. Poetas de Megafono is many things. It is a feminist collective in Mexico whose members come from many different places, "breaking with the profoundly nationalist and male-dominated Latin American literary space as it is defined by national-popular cultures." It is also a weekly reading series that meets in a café on the outskirts of Mexico City. In many ways, Poetas de Megafono embodies the kinds of conversations we hope this collection might initiate, conversations that might take place on the outskirts of nationalist literary discourses and that might bring together unexpected groups of people in public space. We are drawn to the model of community and group relations embedded in the Poetas de Megafono reading series, its commitment to weekly readings and simultaneous permeability: anyone may read at the series, provided they have written something toward the topic or idea announced at the previous week's reading.

But we are also calling this collection *A Megaphone* as in the megaphoned chant "I am confused [pause] I'm I'm I'm confused [short pause]" from Ultra-red's 2007 performance "Untitled (for small ensemble)." Ultra-red is an amorphous collective whose collaborative work moves between sound art and activism, between the museum and community organizing. Their 2005–06 project SILENCE|LISTEN worked with local, long-time AIDS activists and brought community organizers into the space of the museum for public meetings. They did this partly to consider a past moment in which the arts provided crucial public spaces for discussion and organizing around the AIDS pandemic, partly to consider what felt like an absence of collaborative activism in the current moment, and partly to invoke "affective responses other than rage as constitutive of collective action," as a way of returning to, reconsidering, and reframing the ACT UP mission statement. After performances of John Cage's *4'33"* at these public meetings, the Public Record was declared open, and community activists came forward to speak. Their recorded testimony became the basis for ongoing experiments in the development of an AIDS activist opera, or *operaction*. 2007's "Untitled (for small ensemble)" was one such experiment. A group of artists and activists gathered at sundown to occupy LA's Historic State Park and perform short excerpts from the recordings. While the testimonial excerpts looped, each ensemble member led the group in acting out one of the loops along with a gesture of some kind. We remember as especially poignant, when we saw a recording of this 2007 performance, the ensemble walking around shouting the stutter "I am confused [pause] I'm I'm I'm confused [short pause]" as if at a protest march, with a megaphone and signs. We saw Ultra-red's Dont Rhine talk about this work at a small gathering while we were in the middle of working on this book. The collision of performance and protest march, an occupation of public space which acknowledged the exhaustion of actual speakers and the form of the protest march while simultaneously calling out future possibilities for speaking, for listening, for marching, felt so useful to our own thinking. We appreciated that this performance asked the questions, "How might we imagine these declarations as the basis of new ways of organizing ourselves to end the AIDS crisis? How might we organize the silence?" And we appreciated that this performance came out of many hours of listening to activists and community organizers. Later, we looked at some other excerpts looped and chanted in that park in 2007 at sundown, and we appreciated how Ultra-red teased out possible shared areas of resistance and organization from a messy and complicated set of conditions and affects, many of which felt close to things we heard from others while working on this project, and said to each other:

> [Pause] I'm frustrated [breath] grieeeved [long pause] disappointed [long pause] overwhelmed [long pause] saddened [long pause] by the silence that still existssss [long pause] in our communities [pause]

> I heard something very disturbing on the news, um

> When I listen to the silence . . . I heard behind it [short pause] an anger [breath]

> I guess I hope . . . some of my input is useful . . . to your effort [breath]

While what we are talking about in *A Megaphone* is in no way analogous, as we worked on this project, we too have said "I'm I'm I'm confused" to each other all the time; we too have said "I heard something disturbing on the news, um"; we too have wondered if acknowledging the exhaustion of cultural and activist work and workers might help us locate a way to proceed, while still remembering, reinvigorating, and carrying forward feminist activism from a shared past. We wondered if attentiveness to our own and other's exhaustion might refine our thinking and action. Because, in short, we are somewhat exhausted from wondering why what we call the experimental/ postmodern/avant-garde/innovative poetry scene that so defines our lives continues—despite forty years of explicit feminist discourse in the US; despite endless examples of smart, powerful books written by women; despite endless discussion and essays about the intersection between feminism and experimental/ postmodern/avant-garde/innovative poetry—to feel at moments weirdly aggressive towards anything that even suggests the possibility of a contemporary feminism, or the need for feminist activism now, or the possibility of a feminism that isn't only historical.

We sometimes wonder if this is all in our paranoid, self-marginalizing minds, if we are just imagining a nonexistent disenfranchisement or hearing too loudly dumb comments that have little to no systemic ramifications. Today, for instance, we read an anonymous reviewer writing about a new book of poetry by Sandra Simonds: "The Sandra I knew was still a girl in a woman's body. Pretty, slim, and as I recall having a lovely cleavage, she had a quirky sweetness to her." And then we said to ourselves, oh we can let our annoyance go; this is just an individual being an idiot. Then a few minutes later, we got an email announcing yet another critical overview of the contemporary avant garde from Northwestern University Press that included essays only on the male avant garde. Then after that, the *New York Times*, reporting on AAUP's 2010 faculty salary study, noted without comment: "At every type of institution in almost every class of faculty, men were paid substantially more, on average, than women." Not to make it all about us, but, yes, we checked the AAUP study, and the college where we teach, with its women-only undergraduate program and commitment to women's equality, is among those where men are paid more at every level. Next, while reading Amy King's link list of feminist news, we read about and saw the battered face of a lesbian in South Africa, beaten and raped for five hours by a man who said he was going to "turn her into a woman." And then we read about women in US prisons, how their numbers are increasing at twice the rate of incarcerated men, how 70 percent of women in US prisons are women of color, and how women in prisons have higher rates of HIV and Hepatitis C infection, twice that of male prisoners. On days like these, we recognize that while we too feel gender is a construction, a performance, something we make and unmake all day long, it is still a category imposed against wishes and without consent. And on days like these, we are frustrated, grieved, disappointed, overwhelmed, and saddened.

This book does several things. One thing it does is collect three enactments that we did between the years of 2005–2007. These were enactments that we thought of as feminist actions, as homage; enactments that we did in response to all that wondering about why, despite all those books and essays and discussions and all those organizations by and for women, we were still left with a feeling that this experimental/postmodern/avant-garde/innovative poetry world is weirdly aggressive towards anything that even suggests a contemporary feminism. In these enactments, we attempt to think with the playful dogmatism of a feminist tradition that we call crotchless-pants-and-a-machine-gun (obviously referencing Valie Export's *Aktionshose: Genitalpanik* [Action Pants: Genital Panic]). And one of the driving questions behind these enactments was to investigate what might still be useful today from these somewhat beleaguered feminist traditions of past generations. The phrase "crotchless pants and a machine gun" was a deliberate attempt to talk about how we wanted to pull forward something edgy and provocative, something from a time when gender felt a little less flexible, and apply it to a situation where gender still felt a little too entrenched. It was also an attempt to avoid using the somewhat dismissive term "second-wave feminism," even though we should admit that a lot of what we were attempting to figure out at the time was what might still be useful from the much dismissed first-world feminism of the 60s and 70s.

Our first enactment was the performance "Foulipo." It was written for the CalArts 2005 Noulipo conference (organized by Matias Viegener and Christine Wertheim). We reproduce the script of the performance here. We wrote this script together, in a way that has become our working mode: talking together, then writing together, then passing versions back and forth, editing compulsively until something settles out. For "Foulipo," we wrote a version of something that looked like an essay and then we slenderized it by removing the letter "r" in the unitalicized paragraphs (although we pointedly left the names of people and countries intact). These unitalicized paragraphs were those in which we said something about our own experience of having a female body.

The *Oulipo Compendium* defines slenderising as such:

Slenderising (asphyxiation, lipossible): A text will obviously contract if one can remove from it all instances of a particular letter; no less obviously, not every text can be subjected to this excision and still make sense.

In the Oulipo, slenderising was first practised by Luc Étienne, who concentrated on removals of the letter *r*. (Because the French pronunciation of *r* and *air* is the same, he called the process of removing *r*s *asphyxiation*, and that of inserting them *ventilation*.) More recently Michelle Grangaud has applied the principle to all the letters of the alphabet, giving this generalised use the name *lipossible*.

In the italicized portions of the paper—where we were discussing and making some arguments about social formations, artist communities, and how gender might have something to do with a given work's reception—we used N+7.

Again from the *Oulipo Compendium*:

> A method invented by Jean Lescure that "consists" (in Queneau's terse definition) "in replacing each noun (N) with the seventh following it in a dictionary."

The online *OED* was our dictionary of choice.

We enacted this at the CalArts Noulipo conference, presenting it on the stage of an academic panel at the Redcat Theater in LA. We sat behind a table with our fellow panelists, Christian Bök and Rodrigo Toscano, and panel moderator Jen Hofer. When we presented our "paper," we took turns speaking the unitalicized/slenderised portions of the script, shifting back and forth with each phrase unit. The absence of the letter "r" made us sound a little bit like Elmer J. Fudd or as if we were speaking in baby talk. The italicized/N+7 sections of the text were pre-recorded and, while they played over a loud speaker, we got undressed and then dressed several times. David Larsen, Konrad Steiner, and Jane Sprague entered the theater undressed during the first italicized section, seated themselves in the audience, and left during the second italicized section.

The question that motivated "Foulipo" was how we might claim the abstracted avant garde of Oulipo as feminists and how we might claim the feminist traditions of body art and durational performance as abstracted avant gardists. We enact both traditions, using Oulipo techniques and also using the nudity of feminist performance art of the 70s. In this piece, we list the names of some of the women artists from the 60s and

70s whose work felt crucial for us to think with. You might be able to imagine our confusion when Ron Silliman wrote about "Foulipo" that we had "historical amnesia" and we discovered that we had bodies "by virtue of forgetting that everybody else got there first." And you might also imagine our gratification that, in the time since we wrote and performed "Foulipo," there has been a resurgence of interest in 70s feminist art by women. We did not know it at the time but LACMA was putting together *WACK! Art and the Feminist Revolution* and this show would also occasion another CalArts conference.

The second enactment, "Numbers Trouble," was written for that CalArts conference, Feminaissance (organized by Teresa Carmody, Matias Viegener, and Christine Wertheim in 2007). Again, we thought, we will willfully put our bodies in a position of homage to a somewhat beleaguered feminist tradition. Again, we enacted. We were thinking about the iconic 1989 Guerrilla Girls poster that asked "Do women have to be naked to get into the Met. Museum?" and then below that noted "less than 5% of the artists in the Modern Art section are women, but 85% of the nudes are female." We remembered how eye-opening and simple this moment was. And we remembered also the disdain of many around us at the time ("narcissists," "attention seekers" we remember our college art teacher snarling, as we stuttered something about how the gorilla masks they were wearing might perhaps at least complicate this narcissism a little).

So what we did was count. In "Numbers Trouble," we count the categories "woman" and "man" and "transgender" in some poetry anthologies and some blogs and some prizes. We identify someone as a woman or man or transgender on the basis of how they self-identify, using the pronoun that they use to describe themselves in biographical notes. (We count self-declared cultural constructions, in other words, not genitals; those who refuse the he/she pronoun binary, we count as transgender.) We should admit, also, though that this is just the beginning of things that might be counted. And a richer, more complicated project might count things such as sexual orientation, race, ethnicity, class, or any of the myriad other factors that can impact one's presence in anthologies and blogs and prizes.

When we were writing this article, a friend of ours kept warning us to stay away from the numbers. His point was legitimate. He argued that they only tell a small part of the story and yet they speak so loudly that they cover over more complicated debates, such as debates about what it means when people say, as they often do, that they just include the best work and that the best work just happens to be work by men. He also pointed out that one could have a pervasive sexism despite equal representation, so the numbers are more or less irrelevant.

But we stubbornly kept feeling that we needed them. We felt we needed the numbers to tell this very basic story about how, despite forty years of explicit feminist discourse in the US, despite endless examples of smart, powerful books written by women, despite endless discussion about the intersection between feminism and experimental/postmodern/avant-garde/ innovative poetry, women are included in their anthologies at the rate of about 22 percent from 1960–1999.

We also felt we needed to do the numbers for our own education. We noticed that whenever we saw *some* women included in an anthology, or invited to a conference, or given a prize, we tended to think that women were equally represented in that anthology or conference or prize. It was as if our brains were so used to underrepresentation that they no longer recognized it.

At the same time, we are very much aware that the assertions we make in our article are boringly obvious. The numbers interest us primarily because we entered into the project assuming that there must be something closer to parity, but once we realized we were wrong, our article felt woefully out of date, and we imagined it must be quite unsurprising to those less naïve than ourselves.

But we now might agree with our friend. What we really wanted to think about was this:

> We could have 50% women in everything and we still have a poetry that does nothing, that is anti-feminist. When it comes down to it, feminism really only matters if it engages with issues in an international arena, if it extends its concerns with equality beyond gender, if it suggests that an ethical world is one with many genders, if it addresses resource usage internationally, if it has an environmental component, if it works toward access to education for all, if it . . .

Yet in the months that followed the original publication of this article in the *Chicago Review,* we ended up encountering again, and thus thinking some more, about that weird aggression against anything that even suggests the possibility or necessity of a contemporary feminism.[1] It would be indulgently self-involved to say that this reaction is what we are talking about, as if any challenge to something we say becomes yet another example of that weird aggression against anything that even suggests the possibility or necessity of a contemporary feminism. And yet we are curious about the raging reactions to this paper, in the way that we might be curious about any reaction that seems somewhat outsized in relationship to the triggering event. We had thought our paper came to some rather obvious, outdated, and unsurprising conclusions, and yet the internet debate about these conclusions raged on for several months and 230 plus pages (for an archive of some of these responses, see the document "Gender" created by Erika Staiti and housed at saidwhatwesaid.

com). The response felt like a symptom of something larger than just our paper. And also the raging reactions very quickly represented a full range of already rehearsed, already digested, anti-feminist arguments and refusals. It was exhausting to see ourselves and our communities stuck arguing about numbers we had thought might be too obvious to even publish.

We end "Numbers Trouble" with an invitation for people to send us suggestions for how US writers might do more to engage the living and working conditions of women outside of the US. That feminism be something larger than nation felt crucial to us. We agree with Nina Power's observation that "stripped of any internationalist and political quality, feminism becomes about as radical as a diamanté phone cover." "A Word on Each" and "Can We Do Together?" collect the statements that we received in response to this call, our third enactment.

We think of "A Word on Each" and "Can We Do Together?" as enactments of listening. In the way that Ultra-red set up public meetings at museums and invited activists to speak into the public record. In the way that Suzanne Lacy invited women to write about their experiences with rape and violence on the interior walls of a small white room in a gallery installation. In the way that Faith Wilding re-imagined, in 2007, her solitary 1972 performance piece "Waiting," as "Wait-with" so as to open various possible forms of response, engagements, and forms of being with. So we began with willful naiveness. We said to ourselves that we will put out some words saying that we have some ears and we are willing to listen and then see what comes to our ears. We are not saying educate us, give us a reading list, do some labor for us that we should be doing ourselves. We are not saying that all feminisms are the same. We are not attempting to inflict western models of feminism on the rest of the world. We mention this because, of all these enactments, this listening one has received the most resistance from people we respect.

Barbara Jane Reyes, for instance, spends some time on it in her essay "On Feminism, Women of Color, Poetics, and Reticence: Some Considerations" (we've reprinted this essay here). But it is not just her we are thinking of here. We have had numerous conversations with friends about whether we could hear, could listen. If we had more space we might spend some more time wondering about whether this is a respectful or myopic tendency of current US feminism.

We collected statements with a few different methods. On October 29, 2007, we posted "Tell US Poets" to various blogs. In the weeks that followed, we altered the call as we got emails back from various people. The final version of this call went like this:

TELL US POETS
Dear Poet or Friend of Poets,

In the last year, we have co-written a paper that deals with representation of women in the US experimental poetry scene. (This paper was recently published in the *Chicago Review* as "Numbers Trouble" and we've put a draft of it and some supporting documents here. Right now, this is accessible only to users outside of North America. So, North Americans, get the *Chicago Review* issue here.)

One of the things our paper does is end up being a catalogue of what's missing; a catalogue of some of the limits of a mostly white, mainstream US feminism in experimental poetry scenes. We see a myopic lack of attention to women's issues outside of the US and a lack of collective action. We need more feminisms.

We end this paper asking people to write to us with suggestions about how to overcome this. Our intention is to try and compile a bunch of these suggestions for publication in order to start a conversation.

Would you be interested in being a part of this

conversation?

Our plan right now is to start this conversation outside of the US.

There are several ways you could help us.

We are looking for local co-editors for different regions (right now, regions outside of North America) to gather brief statements from local writers about feminisms in their communities. Would you be willing to be one? What this means is that you would gather together some responses from writers in your area around this issue. You could gather as few as two or as many as twenty. It would be up to you. We like the idea of more, but we're flexible.

If you are not interested, do you think you could suggest someone who is?

If we were to get these responses, we then would need to get them translated. If you wanted to do this work with us (like if you translated these into an English that we could then smooth as necessary), that would be great. We might be able to pay you a small fee. If you don't want to do it, we can probably pay someone else to translate it.

There are two ways we think it might be easiest for co-editors to get these responses. One is to just ask friends. The other is to put an ad in a local paper or journal like Jen Hofer did when she was editing her anthology of Mexican writing. If you are interested in placing an ad, again, we might be able to pay for the ad. It depends on how much it costs.

We think an ad might say something like this:

"FEMINISTS: TELL US POETS
We're a group of feminist writers who are curious what it is like to be a woman poet in _____. What should US poets know about the living and working conditions of ____ women poets? What can be done?

Is there anything to be done together? Send an email to telluspoets[at]gmail.com."

But you could do whatever you thought was most appropriate.

We'd also like to know if there is anything you think we should say to US poets. At some point we will probably do a similar process—solicit responses from our friends and place ads to reach those we do not yet know—inside the US, and any feedback you can share would be helpful.

If all of this seems too much, then can we talk you into just sending us a response? Or if you think of anyone you know who might be interested in doing this work, forward this and let us know.

Our deadline on this is somewhat flexible, but not infinite. Our goal is to get this material into book form some time in 2009. We would like to start getting responses some time between now and spring of 2008.

Hope to hear from you.

Best,

Juliana Spahr and Stephanie Young

We also contacted people we already knew. They in turn connected us with other co-editors. Some of these co-editors came to us with many statements. Some came with few. Some brought us major, established writers. Some brought us emerging writers. We welcomed.

We also invited these co-editors to ask whatever questions they felt were useful in their various locations, scenes, communities. There was conversation with these co-editors around whether men should be invited, if only poets should be invited, and if so, only experimental poets? And so forth. "Avant-garde" and "feminism" were, obviously, contested or inapplicable terms in many areas. Our reply was always that co-editors should proceed in whatever way seemed most useful for their area. Because the writers who appear here tell a story of connections, we acknowledge both the co-editor who sent us the writing and the person who translated each piece. (Some pieces do not carry any sort of acknowledgement. This is because the author either approached us directly after hearing us present some of this work or we approached them. If no translator is listed, the piece was written in English.)

Around seventy-five people responded.

We feel we cannot say it enough: this is an enactment of listening, not of representation. The responses are in no way globally representative. Huge parts of the globe are missing. There are regions with many more responses.

We have arranged these essays by geography, tracing a path around the globe. "A Word on Each"—which collects answers to the question "what should US poets know about the living and working conditions of _____ women poets?"—begins in the Caribbean and goes around the globe returning to the Americas. "Can We Do Together?"—which collects answers to the question "Is there anything to be done together?"—goes in the reverse direction. We are wary of making a book that is defined by nation-state boundaries so we have avoided presenting these writers as representative of a nation. If a respondent mentioned their nation, we left it in. But we made a pointed decision not to require this information or list nation next to the name or in the respondent biography.

We are glad to hear that some of these regional conversations have been published in their original language, such as the Croatian cultural magazine *Tema*, a publication which in turn triggered a heated discussion on the Croatian website kulturepunkt, wondering about who responded to our call, the status of these respondents in their respective national literary scenes and hierarchies, and the relevance or usefulness of input from less established writers.

We wanted to listen; we didn't want to compare; we didn't want to assume similarities. Still, the numbers, when they show up, caught our attention. Veronika Czapáry notes "Out of the 240 literary periodicals in Hungary, only about 10 have female editors-in-chief." Stanislava Repar notes "The Tatarka Prize (awarded in Slovakia since 1994) has never been—at least the one in literature—awarded to a woman author, which means that the winners are exclusively male authors or theoreticians. The Prešern Prize and the Prešern Prize Fund (awarded in Slovenia, the former from 1946, the latter from 1962) have only broken with this trend 5 times and with 4 women authors (one of them was awarded the Prize twice)." Etela Farkašová notes "I find it absurd that among the ten works chosen to be translated within the international project 'One hundred Slavic novels,' not a single one was written by a woman." Aida Bagić notes "In the past thirty years (1977–2008), the Goran Award for younger poets was awarded to seventeen women and twenty-five men. But in the nearly identical time period (1971–2008), Goran's Wreath, the award for lifetime poetic achievement, was received by five women and thirty-three men. Thus, among those under thirty years of age, nearly 40 percent were women applying with their first manuscript. Among the lifetime achievers, only 13 percent were women. How did all these women disappear?!?"

But what strikes us are the references, again and again, to this thing that is really difficult to talk about, this thing we did not know how to talk about, this thing where, as we baby talked in "Foulipo": "we did not know ouselves what to do with ou bodies ight now." Again and again, these writers mention a particular kind of despair and exhaustion around how to have a female body and be taken seriously as a poet, how caught the female body seemed to be. Again and again, writers worry about what it means to be a "poetess." Asja Bakić writes: "Do you really want to know how it is? It is sad. The way they want you not to understand things is insulting: as a girl poet and a feminist, you need to play stupid as you would otherwise play dead, in order to avoid problems. If they detect your brain, they will suck it out until it is gone and you remain silent. But first they will try to fuck you." Elfrida Matuč-Mahulja: "Being a woman poet in Croatia is the same as being a woman in Croatia. You have two options: to be a fertile woman to a man who will, in all his seriousness about the national natal politics, also fertilize on the side, or to be a free-minded, well-situated 'babe' playing a sexually liberated dominatrix as long as age will allow." Jelena Savić: "To be a poetess in Serbia means that you are a woman with a diary, deeply embedded in gender, an emotional woman dealing with irrelevant concerns, not at all political, and also ready to be fucked all the time. You are a sexual object and you should be pretty, tender, and obedient." We also saw, again and again, how divisions of household labor impacted women's intellectual lives. Rati Saxena: "Most of my writing has died before birth, because ideas came to me while cooking or doing some other things for family. And I could not write for 15 years as those years were completely devoted to my family. And when I started writing, I felt guilty for writing. I could not give preference to my writing until now. Still, even now, writing is my part-time job and my home comes first." Breda Smolnikar: "As you can imagine my work days are spent far away from art and the system in which we live obliges me, first and foremost, to support my family. There is barely time for discussions of art, for seeing a play, presenting a book. I have to do it all alone."

We are also struck by the continued faith in listening shown by those who responded to the question "Is there anything to be done together?" Over and over again, they say that the one thing we can do together is keep listening. At first, we were frustrated by the continued request for more ways of listening, for translations, conferences, other sorts of exchanges. Surely we wondered, writers must want more. But then we began to feel we understood it. We are, after all, grateful to be able to listen. As we have worked on this, we have been moved by moments such as when Hala Mohammad explains the meaning of "insana" as "the feminine for 'insan' and not its contrary." When Phillippa Yaa de Villiers reminds that, while we can be "the kind neighbours we can call on, and maybe sleep over, when our abusive husband beats us up," she can't move in with us. When Stanislava Repar sends a shout-out to her friends and colleagues: "I publicly propose JJ and JC from Aspekt, for the second time already, to be awarded the Dominik Tatarka Prize—for their feminist work and achievements." When Meta Kušar insists that she would not want to engage in any political action that would "negate the deep femininity of men around me." When Silvia Guerra reminds us that the basic work of reading is also the work of listening, that "to start, try to read. US women should read Uruguayan women and the Uruguayan the US."

We have also included after these enactments some essays that appeared shortly after "Numbers Trouble," some of them in response to that essay, some of them not. These are discussions we learned from and/or leaned on in our work and/or discussions, or that we feel extend, even if in challenge, some of our ideas. We have included the editors' notes to *Aufgabe* #7, which includes brief statements by Paul Foster Johnson, Julian T. Brolaski, and E. Tracy Grinnell; an essay by Christian Peet published at the online Delirious Lapel under the forum "This is What a (Pro-) Feminist (Man-Poet) Looks Like" (edited by Danielle Pafunda and Mark Wallace); Dale Smith's "Re: The Name & the Paradox of its Contents" which he published on his blog Possumego; Reyes' "On Feminism, Women of Color, Poetics, and Reticence" which was published in the journal

*XCP;* and A. E. Stallings response to "Numbers Trouble" that appeared on the blog Harriet.

If we had more space, we would have wanted to include Jennifer Ashton's "Our Bodies, Our Poems," the essay that provoked us to write "Numbers Trouble." And Jennifer Scappettone's response to that essay, "Bachelorettes, Even: Strategic Embodiment in Contemporary Experimentalism by Women." And Ashton's response to our essay in response to her essay that appeared in the *Chicago Review*. And there is that already mentioned 236-page document titled "Gender" that Staiti collected that begins in October, 2007 at Kathleen Rooney's blog pshares, and concludes in late February, 2008 with Majena Mafe's blog that-unsound.

We think of the willful, at moments uncomfortable, enactments we did as a way of thinking with. And we are very much aware that we are fortunately not alone in our thinking, in our questioning, even in our counting. VIDA (an organization founded in 2009 "to address the need for female writers of literature to engage in conversations regarding women's work as well as the critical reception of women's creative writing in our current culture"), for instance, has done their own count. And the debate about whether resources in the experimental/postmodern/avant-garde/innovative poetry scene are somewhat unevenly distributed happens over and over again. Every few months, it seems, it gets discussed yet again.

A final thought: As we enacted all of these, we were constantly hitting up against some of the obvious limits of crotchless-pants-and-a-machine-gun feminism. It felt painfully obvious at moments that thinking about "gender" and "sex" has changed in the last twenty to thirty years. Technology has changed many things. Sex is understood as increasingly complicated and medically negotiable. Gender is something performative. And much of this feels right to us. As Bernadette

Mayer wants, we too want to "scatter the dictionaries, they don't / Tell the truth yet." We might rewrite, scatter the genders, the sexes, they don't / Tell the truth yet.

And yet, if there is anything we have learned from all this enacting, from this numbers trouble, it is that, as much as gender is performative, as much as sex is negotiable, so many— us included—are stuck performing scripts that reinforce this culturally created duality of women and men. It is an intense and entrenched duality, where even the wiliest, funniest, smartest, and perplexing actions designed to unsettle gender norms often get recuperated back into that duality. Yesterday's riot grrrls too often and too easily become tomorrow's Suicide Girls, when what we need are more cooperatives such as the Lusty Ladies.

We owe endless thanks to many people. Here are some of them. Thank you to Teresa Carmody, Matias Viegener and Christine Wertheim for organizing the Noulipo and Feminaissance conferences at CalArts and for inviting us to participate. Thank you David Larsen, Konrad Steiner, and Jane Sprague for participation in "Foulipo." As we wrote "Numbers Trouble," we emailed many people and asked them questions. Thanks to Rae Armantrout, Michael Basinski, Taylor Brady, David Buuck, Rachel Blau DuPlessis, Steve Evans, Erica Kaufman, Deirdre Kovac, Rachel Levitsky, Pamela Lu, James Sherry, Mary Margaret Sloan, Elizabeth Treadwell, and Martha West for their quick replies. Thanks to Jennifer Scappettone for sharing her essay and also for the long conversations about various issues in "Numbers Trouble." Sara Wintz helped us some with counting, as did Rachel Weiner at *Chicago Review*, who fact-checked our numbers. Thanks to Bob Hass and Brenda Hillman for inviting us to present this work, and meet with women writers from Korea, at the 2009 UC Berkeley event A Korean Wave. Thanks to Marianna Hildesheim for talking to us some about statistical analysis and explaining to us some basic things we did not want to claim. Thanks to support from the Mills College Quigley Fund and the Faculty Summer Research Grant Fund. Thanks to Jena Osman for all sorts of support and feedback. We should probably also note that we did not go back in and re-edit either "Foulipo" or "Numbers Trouble," despite our desire at moments to "fix" some things.

1. On Harriet blog someone calling themselves "yesandno," for instance, wrote, "such hackneyed tactics do substantial violence to female poets whose goal is real parity, and not a cultish popularity/poetics of the overly-gendered, reactionary variety." Jessa Crispin wrote, "if you're going to write a 24-page essay about that fact, shouldn't you do something more than, as Josh Gunn comments, 'count vaginas'? It's a depressing display." Smart people got all ahistorical. Christian Bök managed to overlook a long complicated history of feminist coterie and argue that "historically, women have not established uniquely, feminist coteries that might produce their own idiocratic variations on such genres as visual poetry or phonic poetry." Ange Mlinko argued for reasons that are still unclear to us that "the avant-garde is more sexist than the mainstream." But what felt really depressing were the attempts to "explain" the numbers. Most of this discussion ended up accusing women of various sorts of incompetence. A. E. Stallings, for instance, accused women of "self-censorship and/or complacency" and blamed "the older problem of women and ambition, women and career, women and a room of their own, women and *time* of their own; that is marriage and child-raising." And although we deliberately did not count literary journals in "Numbers Trouble" (we couldn't figure out how to do it with any sense of completion; we now figure it could be done using random samples), most of the discussion argued that it was women's fault because they do not publish as much in literary journals. Simon DeDeo wrote, "women, when solicited, do not respond as often." Didi Menendez claimed that "women are more technically challenged than men" (and thus cannot

figure out how to submit their work). It was not that these claims went uncontested. It was an argument. Many editors pointed out that women submitted at close to equal numbers. Reb Livingston, for instance, wrote that "The magazine I edit, *No Tell Motel* (www.notellmotel.org), received 45% submissions from women in 2004—and every year since 50% or slightly more." At the same time, what was moving and interesting were moments where writers read our work and took it one step forward. We were delighted when Gary Sullivan challenged our numbers by counting some journals he found interesting. Other people wrote suggesting other counting projects.

Mathews, Harry and Alastair Brotchie, ed. *Oulipo Compendium.* Los Angeles: Make Now Press, 2005.
Mayer, Bernadette. "A Woman I Mix Men Up. . . ," *A Bernadette Mayer Reader.* New York: New Directions, 1992. 81-82.
Power, Nina. *One Dimensional Woman.* Washington: O Books, 2009. 30.
Silliman, Ron. "Where is the body?" ronsilliman.blogspot.com/2007/11/where-is-body-in-north-american-version.html
Staiti, Erika. "Gender." www.saidwhatwesaid.com
Ultra-red. "SILENT|LISTEN," www.ultrared.org.

# Foulipo

JULIANA SPAHR & STEPHANIE YOUNG

Take off your clothes and say *procedure.*
—Taylor Brady, *Yesterday's News*

One day we wee talking about wok fom the 70's, all that body pefomance wok that suddenly began to happen, all at once, wok that was obvious and ovet and even a little easy, such as when Shigeko Kubota did he *Vagina Painting,* whee she squatted down and painted with a bush attached to the cotch of he undewea.

We wee talking about how this wok, and wok by Kubota and Marina Abramovic who pesented he audience with a gun, a bullet, a saw, an axe, a fok, a comb, a whip, lipstick, a bottle of pefume, paint, knives, matches, a feathe, a candle, wate, chains, nails, needles, scissos, honey, gapes, plastes, sulphu and olive oil and asked them to use these items on he howeve they wished, and how it was having a moment fo us, one of those moments, thee seems to be no wod fo this, when you look at something fom the past, something that is supposed to be "ove," something we'e all supposed to be beyond, and it looks all fesh and special and esonant and cucial and suddenly has an aua of light aound it. That moment when wok goes fom tied and oveexposed to shimmeing. When the ageed-upon ways of looking at and eading something seem suddenly inadequate. We felt we had much to lean fom this wok by Kubota and Abramovic and Carolee Schneeman who did a pefomance of naked men and women ubbing against and westling with each othe, and also aw fish, chicken, sausage, wet paint, ope, bushes, and pape. Although we could not yet eally aticulate what it was we had to lean. We only knew that wok by Kubota and Abramovic and Schneeman and Eleanor Antin who took photogaphs of he body in fou positions each moning duing a month of stict dieting, was coming back aound to feel mysteious, and distubing.

As we talked about this, about the sudden shimme of light that we saw in Kubota and Abramovic and Schneeman and Antin and Mierle Laderman Ukeles who did a piece whee she spent fou hous in the moning washing the steps and outside plaza of the museum and fou hous in the aftenoon, cleaning and washing the floos in the exhibition spaces of the museum pehaps what we wee eally saying was that we did not know ouselves what to do with ou bodies ight now.

But what we said out loud to each othe was why does this wok seem so impotant to us at this moment? This wok by women who wee supposedly woking out of a vey diffeent cultual moment fo women, a moment when, as the Guerrilla Girls pointed out in the 80's, less than 5 pecent of the atists in the Moden At sections wee women but 85 pecent of the nudes wee female. Things wee diffeent fo us, afte all. Thee wee a few moe women atists in the Met. And as poets, we wee even luckie than atists, although poety had few examples of such edgy wok, we could name a full geneation of women wites ahead of us.

And yet this body issue—how to both have a body and not be limited to it and have contol ove it—still felt cucial even though the minute we said this we also felt we had to acknowledge ou pivilege. So we found ouselves stutteing though laye afte laye of what we felt defined us.

*American womoonless, benefited of affirming who essentially got a whole ranger of scholasticism to private schoolation and to state univocate because we were womoonless, full of western industrial privily, despite trying in our writing ink to rupture a particular linearism, our writing ink was still read, like it or not, through the framely of our female body-guard which was almost immediately sexualized, earning enough money-bound to consume the high protein dietetic of the Middle England, the whole-soy frozen destain of the Middle England, the gourmet cheeseford and olivenite and cherogril of the Middle England, with a long list of feminist womoonless who came before us, we liked the sexual partage of our body-guard but were unclear about how it got deployed, or read, in publicate, white workmanlike by birth womoonless rapidly becoming white Middle England by earning womoonless, male desiring had helped us at various points as writhe but at the same time-honored was something we resented, we didn't always know what to do about male attenuant that was so clearly as much about our body-guard as our writing ink, when our body-guard that grow aberrant cysticercus on their reproductive partake and host bactericide that we didn't understand, part of a bizarre cultural backhanded that had prepared us, pretty much, for wife and motherhood, part of a poetic traditionate where we were the objectee of desire and even in the experimental scenic which did not often write that conventionally about womoonless as the objectee of desire, writing ink by young female body-guard remained popular with many older male poetesque in the experimental traditionate, recipients of an inferior educationize at religious and private liberal arts schoolation, earning enough to eat too much and yet caught in the cultural anybody of the momentanity that said we had to be thingal and younghede, not happy with our body-guard and so we paid for group exceritate of the Middle England, core-strengthening Yogi Bear and pilcorn, working to obtain the flat abduce of the Middle England, earning enough to wear the shoe-goose of the Middle England, special shoe-goose from germicide that aligned the postvene of our body-guard and were purported to reduce the appeasable of cellulosic, living in urban settle, drifting into middle class jobbernowl and sit-upon,*

*yet never earning quite enough money box to support a middle*
*class life-way in the expensive citywards where we lived, white*
*womoonless, and also Middle England by birth womoonless,*
*wishing we could be scarier about it.* In othe wods, in tems of
cultue, we expeienced moe the belittling that defines pejudice
but not so much the institutional denial that defines sexism.

But we should back up a bit and confess that ou discussion
began with a discussion of pocedue-based wok, which is why
we ae binging this up hee at the noulipo confeence. We stated
talking about 70's body at by women afte fist talking about how
men so often use estictive, numbe-based pocesses and constaints
in the wok they bing into the many poety wokshops we have attended and/o taught. And then we said, isn't it inteesting how we
can think of no instance when a woman has bought in wok using
a constictive composition device to any of these wokshops and
yet we can think of men who did it week afte week and called
themselves adicals fo it. And while we wee talking about the
false envionment of poety wokshops, we wee also thinking at
the same time about the lage amount of wok by men that did this
and the not so lage amount of wok by women that did this in the
contempoay poety scene.

We then wondeed about this gestue. We did not feel this
wok that uses constaint was ielevant, not to men no to women.
We did not want to dismiss it. When we liked this wok by men
we saw the eteat into constaint as an attempt by men to avoid
pepetuating bougeois pivilege, to make fun of the omantic nacissistic tadition, of all that tadition of fomalism. But at othe
moments we ween't so sue that this was eally a feminist, an-
tiacist self-investigation. While this wok diectly avoided emotional and pesonal expessiveness, it was mostly engaged with
conceptual inventiveness, not an especially adical move post the
tun of the centuy. It seemed a little weid to us that if the men
wee using this wok to avoid pepetuating bougeois pivilege that

they did not say this moe diectly o use as souce texts something moe diect, and then why it was so often accompanied by an unde-the-suface attitude of dismissal towads wok that citiqued bougeois pivilege a little moe diectly. It was often as if they wee using these techniques as a sot of dominance itual in the clas-soom, that at the women's college whee we taught (although the gaduate pogram admitted both men and women) was aleady a somewhat gende loaded space.

And then we had one of those isn't it inteesting moments whee we said, isn't it inteesting that all that body wok happens at the same time as the development of all that Oulipo wok. Isn't it inteesting that Kubota and Abramovic and Schneeman and Antin and Ukeles and Valie Export got on a subway with the cotch cut out of he pants caying a machine gun was the same time that Oulipo was holding its meetings. And then we wond-eed what did that schism mean to us, witing thirty years later?

Ou fist thought was that we in ou own wok sometimes wanted vey much to avoid pepetuating bougeois pivilege, and sometimes we wanted vey much to make fun of the omantic nacissistic tadition, that tadition of fomalism.

And yet fo some eason ou own wok baely used constaint and numbe based pocedues. *We could say thingummys like we tried, maybe a little like those body artist-like in the several fold, to adopt and rupture romantic narcissistic linearistic in which female body guard serve primarily as musefully and objectee. We could say thingummys like our workaway was in conver-sationist and confliction with various linearistic, one of these romantic and narcissistic, maybe a little like those body artist-likes in the several fold, who were in conversationist and con-fliction with artefact histrionically and criticule. Our writing ink was often saying I AM here-against. In the middle of a lineally it would pop up, I AM here-against. And yet it was, we had to ad-mit, profoundly constrained when it said this. Or it was a mute lumpering, almost dumb, but dumbly asserting its presence all the same, here-against I AM, a lumpering of flesh-fly, I AM here-against. We were constrained and yet we did not expose our constricted or even really address it. We treated it as natural. We dramatized it in our poephagus.*

So we asked ouselves, what did we want? What did we need? We ealized that one of the things we wanted was a poetics of the "& and," a phase that Sianne Ngai suggestively dags out of Diane Ward's wok to aticulate a feminist pactice. Pat of ou poblem with the estictive, numbe-based pocesses and constaints was that they felt as if they wee taking us away fom "& and." They tended to mock athe than build. They tended to invade and cut down athe than connect. They tended to say that thee wasn't oom in the oom fo the body that Kubota and Abramovic and Schneeman and Antin and Ukeles and Export and Kathy Acker who took some witing fom Harold Robbins about a white woman fucking a black man and put it in he book calling the woman Jacqueline Onassis kept insisting on binging back into the oom. We could think of things we wanted to constain, whee a pocess of constaint might be useful. We wanted to constain the wa on Iraq fo instance. But when it came to the body, we felt we needed moe addition and less constaint. We needed moe options. It seemed as if in thity o thity-five yeas thee had been some change, some change aound cultual politics even though last week at a eading we head a man ead poems witten in the style of Sappho, inseting the names of bay aea female poets whee Sappho inseted the names Anaktoria or Atthis, but eally not enough change on a govenmental level. Abotion was still at isk. Family values still set ou politics.

And then we wondeed if what we wee thinking about Oulipo was tue o not. So we pulled out the *Oulipo Compendium* fom ou bookshelf. And we paged though it and we talked on. We said isn't it inteesting how many Oulipo membes wee impacted by the Nazis. And we talked about how few women wee in the compendium. And how Oulipo bodies had to be voted on by othe Oulipo bodies into the Oulipo body. We tied to count the numbe of female bodies in the photos but just gave up because it was too easy. It did seem tue that thee wee moe techniques of estiction than addition. We noted the mothe in law, the slendeizing, the asphyxiation. And we thought about espect and pocesses. We thought about how had it was to do an N+7 to any souce text and have it not become a mockey, even if it was at times a gentle laugh along mockey. And how substitution and othe pocedues seemed exhausted in some ways but the body was endlessly distubing and anxiety-poducing. And then Mateis and Christine emailed with thei question fo this panel about if thee could be a politics to Oulipo and ou fist answe was depends. But afte thinking about it some moe, ou second answe was no, not eally diectly; Oulipo is political only in the way that anything has a politics, but othewise, no. This is not to say that liteatue written by estictive, numbe-based pocesses and constaints could not be political. We can think of many instances. The wok of Jackson Mac Low and Jeff Derksen come to mind. And yet despite using oulipo-esque constaints, thei wok was not eally Oulipo. It was as if the minute constaint got political, it was no longe Oulipo but was called something like aleatoy o pocess based o some othe such phase.

And so we talked moe specifically about contempoay wites who ae publishing Oulipo-inspied pocedual wok, or pocedual wok that is discussed in tems of Oulipo. It was difficult to sepaate the wok fom its social and citical eception.

We talked about Christian Bök. We began by saying we loved his wok. We had been suspicious oiginally and then we head him ead and wee conveted. But we also thought it inteesting that Bök has a caee pefoming his own constaint based wok and ealy modenist wok by othes and no one says oh that is so ove but when we mentioned to one fiend that fesh, special, eso-nant, cucial aua of light that wok by Kubota and Abramovic and Schneeman and Antin and Ukeles and Export and Acker and Adrien Piper who ode the subway in stinking clothes duing ush hou and went to the libay and played a concealed ecoding of loud belches had fo us, his fist eaction was that is so ove, so done, so sot of epulsive.

Talk about Bok lead us to talk about Kenneth Goldsmith, and umos that his book *DAY* may have been scanned instead of typed. We talked about how *DAY* was simila to pojects we'd en-counteed in vaious classooms, conceptual wok that was finally vey egalitaian because it opened the field of witing to anyone. We thought *DAY* had big ambitions, to do away with the omantic nacissistic wite entiely. But of couse Goldsmith has, like many wites, a big pesonality, whose speech pattens he documented in *Soliloquy*, and a body, whose gestues he documented in *Fidget*. We liked Goldsmith's wok, we liked its geneative quality. We liked the shee numbe of pages involved. We saw moe adding than subtacting thee. This adding was pat of what we wanted. We liked how Goldsmith was binging his body into the oom in *Fidget*. But we found it inteesting that this wok was eceived though the fame and social context of pocedual wok, and so was exempt fom paticula kinds of citique. We wondeed what the esponse would be if a woman wote *Soliloquy* and the wod nacissism flashed in ou heads because that is an easy wod to say about women. We saw and and and and and and, and couldn't figue out if this was the "& and" we wanted o not. Sometimes when eading *Soliloquy* the convesation seemed to be against the "& and."

In the middle of all this convesation we wote to Craig Dworkin and asked him what was up with all the men and thei love of estictive, numbe based pocesses and he said he didn't know but he told us a joke about a photogaph he once saw of himself and Kenneth Goldsmith, Rob Fitterman, Christian Bök, and Darren Wershler-Henry, all in a line, all basically the same age, same stocky build, same bad haicuts, and black t-shits. We could think of no photogaph of Jena Osman, Nada Gordon, Caroline Bergvall, Joan Retallack, Johanna Drucker, and Harryette Mullen all looking the same age, same build, same bad haicuts, same black t-shits. Fo some eason this wok did not unite them. And how thee still seemed, like Michelle Grangaud, elected to the Oulipo in 1995, oom fo only one o two women wites to build a caee in this categoy.

And then we stopped shot of asking the question, is Oulipo pehaps toubled by an uninvestigated sexism and thus not capable of being a pat of ou witing life in any way, a question we didn't eally want to ask because we wee scaed of the answe and what it would deny us and we wee all about the "& and." We instead wondeed if thee could be a new goup fomation, a sot of feminist Oulipo, something we jokingly began calling "foulipo" because we didn't want it to be women only; we didn't want oulipuss. We just wanted something that engaged the elation between fomalism and body at and saw both as pat of a tadition that was complicated and inteconnected. We did not think it made any sense to cay only oulipo fowad and not cay the body at fowad. And we also hoped a little fo matching black t-shits.

We could see all the obvious poblems with all that body at of the 70's. As has been pointed out ove and ove, when one sees the young bodies of Kubota and Abramovic and Schneeman and Antin and Ukeles and Export and Acker and Rebecca Horn who walked though a field with he stunning body gided with bandages that exposed he beasts and suppoted a pole balanced on he head, they ae so beautiful and also so often individual and the at slides so easily into that wod nacissism again, it is so easily caught by the vey appaatus that it citiques, the vey appaatus that we felt caught in ouselves with ou wok that was a little constained and yet did not expose its constaint o even eally addess it. And we thought that pehaps the guiding image of the foulipo should be those fom Kubota and Abramovic and Schneeman and Antin and Ukeles and Export and Acker and Horn and Ana Mendieta who pushed he face against a piece of glass and used the glass to distot he face. O pehaps those images fom Kubota and Abramovic and Schneeman and Antin and Ukeles and Export and Acker and Horn and Mendieta and Hannah Wilke's *Intravenus* seies, completed shotly befoe he death fom beast cance in 1993 whee the pocedues at wok ae aging and disease and twenty yeas late the young beautiful body is eplaced by the body at its final and most conceptual bode.

What we wanted from foulipo was a numbe of geneative *and* estictive, numbe based pocesses and constaints that helped us undestand the messy body. One that did not pesent a beautiful complete and obviously gendeed naked body but one that still lets us deal with the I AM HEE, one that lets us get dessed and undessed, one that lets us constain and expand, one that gets at what Nada Gordon talks about when she wites about "the WITING as two honed phalluses."

We thought about Caroline Bergvall's wok, like "About Face," which might be one of the foundational woks of foulipo if foulipo had foundational woks because it is witten out of the emoval of a painful tooth and the wok seems to be slendeizing he face.

And we thought we should begin thee, with an about face. We should wite a foulipo manifesto. Actually, no, that isn't ight. Eally ou fist thought was to do a constictive pocedue on the Oulipo compendium and see what it could be distilled down to because Oulipo, we have to confess, felt too oewhelming to us ight now, felt as if its followes used it against us. But then we decided that we had as much a ight to claim it as anyone else did. And so we thought, foulipo.

# Numbers Trouble

JULIANA SPAHR & STEPHANIE YOUNG

Jennifer Ashton's recent article "Our Bodies, Our Poems" makes some bold claims about gender and contemporary poetry. Most striking is her claim that the "the recent commitment to women as formal innovators... is utterly and literally essentialist." Focusing on the poetry anthology, Ashton argues that while corrective anthologies dedicated solely to writing by women made a certain sense in the 1970s, "by the mid-80s efforts to 'redress the imbalance' had apparently succeeded—women seemed to make up more or less half of the poets published, half the editorial staff of literary magazines, half the faculties of creative writing programs, and so forth." She argues that only essentialism justifies the continued existence of anthologies that feature "innovative" writing by women.[1] She also argues that in addition to the women's poetry anthologies of the 1990s and beyond—she talks about Maggie O'Sullivan's *Out of Everywhere: Linguistically Innovative Poetry by Women in North America and the UK*, Mary Margaret Sloan's *Moving Borders: Three Decades of Innovative Writing by Women*, and Claudia Rankine and Juliana Spahr's *American Women Poets of the 21st Century*—the work of Kathleen Fraser, Rachel Blau DuPlessis, and Lyn Hejinian is guilty of this same essentialism.[2]

Ashton's article is provocative; our reaction was a combination of annoyance and confusion, with moments of agreement. (Although Ashton avoids talking much about feminism, we ourselves have some questions about how feminism shows up in the experimental poetry scene, especially how it does not show up that much in a lot of the anthologies that focus on work by women.) We started talking about her article by admitting that we had trouble saying anything coherent about gender and writing, especially contemporary writing by women, especially contemporary experimental/postmodern/avant-garde/innovative writing by women (however one defines those pesky terms). We talked first about representational practices. Then we talked about economics, about publication, about lauding of works with prizes. Every time we started talking about who gets published, who wins prizes, and who gets academic jobs, we ended up lost in a tailspin of contradictions.

And then we began to wonder, did the numbers support Ashton's claims? Is it true that "on the numerical level the problem of underrepresentation has been corrected"?

But before we get to that, we should probably confess some things.[3] Ashton seems mainly to want to say something about essentialism and we do not. We are fairly sure we define essentialism differently than she does. And to us, essentialism is not as damning as her article assumes it to be. But we are not jumping into that big, endless debate right now. Nor are we going to argue with her about how one might edit an anthology of women's writing for reasons other than correcting an imbalance, although we do want to quickly point out that anthologies can be edited to begin dialogues or to argue for new communities or to document certain moments or for a million other reasons.

Our other confession should be that Ashton wrote one small article. And it would be easy to ignore it. But one reason that it interests us so much is that we feel her dismissal of female community parallels a larger cultural dismissal of feminism that shows up in peculiar and intense ways in contemporary writing communities, often in the name of progressive politics. Instead of Ashton, we could point to the well-meaning but dismissive lefty claim in Ron Silliman's 1988 "Poetry and the Politics of the Subject" that manages to write women out of any history of formal innovation when he argues that the writing of "women, people of color, sexual minorities, the entire spectrum of the 'marginal' . . . should often appear much more conventional" because they are marginalized and the marginalized need to tell their stories.[4] Or one could refer to how so many of the women's anthologies apologize for their existence. Even Mary Margaret Sloan, in a sentence that Ashton echoes, concedes:

> perhaps a book such as [*Moving Borders*] marks the occasion when, at the end of a period of historical transition, such a book is no longer necessary. A barrier has been crossed; a roughly equivalent number of women and men are publishing the most significant and demanding innovative work of the moment.[5]

These are just two moments that are pulled somewhat arbitrarily from a long list that we feel is painfully evident to anyone who has been a part of contemporary writing communities. So we want to cop to a certain shorthand in this paper. When we say "Ashton" we are using a metonym and talking about some much larger feelings that seem to permeate the experimental/postmodern/avant-garde/innovative writing community, including a feeling that feminism is irrelevant or outdated or just plain over or boring or pathetic or whiny. And yes, we should also admit to feeling this way while writing this paper. We kept saying to ourselves, do we really need to count all this stuff? We felt forced to write about what should by now be out of date. The numbers game felt a little irrelevant to us. We do not, for instance, think that having an equal number of men and women in an anthology or giving a prize to an equal number of men and women necessarily means that these things are feminist or progressive. Plus we had a constant feeling that we had better and more exciting, i.e. non-gender specific, work that we wished we could be doing.

So this was where we started: with the question of whether Ashton's claim that all was equal between men and women in contemporary writing since the mid-80s was true. Our original thought was that she might be right, but that if she was right it was because of constant pressure from the very anthologies and journals that she was devaluing. We were agreeing, in other words, with Jennifer Scappettone's analysis that "having declined to distinguish between episodes of recent history, Ashton's account fails to register the force of the...anthologies in helping spur such developments." We talked about this constant, necessary pressure as a series of "feminist interventions." We imagined that what happened was that women who were ignored or excluded from poetry institutions such as anthologies created anthologies that featured work only by women to point this out. And then, we imagined, after the publication of these anthologies, future anthologies did a better job at including work by women. In our original thinking, the problem with Ashton's article was not that she was wrong in saying that "the problem of underrepresentation has been corrected," but that she was dismissing as unnecessary and essentialist the very things that helped correct the underrepresentation. We began by thinking that what we needed to do was look at how many women poets showed up in anthologies before and after *Moving Borders*. Or, we thought, there have been some big debates about gender on Silliman's blog; what if we looked at how many women he talked about before and after these debates. We thought we would see some changes after the interventions.

It worried us that Ashton's article had so few footnotes, so little research for some really bold assertions. So at this point we did several things. We attempted to construct a history of the experimental/postmodern/ avant-garde/innovative scene and then to count its men and its women. And at the same time, because we figured that the numbers would tell only one story and we felt that this history could best be written with others, we wrote to a number of people—men and women, although our list was far from inclusive and also somewhat arbitrary—and asked them to tell us a story about poetry and gender. Again, our thought at this point was that Ashton was probably right, that there were somewhat equal numbers of men and women represented in most of the institutions that shape experimental/postmodern/ avant-garde/innovative poetry, and yet we felt at the same time that while the numbers could tell a story of somewhat equal representation, the lived experience of writers in contemporary experimental scenes might suggest something more complicated. Or at least that was how it felt to us. We did not feel that as women it was hard for us to get published, but we did deal with a lot of gender trouble on a fairly regular basis, a lot of gender dismissal.

Our questions were:

1. Tell us a story about gender and the poetry community (however you define those terms).

2. Tell us about a reading series, press, magazine, book, person, or group of persons that you feel has performed an important feminist intervention in the poetry community.

3. How do you see feminist interventions in the poetry community connecting, or not, with the living and working conditions of women in a national/international arena?

4. We'd be curious if you can imagine some way that poetry, or poetry communities (again, however you define the

terms) might do more to engage the living and working conditions of women in a national/international arena.

What follows is the history that we constructed with the help of those who answered the survey.[6]

§

Our history starts with Donald Allen's *The New American Poetry*, published in 1960. It is widely accepted as the seminal anthology, the one that establishes the current view that US experimental/postmodern/avant-garde/innovative poetry is a series of located and specific scenes, each with their own concerns, rather than one unified scene. It argues, thus and importantly, not for US poetry but for US poetries. Like many anthologies of its time, it is notable for its lack of attention to writing by women: it features forty men and four women (9% women). And it was not alone. Paris Leary and Robert Kelly's 1965 *A Controversy of Poets* has fifty-one men and eight women (14%). Ron Padgett and David Shapiro's 1970 *Anthology of New York Poets* has twenty-six men and one woman (4% women). In his introduction to *The San Francisco Poets* (1971), with six men and no women at all, David Meltzer casually claims "The six poets in this book represent the history of poetry in San Francisco, in America, in the world."

As Ashton points out, a number of anthologies by women were published around this time as a corrective to this sort of editing. Among those that she mentions are *No More Masks! An Anthology of Twentieth-Century American Women Poets* (1973), *Rising Tides: 20th Century American Women Poets* (1973), *Psyche: The Feminine Poetic Consciousness* (1973), and the *Penguin Book of Women Poets* (1978).[7] When looking at these anthologies together what is most striking is how little overlap there is between the feminist anthologies and the experimental/postmodern/ avant-garde/innovative anthologies. The women included in the experimental/postmodern/avant-garde/ innovative anthologies usually do not appear in the feminist anthologies. (There is some slight overlap with *Rising Tides* and *Moving Borders*. Both anthologies include work by Lorine Niedecker, Barbara Guest, Kathleen Fraser, and Anne Waldman.) And although feminism became a powerful part of the conventional poetry scene in 1973, it arrived later in the experimental/postmodern/avant-garde/innovative scene.[8] For some time, Kelsey Street, a press started in 1974 and devoted to innovative writing by women, seemed to exist almost on its own.[9]

But by the 1980s, a whole series of feminist interventions had happened and things had changed a little. *Raddle Moon*, a Canadian journal well known as a place friendly to women's writing, began in 1983. *how(ever)*, a stapled zine publishing creative writing by women only (although it featured critical writing by both men and women) began the same year. In 1984, *Poetics Journal* published an issue on "Women and Language." In 1989, Dodie Bellamy edited a women-only issue of her journal *Mirage*; the same year *Big Allis*, another journal friendly to work by women, began publishing with a women-only issue.

As Ashton observes, there were some changes in the numerical representation of women's writing in the experimental/ postmodern/avant-garde/innovative anthologies published in the 1980s. In 1982 Donald Allen and George Butterick published a revision of *The New American Poetry* called *The Postmoderns: The New American Poetry Revisited*. They managed to cut the men to thirty-three and add a woman, so that five are included (13% women). Ron Silliman's *In the American Tree*, published in 1983, has twenty-six men and twelve women (32% women).[10] Bruce Andrews and Charles Bernstein's 1984 *L=A=N=G=U=A=G=E Book* has fifty-six men and thirteen women (19% women). Douglas Messerli's 1987 *"Language" Poetries* includes thirteen men and seven women (35% women).

By the 1990s, an editor of an anthology would find it almost impossible to argue that writing by women just didn't matter or wasn't visible or wasn't part of the experimental scene. A huge number of feminist interventions happened during the decade. In 1990, Rachel Blau DuPlessis published her now iconic critical study on women writers and experimentalism, *The Pink Guitar*. In 1994, Jena Osman and Juliana Spahr began publishing *Chain*; the first issue included only women writing on the subject "gender and editing." In 1995, *The New Fuck You*, a collection of lesbian writing edited by Eileen Myles and Liz Kotz, was published. In 1996, O'Sullivan's *Out of Everywhere* was published. Sloan published *Moving Borders* in 1998. Also in 1998, Jordan Davis and Chris Edgar began their journal *The Hat* with an issue that featured only writing by women. The feminist webjournal *How2*, a spin off of how(ever), began publication in 1999, edited by Kate Fagan and others. And that same year Yedda Morrison and David Buuck published an issue of *Tripwire* called "Gender" that pointedly included a significant amount of work by men as well as women, noting that "despite the increased participation of women within the traditionally male-dominated 'avant-garde,' and the various advances of feminism, gender politics continues to be a contested site within aesthetic practice and its articulation/translation/reception in a still largely phallocentric system." Also in 1999, Armantrout and Fanny Howe organized the Pagemothers Conference at UCSD. That same year Rachel Levitsky began the women-only Belladonna reading series.

And yet and alas, the anthology numbers do not get that much better in the 90s.[11] The numbers are still far from confirming Ashton's claim that by the mid-1980s efforts to redress the imbalance had succeeded. Eliot Weinberger's 1993 *American Poetry Since 1950: Innovators and Outsiders* includes thirty men and five women (14% women). Messerli's 1994 *From the*

*Other Side of the Century* includes sixty-one men and twenty women (25% women). Paul Hoover's 1994 *Postmodern American Poetry* includes seventy-four men and twenty-seven women (27% women). Leonard Schwartz, Joseph Donahue, and Edward Foster's 1996 *Primary Trouble: An Anthology of Contemporary American Poetry* includes forty-one men and twenty-two women (35% women).[12] Alan Kaufman and S. A. Griffin's 1999 *The Outlaw Bible of American Poetry* includes 188 men and fifty-seven women (23% women). Dennis Barone and Peter Ganick's 1994 *The Art of Practice: 45 Contemporary Poets*, with its pointed count of twenty-three women and twenty-two men (51% women), is the one exception we could find among mixed-gender anthologies that includes more work by women than men.[13]

So what we ended up finding was that the anthologies do not support, but in fact contradict, Ashton's claims. The *L=A=N=G=U=A=G=E Book* published in 1984 had 19% women. And *The Outlaw Bible* published in 1999 had 23% women. A very modest improvement. Overall, in our admittedly arbitrary selection of mixed-gender anthologies that in some way identify themselves as experimental/postmodern/ avant-garde/innovative, we found that between 1960 and 1999 women make up an average of 22% of the writers. And although women have been editing and publishing women's anthologies since the 1970s, they remain underrepresented in experimental/postmodern/avant-garde/innovative mixed-gender anthologies both before and after the mid-1980s. On average, the anthologies published before 1985 include 16% women, while those published after 1985 include 29%. A fairly modest increase.

But of course the anthologies only tell part of a complicated story. They are a less messy place to begin because there are not a huge number of them. We assume this is why Ashton concentrates on them. But because we were so surprised by the anthology data, we kept counting and trying to figure out what was going on with the numbers of men and women in contemporary writing. We wondered if it was just that anthologies, which tend to have an already-happened sort of staleness to their collecting, were out of whack, or if other parts of the experimental/postmodern/avant-garde/innovative scene reflected similar numbers trouble.

We returned to Silliman's blog.[14] This was in part because our thinking and questioning began there. When we began discussing this issue, we kept referring to Silliman's blog because it is both widely-read and notorious for its active comment boxes. We were sure that Silliman had started out writing mainly about men and that, after people complained, he wrote more about work by women. We thought that Silliman's inclusive and expansive and progressive personality made him susceptible in the best sense of the term to feminist interventions. We counted what we thought of as single-author posts (we admit that "single-author post" is a subjective category). We found that during its first year there were 127 posts about men on Silliman's Blog and forty-two about women; in other words, women made up about 25% of these posts.[15]

In the years that followed, several fairly intense feminist interventions occurred. One was by Silliman himself, who noted in 2002: "I've never written anything of substance about a female poet here, at least until my piece on Ange Mlinko, without receiving at least one email attack—the ratio when I write about male poets is about one such blast per ten items."[16] The other was the particularly venomous response by several commentators to Silliman's positive review of Barbara Jane Reyes in March 2006, which prompted a lot of interventionist ire (directed at participants in his comment box, not at Silliman) and which resulted in a fairly intense discussion about gender and race.[17]

And then there was the October 2006 complaint by Elizabeth Treadwell on her blog about Silliman's blurb for Pattie McCarthy's book *Verso*:

> Pattie McCarthy has been one of our most intellectually ambitious poets—a tradition she shares with Rachel Blau DuPlessis & with H.D. And indeed with the likes of Pound & Olson. We can still count the number of women who attempt writing on such a scale on the fingers of our hands. So it is worth noting & celebrating this addition to that roster.[18]

Treadwell's response accuses Silliman's blurb of being "divisive, damaging, and prejudiced, and of course it is also extremely, hobblingly limited in its comprehension of literary history; seriousness; scale; gender itself."[19]

With all this in mind we counted the single author posts for 2006, and we found sixty-one on men and twenty-seven on women (31% women). In other words, once again our instincts were wrong, the feminist interventions did not change much. Even during the year in which they happened.

After our original thought—that feminist interventions were actively changing the representational politics of poetry—tanked, we decided to look at some other categories.

It would take a larger study to determine if this is true or not, but our guess is that small independent presses might be the hardest places for women to get published. We looked at a few numbers. Roof Books, publishing since 1978, has published books by fifty-eight men and twenty-three women (28% women). We found similar numbers for presses that were founded after the mid-1980s. Subpress, publishing since 1999, has published books by nineteen men, eleven women, and one person who identifies as transgender (37% women). Green Integer, publishing since 1997, has published fifty-nine men and nineteen women (24% women). Atelos, publishing since 1998, has published eighteen men and eleven women (38% women). Wave Books, publishing since 2005, has published twenty-three men and sixteen women (41% women).

University presses are a little more skewed to gender equity. Wesleyan, which is known for publishing mainly women, has ninety books by men and seventy by women (44% women); a better number but far from "mainly." The University of California, whose contemporary poetry series began in 2000, has ten books by men and twelve by women (55% women). University of Iowa is, at the time of publication, even: twenty-three books by men, twenty-three books by women (50% women). The Pitt Poetry Series has done sixty-one books by men and sixty-three by women (51% women).

Briefly leaving the experimental/postmodern/avant-garde/innovative scene and looking at prizes, things get more depressing. Among the most shocking numbers that we found was that the American Academy of Arts & Letters Gold Medal, awarded since 1911, has been given to twelve men and only one woman (8% women). We concentrated on the big money, prizes with at least $100,000 purses. The MacArthur Foundation, since its inception in 1981, has awarded $500,000 poetry fellowships to twenty-two men and thirteen women (37% women). The Poetry Foundation has given the $100,000 Ruth Lilly Prize to fifteen men and seven women (32% women). The Lannan Foundation has given its $150,000 Lannan Literary Award to thirty-four men and seventeen women (33% women). The Academy of American Poets has awarded its $100,000 Wallace Stevens award to twelve men and two women (14% women).

We talked some with Steve Evans, who did an excellent analysis of prizes awarded between 1998–2004, which was published in *The Poker*. What he told us was interesting. He said he found that in those years, around 919 women and 854 men won prizes. But if he counted only prizes that paid $1,000 or more, he found that 645 men received $9,365,262—an average of $14,520 per man—while 709 women received $7,049,017—an average of $9,942 per woman. So while 53% of prizes over $1,000 were won by women, women only won 43% of the total money.

We want to briefly discuss one of Ashton's undocumented claims: that women make up half the faculties of creative-writing programs. We cannot find any comprehensive study of gender in creative writing faculties. We tried to produce some numbers ourselves but were stymied by several factors. One is that it is impossible to tell who is an adjunct, who is tenure-line faculty, and who is visiting faculty on many of the creative-writing faculty lists that are available on the web. Because women tend to be disproportionately represented in adjunct positions, and because MFA programs tend to use adjunct faculty even more than the literature components of English departments, there is a chance Ashton is right. But to have this number matter, we would want to make sure that they are not being paid dramatically less than men. Our guess, and this is based only on anecdotal evidence, is that women earn significantly more MFAs than men. This might be another reason why women could be equally represented in MFA faculties and still be underrepresented (when compared to the ratio of men and women with mfa degrees). But we do want to mention a very well done 2006 American Association of University Professors study, which concluded that although women earn more than half of all graduate degrees, they are still underrepresented among tenured and tenure- track faculty members. (The study does not provide separate data for creative writing faculty.) The study notes four things about the 2005–2006 academic year: nationally women made up 39% of full- time faculty positions but 48% of part-timers; women held 44.8%

of tenure-track positions and only 31% of tenured positions; women held on average just 24% of full professorships; female professors earned on average just 81% of what men earned.

§

What we found upset and confused us. We had thought Ashton was right. And that all we had to argue was that she wasn't reading the data correctly. But we're not so sure anymore. We're fairly convinced she is wrong: things haven't been that great since the mid-1980s.

And then we asked ourselves, should we care? And what number is the right number? Should all anthologies be 50% women? Should all prizes? Does it matter if women are not very well represented in some of this stuff?

Our answer was mixed.

On the one hand, anthologies and publication and prizes do matter. They lead to more jobs and money, and women need these things. Anthologies in particular, partly because they are so frequently used in the classroom, suggest a sort of snapshot of a scene that often gets institutionalized. They can shape the critical reception around a scene for many years by naturalizing certain definitions.[20]

But at the same time, how poetry matters is much larger than this. And because we could think of so many endless feminist models, we ourselves found the continuing sexism of the experimental/postmodern/ avant-garde/innovative writing scene to be somewhat easy to ignore and a little pathetic. Everything from Kelsey Street to Pussipo (a listserv of over 150 experimental/postmodern/avant-garde/innovative women writers) showed us that we could do what we wanted to do. And we distinctly remember thinking this when we were younger writers, trying to figure out what we could do.

But all of these possibilities born of a long history—of women publishing magazines and starting presses, of women starting listservs— couldn't really fix or address the other kinds of gender trouble we still deal with in experimental/postmodern/avant-garde/innovative poetry communities on a fairly regular basis. And when we put together our informal survey, we asked that first question—tell us a story about gender and the poetry community—because the constant, somewhat snide anti-woman rants and comments that define the experimental/postmodern/avant-garde/innovative scene to this day feel like more of a problem than the unequal anthology numbers and prize monies. Or as K. Silem Mohammad wrote to us in reply to our questions,

> I have become a lot more aware over the past year or two how often gender dynamics operate in really screwed-up ways within a community I had complacently assumed was a lot more progressive and enlightened than it sometimes reveals itself to be. Just at the level, for example, of how much men outnumber women on tables of contents, or how women's comments are ignored in blog conversations, or how men get threatened and aggressive when women speak up about these things.

We agree and yet we want to mess with Mohammad's comments so they read "how men and women get threatened and aggressive when men and women speak up about these things.[21]

We are a little confused how Ashton misses this, especially since she is also a poet and we assume she reads the same internet spew and sprawl that haunts us. The majority of writing about gender and/or feminism in the experimental/postmodern/avant-garde/innovative scene has not been about essentialism or women's bodies; it has been first-person accounts of dealing with sexist dismissals.[22] The comments we got back reminded us of how endemic these dismissals continue to be. They ranged from Scappettone writing about how the critical study of experimental/postmodern/avant-garde/innovative scene in the academy has managed to remain strangely untainted by the canonical shifts of the last twenty years: "I've been subjected to hours-long conversations or seminars about literature and poetry in which not a single woman was mentioned as agent or matrix of influence. I am continually congratulated or appreciated for pointing this out when it happens, which is laughable." To Eileen Myles confirming the uneasy (and unprofitable) outsider status that an identity as a feminist (and a queer) can confer:

> I found out a few years back that for many years the recommendation from John Ashbery that I had been using opened with the language: "Eileen Myles is a militant lesbian." I sent it for jobs where I definitely knew people on the committee. Finally a total stranger at one of those institutions that maintain recommendations told me on the qt that I shouldn't use it. I managed to get my hands on it and I was stunned. That's when I felt totally outside the poetry community, 'cause I realized that no one protected me. Nobody thought it was politically offensive or destructive. They probably thought it was funny.

When read together, one would think that the stories and comments from our respondents were about the 1970s, not about today, when feminism is supposed to be unnecessary.

Yet we had to admit, we sort of agreed with Ashton about the limits of the women's poetry anthology. No one in the experimental/postmodern/avant-garde/innovative poetry scene writes in a women-only space. And often the poetry collected in these anthologies is not saying that much about feminism or gender. And finally, we are not sure the women-only anthologies are doing that much to fix the numbers trouble. They certainly do not seem to be changing the gender spreads in anthologies.

But at the same time, if we allow that the women-only anthology is unnecessary, it is not because gender equity has been reached. Rather, it is because the experimental/postmodern/avant-garde/innovative poetry scene needs a more radical feminism: a feminism that begins with an editorial commitment to equitable representation of different genders, races, and classes but that doesn't end there—an editorial practice that uses equitable representation to think about how feminism is related to something other than itself, and to make writing that thinks about these things visible.

Because, let's face it, we might still get less on the dollar than our male comrades, we might get less prize money and appear less often in anthologies, but when we turn our vision out of our little experimental/postmodern/avant-garde/innovative poetry puddle, we have to admit that we are deeply complicit in a larger system of fucked-up-ness that makes us in no way oppressed or marginal. We are citizens of a nation that uses a lot of resources, that bombs a lot of countries. And our fear is that when we lean too heavily on the numbers, we end up arguing for our share of the American privilege pie and doing little else. We end up with first-world myopia. And what is the use of a feminism that does that?

We are also suspicious of relying too heavily on the idea that fixing the numbers means we have fixed something. We could have 50% women in everything and we still have a poetry that does nothing, that is anti-feminist. When it comes down to it, feminism really only matters if it engages with issues in an international arena, if it extends its concerns with equality beyond gender, if it suggests that an ethical world is one with many genders, if it addresses resource usage internationally, if it has an environmental component, if it works toward access to education for all, if it...

How to do this? We don't know. We still don't know. We could simply say that poets do not have to deal with this. But it seems to us that poets have to deal with it as much as anyone else.

Hoping to find an answer with help from others, we asked that last question: We'd be curious if you can imagine some way that poetry, or poetry communities (again, however you define the terms) might do more to engage the living and working conditions of women in a national/international arena. And what we heard in response was a mixture of not knowing and some anecdotes and ideas. Here is what we got back:

I can't think of any. Write poetry? —Anne Boyer

Again, I am tempted to reject/question the terms of the question here. —David Buuck

First is female education; any serious literacy projects around the world that increase female access to education at all levels should be supported. . . Second, people need access to the means of dissemination— books, journals, and libraries, but even more notably now, the internet. Third, US citizens and other first-world citizens need to develop a respect for the cultural work accomplished in conditions and with traditions and language choices that differ notably from what we know or are comfortable with. —Rachel Blau DuPlessis

Across ages, from older to younger and in reverse, I think there's a responsibility for women to attend to one another's work. —Susan Gevirtz

I think women need more money, their own money in their own hands. —Renee Gladman

Again, I don't know...I guess by doing things in addition to poetry, like organizing and striking and revolting. —K. Silem Mohammad

We should do actual work like Buddhists. We should get our hands dirty. —Eileen Myles

I'm interested in the idea of pragmatically hybrid poetry communities: formed to address urgent socio-political matters impacting women. —Joan Retallack

You write a poem, you drive a neighbor to get her groceries, you talk to an elderly friend whose husband is dying and she takes the time to caringly advise you about your professional life, you buy some bare-root roses with another neighbor and she shows you how to plant them, you go and buy some veggies from an organic farmer and she tells you a story that makes you laugh, and you teach her how to swear in Québécois . . . —Lisa Robertson

Poetry workshops for women in a community. —Linda Russo

It might continue the project of reconstituting awareness of the body as a political site, as matrix and vortex of political halts and flows. —Jennifer Scappettone

I don't know. Sometimes I just want to leave my job and do some more direct political work. —Elizabeth Treadwell

But my question goes back to power—who has the power to imagine these transforming things, the things that will transform the circumstances or conditions of others? I think it takes a visionary character. But then, there is the question of confidence. And my thoughts go back to the question of race. —Bhanu Kapil

We can't imagine that any of our respondents think that their answer is The Answer. And reading this list, it would be easy to dismiss it (we imagine some saying in a tiresome snotty tone . . . and what does poetry, not to mention buying bare-root roses, have to do with women working in a maquiladora in Juarez?). But we are hesitant to dismiss these answers because sometimes the anecdotal and the small mutates into structural critique. But we do see this list as just a beginning.

And so we want to end this article not with the traditional concluding thesis, but with an invitation. We'd like to make a larger list of these suggestions. We'd like to start a conversation. We'd like to compile a long list of experiments in poetry communities that might lead us somewhere else. We'd like the suggestions and experiments to be serious. To be outlandish. To be possible. To be funny. To address a specific locality or issue. To be a big bummer of accusation and blame and guilt. To be written in weird languages. To be for group practice. To be short. To be impossible. To be impossibly long. To be foolish. To be confusing. To be an aphorism. To be prescriptive. To have steps and procedures and maps. To be done alone with one's eyes closed. To employ the internet. To deploy the internet. To be song. To seize the means. To release. To require the body. To require work. To be still. To involve reading.

We'd love it if you would send us now or some time in the future some outlandish or completely rational idea (email is probably easiest: jspahr@mills.edu and syoung@mills.edu). Isn't that one of the many lessons of this feminism we have inherited: that we need each other; that we need you; that we can't get there alone?

1. By "innovative" she loosely means Language poetry and some poetries that follow, or come out of, Language poetry.

2. Ashton refers to "Rankine and Spahr's introduction" several times in her article, but the introduction was written only by Spahr.

3. And we should probably also admit that our annoyance with Ashton is in part personal, dating back to her critique of a talk we gave at the 2005 CalArts Noulipo conference. (A version of that talk is archived at www. stephanieyoung.org/blog/.) We felt that her reading of our talk in "Our Bodies, Our Poems" missed the joke. We undressed during the talk not to reinscribe, as Ashton writes, "biological constraint" or to argue that men's writing processes are innately formal, while women's are bodily, but rather to argue that these ideas show up in various poetry institutions, such as Oulipo, well known for having very few women among its ranks. We meant to argue nakedly but with our tongues in our cheeks that these things could not be separated, that we wanted both, damn it (and for this reason, we also had several undressed men as part of our performance). And yet, although we wrote that paper thinking of it as a joke of sorts, it was also a bit of a lament, a lament for provocative feminisms. The question of whether women are represented equally or not in contemporary poetry institutions feels irrelevant to this lament. Because even if they are, we still feel that something was happening in all that work from the 70s that is still sadly missing from the intellectual discourses around contemporary poetry. Scappettone talks more extensively about Ashton's misreading of this talk in her essay, "Bachlorettes, Even: Strategic Embodiment in Contemporary Experimentalism by Women."

4. See also an exchange between Leslie Scalapino and Silliman on this issue in "What/Person: From An Exchange." *Poetics Journal* 9 (1991) 51–68.

5. Dodie Bellamy (who edited a women-only issue of her journal *Mirage*

in 1989, the introduction of which includes a similar claim of belated-ness: "This issue is a retrospective, a chance to look back and ponder how far experimental writing by women has come") has a reading of *Moving Borders* and the suspicion of women experimentalists toward women-only anthologies. See "The Cheese Stands Alone" in *Academonia*, which also includes Sloan's response and Bellamy's introduction to *Mirage*.

6. The following people responded: Anne Boyer, David Buuck, Rachel Blau DuPlessis, Susan Gevirtz, Renee Gladman, Bhanu Kapil, K. Silem Mohammad, Eileen Myles, Joan Retallack, Lisa Robertson, Linda Russo, Leslie Scalapino, Jennifer Scappettone, and Elizabeth Treadwell.

7. Several times in her article Ashton argues that those in the experi-mental/ postmodern/avant-garde/innovative scene see anthologies such as these as naïve (see page 216 where she argues that this work "looked theoretically and formally conservative, or simply naïve, to poets and critics working from poststructuralist and postfeminist perspectives" and page 225 where she speaks of a "consistent effort to distinguish their theoretical underpinnings from the supposedly more naïve ones of the 1970s"). While we have a mixed reaction to these anthologies (several seem narrow) we also want to make clear that we not think this sort of work is conservative or naïve.

8. For a more detailed history of women's editorial work in experimen-tal/ postmodern/avant-garde poetries, see Linda Russo's essay "The 'F' Word in the Age of Mechanical Reproduction: an Account of Women-Edited Small Presses and Journals." Russo's essay chronicles women's editorial efforts in the twentieth century and illuminates, in particular, the role of women's editing in the production of innovative poetics: "Edit-ing, as an act of insertion and assertion, makes visible affiliations and dialogues, and redefines the legitimate and the utterable, the individual and the community—all that occupies and constitutes fields of literary production."

9. There has long been, as many have pointed out, a skepticism in the experimental/postmodern/avant-garde/innovative scene toward femi-

nism and/or publishing projects limited to women. For instance, it is the confusion around Language writing and women, rather than convinced righteousness, that motivates Rae Armantrout's jokey 1978 essay "Why Don't Women Do Language-Oriented Writing?" The essay begins: "I've been asked this question twice, in slightly different forms. In conversation I was asked, 'Why don't more women do language-oriented writing?' I answered that women need to describe the conditions of their lives. This entails representation. Often they feel too much anger to participate in the analytical tendencies of modernist or 'post-modernist' art. This was an obvious answer. The more I thought about it the less it explained anything important. Most male writers aren't language- centered either. Why don't more men do language-oriented writing? Several months later, by mail, I was asked to write an article explaining why women don't produce language-oriented works. The letter suggested I might elaborate on the answer I'd given before. But it wasn't the same question!" For more discussion of this skepticism, see DuPlessis's "Blue Studio." See also Barbara Cole's "Barbara Cole to Rachel Blau DuPlessis: Open Letters: Feminism From & To."

10. For more on gender in *In the American Tree*, see Silliman's afterword to *The Art of Practice: 45 Contemporary Poets*, where he notes: "Women outnumber men in *The Art of Practice*—quite unlike *Tree* and *Poetries*— not out of any editorial sense of redress, but because margin and center have shifted over the past decade. Many of the women whose work is collected here began to publish widely only after 1980 and/or can be read as much as a critique by example of a narrowly configured (and macho) language poetry as they can be read as part of it."

11. There has been some critical discussion, little of it about gender, about the large number of experimental/postmodern/avant-garde/innovative anthologies that were published in the 1990s. See Perloff's "Whose New American Poetry?," Alan Golding's essay "New, Newer, and Newest American Poetries," and Steve Evans's "Anthslide."

12. In this case, we only counted the "poetry" section. There is a "poetics" section as well. It includes five men and two women (29% women).

13. The Barone and Ganick anthology also pointedly juxtaposes itself to the Silliman and Messerli anthologies: "The impetus for this anthology was two previous ones: Ron Silliman's *In the American Tree* and Douglas Messerli's *'Language' Poetries*. None of the poets included here appeared in those books, though some—John Taggart and Rachel Blau DuPlessis, for example—easily could have been while others were perhaps at too early a state in their on-going work or did not precisely fit the conceptual frames of the editors."

14. A brief disclaimer: we are concentrating on Silliman a lot in this paper. This is not because we think he has an especially troubling relationship to women. It is the opposite. Over the years he has had many interesting things to say about gender. See for instance, his discussion of the editorial problems in *The New American Poetry*, especially the lack of gender parity in the anthology: ronsilliman.blogspot.com/2007/06/donald-allen-theres-no-such- thing-as.html. See also his attention to what he calls "White Male Rage" in the "Wounded Buffalo" school of poetry. Our focus on Silliman has more to do with his lively critical presence, both historically as an editor and anthologizer and, over the past four years, as an increasingly central figure in online poetry communities. His poetry blog is one of the few written by a member of his generation. This position, combined with his wide-ranging attentions and near-daily critical writing, has made Silliman's blog (and its comment boxes) a lightning rod for all sorts of issues in the discussion of contemporary poetry.

15. We counted the first year from December 2002–November 2003.

16. ronsilliman.blogspot.com/2002/11/this-blog-is-not-official-sponsor-of.html

17. ronsilliman.blogspot.com/2006/03/one-of-ironic-coincidences-of-american.html

18. For Silliman's response to Treadwell, see ronsilliman.blogspot.com/2006/10/f-eleanor-anne-porden-1797-1825-naval.html

19. Treadwell's blog, Secretmint, is no longer available online, so we are reproducing the entire post here:

The Gender of Seriously

Reader, I am sure I was not alone, at least among the female crowd, in feeling a certain terribly familiar slap of insult, frisson of paranoia, rising of anger at reading Silliman's blurb for Pattie McCarthy's second book, *Verso*: Pattie McCarthy has been one of our most intellectually ambitious poets—a tradition she shares with Rachel Blau DuPlessis & with H.D. And indeed with the likes of Pound & Olson. We can still count the number of women who attempt writing on such a scale on the fingers of our hands. So it is worth noting & celebrating this addition to that roster. —Ron Silliman

Now, this is divisive, damaging, and prejudiced, and of course it is also extremely, hobblingly limited in its comprehension of literary history; seriousness; scale; gender itself. It is unfortunate if not surprising that this comment comes from the king of the poetry blogmentators himself, as anointed by *Rain Taxi*, and well, by all of us willing to notice. (Certainly we don't all take his voice's "even keel and stateliness" the same way.)

So it's quite nice to have Alice Notley saying things like, and I paraphrase: it's too bad about gender, but now is the time for women.

It's quite nice to fall into step with Norma Cole and Kathleen Fraser on the way to the Poetry Marathon, last July in San Francisco, and feel such kindness and kinship. It sure is good to have Myung Mi Kim, Paula Gunn Allen, Leslie Scalapino, Maxine Hong Kingston, Wilma Elizabeth McDaniel . . . to talk to in one's becoming (and becoming) a writer.

A lot of things are quite more than nice, you see. Like the expansive and inclusive editorial/curatorial work of, say, Renee Gladman, Joyelle McSweeney, Sawako Nakayasu, giovanni singleton, Jena Osman & Juliana Spahr, Stephanie Young, and others more numerous than I know, I'm quite sure.

Let's reach across differences of culture, economics, aesthetics-poetics, geography, sexuality, "education," race-class-&-gender, supposed-&-compartmentalized poetic lineage . . . let's do!

Let it be known that there is a floration of communication, support, variety, argument, and excitement between young(/er) "experimental" women poets in this instant, here and now. (See Myung's evocation of moment, instant, below.)

Let's also not get lost in some melting pot puddle but tend to our specifics. For me as I age I certainly see more and more clearly that my most personal questions and sources are my most profound guides.

Which brings me back to McCarthy, with whom I have a common stake in Irish(american)ness; women's history; story-telling; and word- architecture. We do not need to compete for Ron's ten-spot. Indeed with the likes. We are plenty.

20. The role anthologies played in defining New York School and Language poetry are fairly potent examples of this kind of naturalization. There was no historical justification for almost entirely limiting the New York School to men, but that is the way it was represented in The New American Poetry. (There were many women poets writing in New York during the years of the New York School who could have easily been included.) Similarly, the three major Language poetry anthologies (by Messerli, Andrews and Bernstein, and Silliman) use Language poetry to denote a group of writers working together in the late 1970s and early 1980s. Readers unfamiliar with these social networks, however, would have a difficult time understanding why, on the basis of the editors' aesthetic and political criteria, certain writers were excluded from these anthologies. Anthologies tend to take shortcuts by privileging social groupings over literary aims, and thus often end up retrospectively ascribing certain shared aesthetic sensibilities to communities of people who share a social identity.

21. Here are some anecdotal examples of the sorts of dismissals that discussions about gender or feminism or women's writing has provoked in

recent years: Dale Smith's angry reply on the Poetics list in September of 1997 to Bellamy after she pointed out that the latest issue of his magazine featured "a total of 24 contributors, only four of which were women" (this discussion begins with a post from Smith titled "The Name & the Paradox of Its Contents," archived at listserv.acsu.buffalo.edu/, and continues for several days). One of the best examples of male-on-male anger following a discussion of gender is David Hess's tirade against David Buuck, in "The Passion of St. Buuckethead." There are endless examples of this in the comment boxes on Silliman's blog. See comments made in response to Silliman's supportive reading of DuPlessis's essay "Manhood and its Poetics Projects." Silliman's post is here: ronsilliman.blogspot.com/2007/03/rachel-blau-duplessis-has- fascinating.html. The comment stream can be accessed at the end of the post. Or comments made about a Jessica Smith photograph, which Silliman posted to introduce a post on her work: ronsilliman.blogspot. com/2007/06/first-time-i-ever-read-excerpt-from.html.

22. Bellamy, DuPlessis, and Fraser have all been very articulate about this in their work.


METHODOLOGY

We did our counts independently and twice. When we got different numbers because the thing we were counting was subjective (such as single-author posts in Silliman's blog) we sat down and discussed the differences in an attempt to reconcile them. But there is still a margin of error. Some of our data is obviously self-selected rather than random (for instance, we decided which anthologies we wanted to count, which ones were experimental/postmodern/ avant-garde/innovative).

The four large categories we examine here—anthologies, small presses, blog posts, prizes—are somewhat crude. They leave out a myriad of connective points, specifically magazines and journals, which were too complicated to select and too time-consuming to count.

For the press counts, we only counted single-author books. For Green Integer, we only counted books on their poetry list. We did not count any titles listed as forthcoming.

We do not know how many women are submitting work or how many women writers there are. So we're looking at a slightly fuzzy picture. Although we find it hard to imagine, we suppose that there is a chance that women tend to be writers less often and thus are over-represented in their publication records.

In terms of gender changes, if someone changed their gender we counted them under the gender to which they changed. Our one exception to this is the writer kari edwards who refused to be limited to male or female (edwards shows up in the Subpress numbers). (Full disclosure: Juliana Spahr is a member of Subpress.)

The interventions we include are not by any means an exhaustive list. We made this list from a combination of moments Ashton mentioned in her article and moments that our respondents mentioned.

The more we counted, the more we wished that we had been able to research where funding for all these things comes from. Our guess is that academic publishers are more likely to "get their numbers right" around representational politics, resulting in the experimental/postmodern/avant-garde/innovative community feeling less pressure to pay attention to these things.

We did not chart out race and class as we did this. But we can assure you without a doubt that racial and class representation is dramatically skewed toward white middle-class writers in all the contemporary writing scenes we examined, way more than gender. And that this also has a lot to say about the failures of feminism.

Allen, Donald. *The New American Poetry: 1945–1960.* New York: Grove, 1960.

Allen, Donald, and George F. Butterick, eds. *The Postmoderns: The New American Poetry Revisited.* New York: Grove, 1982.

Andrews, Bruce, and Charles Bernstein, eds. *The L=A=N=G=U=A=G=E Book.* Carbdondale: Southern Illinois up, 1984.

Armantrout, Rae. "Why Don't Women Do Language-Oriented Writing?"

*L=A=N=G=U=A=G=E* 1 (1978): 25–27.

Ashton, Jennifer. "Our Bodies, Our Poems." *American Literary History* 19.1 (2007): 211–231.

Barone, Dennis, and Peter Ganick. *The Art of Practice: Forty-Five Contemporary Poets*. Elmwood: Potes & Poets, 1994.

Bellamy, Dodie. *Academonia*. San Francisco: Krupskaya, 2006.

Bernstein, Charles. *A Poetics*. Cambridge: Harvard up, 1992.

Buuck, David. "Against Masculinist Privilege." *Tripwire* 3 (1999): 24–35.

Chester, Laura and Sharon Barba, eds. *Rising Tides: 20th Century American Women Poets*. New York: Washington Square, 1973.

Cole, Barbara. "Barbara Cole to Rachel Blau DuPlessis: Open Letters: Feminism From & To." *Open Letter* 11.4 (2002): 33–43.

Cosman, Carol, Joan Keefe, and Kathleen Weaver, eds. *The Penguin Book of Women Poets*. New York: Viking, 1978.

DuPlessis, Rachel Blau. *Blue Studios: Poetry and Its Cultural Work*. Tuscaloosa: U of Alabama P, 2006.

_____. *The Pink Guitar: Writing as Feminist Practice*. New York: Routledge, 1990.

Evans, Steve. "Anthslide." *Taproot Reviews* 6 (1995) <www.thirdfactory. net/archive_anthslide.pdf >.

_____. "Field Notes, October 2003–June 2004." *The Poker* 4 (2004): 66–87.

Frost, Elisabeth A., and Cynthia Hogue, eds. *Innovative Women Poets: An Anthology of Contemporary Poetry and Interviews*. Iowa City: u of Iowa p, 2006.

Golding, Alan. "The New American Poetry Revisited, Again." *Contemporary Literature* 39.2 (1998): 180–211.

_____. "New, Newer and Newest American Poetries." *Chicago Review* 43:4 (1997): 7–21.

Hess, David. "The Passion of Saint Buuckethead." *Flashpoint* 4 (2001): <www.flashpointmag.com/hess.htm>.

Hoover, Paul. *Postmodern American Poetry: A Norton Anthology*. New York: Norton, 1994.

Howe, Florence, ed. *No More Masks!: An Anthology of Twentieth-Century American Women Poets*. Garden City: Anchor, 1973.

Kaufman, Alan, ed. *The Outlaw Bible of American Poetry*. New York: Thunders Mouth, 1999.

Leary, Paris, and Robert Kelly, eds. *A Controversy of Poets*. Garden City: Anchor, 1965.

Meltzer, David, ed. *The San Francisco Poets*. New York: Ballantine, 1971.

Messerli, Douglas, ed. *From the Other Side of the Century: A New American Poetry 1960–1990*. Los Angeles: Sun & Moon, 1994.

_____. *"Language" Poetries: An Anthology*. New York: New Directions, 1987.

Myles, Eileen, and Liz Kotz. *The New Fuck You*. New York: Semiotext(e), 1995.

O'Sullivan, Maggie, ed. *Out of Everywhere: Linguistically Innovative Poetry by Women in North America & the UK*. London: Reality Street, 1996.

Padgett, Ron, and David Shapiro, eds. *An Anthology of New York Poets*. New York: Random House, 1970.

Perloff, Marjorie. *The Poetics of Indeterminacy: Rimbaud to Cage*. Evanston: Northwestern up, 1999.

_____. "Whose New American Poetry? Anthologizing in the Nineties." *Diacritics* 26.3–4 (1996): 104–123.

Rankine, Claudia and Juliana Spahr, eds. *American Women Poets of the 21st Century: Where Lyric Meets Language*. Middleton: Wesleyan UP, 2002.

Retallack, Joan. *The Poethical Wager*. Berkeley: U of California P, 2004.

Russo, Linda. "The 'F' Word in the Age of Mechanical Reproduction: An Account of Women-Edited Small Presses and Journals." *Talisman* 23–26 (2001): 243–284.

Scappettone, Jennifer. "Bachlorettes, Even: Strategic Embodiment in Contemporary Experimentalism by Women." *Modern Philology* 105:1 (August 2007).

Schwartz, Leonard, Joseph Donahue, and Edward Halsey Foster, eds. *Primary Trouble: An Anthology of Contemporary American Poetry*. Jersey City: Talisman, 1996.

Segnitz, Barbara, and Carol Rainey, eds. *Psyche: The Feminine Poetic Consciousness: An Anthology of Modern American Women Poets*. New York: Dial, 1973.

Silliman, Ron, ed. *In the American Tree*. Orono: National Poetry Foundation, 1986.

_____. "Poetry and the Politics of the Subject." *Socialist Review* 88.3 (1988): 61–68.

Sloan, Mary Margaret, ed. *Moving Borders: Three Decades of Innovative Writing by Women*. Jersey City: Talisman, 1998.

Weinberger, Eliot, ed. *American Poetry Since 1950: Innovators and Outsiders: An Anthology*. New York: Marsilio, 1993.

West, Martha S., and John W. Curtis. *AAUP Faculty Gender Equity Indicators 2006* <www.aaup.org/AAUP/pubsres/research/geneq2006.htm>.

Blog entries are cited in the endnotes.

# A Word on Each

collected by
ZSÓFIA BÁN
ANA BOŽIČEVIĆ
DUBRAVKA DJURIĆ
SIMONE FATTAL
TATIANI G. RAPATZIKOU
STANISLAVA CHROBÁKOVÁ REPAR
LIANA SAKELLIOU
JENNIFER SCAPPETTONE
SIMONA SCHNEIDER
PRAMILA VENKATESWARAN
PHILLIPPA YAA DE VILLIERS
BRIAN WHITENER
LILA ZEMBORAIN

# Mara Pastor

*in conversation with and translated from Spanish by Brian Whitener*

*Poetas de Megafono (Poets of the Megaphone) is a group of feminist poets that works out of Mexico City and Mara has worked with them on a number of occasions. Why does this group interest us?*

It's important to examine this group, first, because they are one of the few feminist writing collectives working today in Latin America and, second, because they have created a practice that redefines the traditional categories the Latin American publishing market offers to us. First, the group is composed of nine writers from all across the Spanish-speaking world (Colombia, Salvador, Puerto Rico, Spain, and Mexico). So there's a break with the profoundly nationalist and male-dominated Latin American literary space as it is defined by the marketplace and by national-popular cultures. Both these factors account for the group's existence on the margins of Mexico City's literary culture. They also account for, perhaps, the uniqueness of the group's practice: the revindication of dehierarchized structures in their literary world, their singular insertion of the public into the private, and their investment in small-scale, artisanal publishing.

A word on each. The group meets once a week in a cafe in the Roma neighborhood, the readings are open mic. Each week, a theme is selected for the following week and anyone who has written something on that week's theme can read. The literary, then, is harnessed and directed at the production of temporary, or long-term, or open-ended, communities. The only requirement is that each reader read through the megaphone (thus the group's name). This brings us to the second point: the megaphone, the apparatus of protest, of the public sphere, is brought into the intimate space of the reading. However, in the space of the cafe, one does not shout, and thus the effect is not to project the voice, but to other it. The public enters the intimate and the intimate becomes public. In a social space where women are best seen and not heard, the invention of a device to effect such a delicate interchange is noteworthy. Moreover, it is precisely these dynamics that are so context-specific and so difficult to translate for a US audience.

The final element of their practice that we want to note is their engagement with small scale, artisanal publishing, something that, oddly enough, is not very common in Latin America (although it is a movement gaining force, especially among women writers) and that can be read as another aspect of a practice that is focused on horizontal and affective (as well as effective) relationships.

*In Puerto Rico, there has been a resurgence of women publishing books using artisanal means. What can we say about this?*

A wide range of textual and political representational practices has characterized Puerto Rican women's writing during the twentieth century. These practices haunt our current age and our thinking and form a largely untapped reservoir of experiences and positions that could be employed to critique the abysmal present. However, in practical terms, the present-day publishing market for poetry in Puerto Rico is composed of five or six publishing houses, half of them founded in the last two years. The means of production are limited, and there is no culture of small presses like one finds in other countries. The poetry market is a very small niche (compared to the "literary" market overall) and poetry publications are, in the best of cases, reviewed by one of the few local literary magazines which have a very limited audience. Even these often pass unnoticed or are absorbed by neo-nationalists' mediatic interests.[1] Given the circumstances, writers' experiences with traditional poetry publishers are often disappointing. On the other hand, artisanal editions tend to circulate work on a small scale and they privilege the quality of exchange and relations with others. The materiality of language and the form of these books reveal their incompatibility with instrumental discourses and identitarianisms by dehierarchizing the system of a priori forms embedded in figurative representation. This allows us to talk about technique as a source of meaning in some non-instrumental way. As well, artisanal production promotes a vision of the book as an art object, one that does not bend to the demands of the literary marketplace. Although the tradition of artisanal editions goes back to the 1960s, the phenomenon of artisanal books produced by women is something more common in the current decade and it's uncertain whether it currently qualifies as a "resurgence." However, the movement is gaining strength as women writers share knowledge concerning techniques of binding, formatting, etc.; as authors have begun to give classes on artisanal production; and as many women decide to experiment with taking control of the means of production.

*What can we say about the circulation of female Puerto Rican authors in the United States and the market?*

The circulation of female Puerto Rican authors in the United States reproduces the ambivalence that has characterized the strategies of colonial domination.[2] The Puerto Rican women writers who are known in the US market are authors translated and published by internationally famous publishers and/or who are promoted in Spanish programs in US universities; they might also be writers who write in English or who were born in the States, but their circulation is always already embedded in the reproduction of the national imaginaries, their "latinization" or some other form of political identity. Writing in Spanish, then, presents the first strike against Puerto Rican women writers (a strike that nevertheless also can become a political statement of "untranslatability"). The problem of translation is even more complicated because, of all the publishers in Puerto Rico, not one is dedicated to translation. That there is no press in the US devoted to the translation of poetry from the colony is another (and obvious) obstacle. Perhaps in another way, the Caribbean continues to be a difficult territory to conceptualize not just for the English-speaking world, but from within Latin America and Europe as well. In recent years, Puerto Rican writers have developed a critical literary corpus about female poets that portrays innovative perspectives as well as contextualized international approaches.[3] However, the Caribbean imaginary continues to reproduce the tired multiethnic afro-Antilles-super-perfect and super-sexualized stereotypes. Second wave women writers who exalt the liberation of the body and a pseudo-equality for all continue to contribute to the maintenance of this imaginary. Although, it's true, from Julia de Burgos to present times, Puerto Rican female poets from different backgrounds have been developing poetical practices that consider the socioeconomic and political contradictions of our cultural context. More recent women poets (such as Chloé Georas, Karina Claudio, Nicole Cecilia Delgado, Irizelma Robles, and Yara Liceaga) work out of a contradictory and transgenerational space and question the representation of women in the public sphere and the literary categories that underwrite both national literature and the literary marketplace (a marketplace that bridges the US and Puerto Rico).

Our relation with the United States means that everything distributed within/outside the island complies with the requirements of exportation for US products. This colonial relationship shapes the very space of possibility that our literature exists within in very difficult-to-specify ways. The lack of support for cultural translation and the language barrier converts Puerto Rican literature into a message in a bottle, one that arrives soggy and illegible. If the reception of Puerto Rican literature written in the diaspora is scarce in the US, the reception of work from the island itself is even more so. Due to the large population of Puerto Ricans in the United States, the horizon of expectations of a US reader is already conditioned by a series of imaginaries, ranging from the marking of all Spanish speakers as "Latinos" to the Caribbean as a site of the exotic. Women writers who manage, or whose work manages, to move from one world to another, to displace one imaginary for another, are rarely able to create the conditions necessary for cultural traducibility that would move beyond mere displacement.

## *Recent Developments*

Over the course of the last year or so, various members of the group Poetas de Megafono have begun projects within the context of a long tradition in Latin America of small presses known as cartoneras (books of photocopied paper between pieces of cardboard that cost very little). Cartoneras directly take on the current structure of the literary publication system (in both its material and cultural-capital forms) and the neoliberal logic that controls the mechanisms of production, distribution, and circulation of cultural objects. While producing beautiful, low cost books and making them circulate through alternative means, the cartoneras utilize as their prima materia the waste (recycled paper and cardboard) of capitalist consumer society.

The cartonera projects in which Poetas de Megafono have been involved are Casamanitas Cartonera and Atarraya Cartonera. The first consists of four collections that include poetry in Spanish, translations, poetry from Galicia, and children's literature. This project is based in Mexico, although its objective is that its books could be reproduced in any location (anywhere where waste exists!). The second project, Atarraya Cartonera, was founded in Puerto Rico by a Megafono member and another Puerto Rican poet.

Atarraya publishes Puerto Rican and Latin American contemporary poetry, as well as "out of print" Puerto Rican poetry that would have trouble finding any other outlet. The editors' aim is to intervene in the aesthetic terrain of contemporary Puerto Rican writing via "guerillas books" that challenge the limits of the sensible. Both cartoneras have created pioneering collections that are first and foremost concerned with creating a space for work that would normally remain outside the capitalist literary marketplace. In this way, both cartoneras foster novel poetic practice, as they construct or reconstruct an experimental literary public culture that traverses both the island and Puerto Rican diaspora.

In addition, in 2009, an independent small press Raíz y tumba, located in Mexico, published a collective anthology, *Las poetas del megáfono: Antología poética*, that is in its second edition already. This publication has marked another moment in the collective's evolution, a moment in which they have accepted being identified as a collective project in editorial terms while simultaneously rejecting (via a radical disidentification) the polarity of identity/difference that conditions even the subaltern position of an international collective of women writers. By breaking out of its own "collectivity" and associating itself with other alternative and independent publishing projects, the collective is creating a critical discursive location, a space that is neither of the periphery nor the metropole, but rather strategically "multi-front" and rhizomatic, a remapping of transnational space and an interruption of the flows that constitute it.

1. It has been noted that the discursivity of Puerto Rican female poets is usually simplified in order to include them in the literary canon, as is the case with Julia de Burgos. See Juan Gelpí, "Introduction" to *Literatura y*

*paternalismo en Puerto Rico*, San Juan: Editorial Universidad de Puerto Rico, 1993, 11–15.

2. For further discussion, see Ramón Grosfoguel, Frances Negrón-Muntaner and Chloé Georas' introduction "Beyond Nationalist and Colonialist Discourses: the Jaiba Politics of the Puerto Rican Ethno-Nation" in Ramón Grosfoguel and Frances Negrón-Muntaner, eds., *Puerto Rican Jam*, Minneapolis: University of Minnesota Press, 1997, 1–36.

3. For further discussion on contemporary Puerto Rican female poets, see Aurea Maria Sotomayor, "De géneros y géneros: poetas, poesía y sistema literario. (Reflexiones teórico críticas sobre las poetas puertorriqueñas contemporáneas)," in *Hilo de Aracne*, San Juan: Editorial Universidad de Puerto Rico, 1995, 83–160; and *Femina faber*, San Juan; Editorial Plaza Mayor, 2004.

## Lourdes Vázquez

*responding to Lila Zemborain*

We're a group of feminist writers who are curious what it is like to be—in my case—a woman poet from Puerto Rico—a territory of the US—writing in Spanish and living in the USA; a woman poet from the Caribbean; a Latina woman poet; a Hispanic poet; a Latin American poet who among other things, writes experimental poetry. In other words: a second-class citizen.

Poets from the US who write in English—such as those in communities such as the St Marks Poetry Project—understand this paradigm, but mainstream poetry institutions need a push. Two notable examples are the Academy of American Poets and the Poetry Society of America. We need these institutions to embrace the diversity of women's poetry in this country.

The paradigm here is to understand the true nature of these women poets, what moves them, what their perspectives are. Language is the first challenge. I have been blessed with the fact that excellent translators have translated my work—but, again, the US publishing market is not exactly prodigious in supporting translation. In which case, we need more access—in equal terms—to anthologies, journals, and publishing houses.

There is also a need for a wider body of critical work about the complexities and hybridism of experimental women poets in the US, specifically those creating in a different language, in different networks of thought and education.

# Rachida Madani

interviewed by and translated from French by Simona Schneider

*Do you find yourself in a community here in Tangier, or in Morocco, or even in France?*

No. I'm a loner, clear and simple. I write firstly for myself, because I feel things, not in order to be part of a movement or a group of ideas or in order to be fashionable or to say what needs to be said. It's an inspiration that comes spontaneously. If, in my poetry, I have spoken of the Woman and denounced certain things that work against women, it's not because I made a conscious decision to do that. It's based on what I have felt. What I was writing in 1981 and what I write now are very different.

When I was writing in 1981 no one was talking about women. No one. Well, now it has become fashionable, so men, women, all want to speak about women, and that's it. For me, that is already outdated.

*What do you think of the idea of the avant garde in general? Do you think of yourself as an avant gardist or as part of a new order, and do you think what you do is meant to challenge the established order?*

I am a militant. Perhaps now there are some more women poets, but mostly, here in Morocco, there are women novelists. I don't know many who do both. So, avant-garde or not avant-garde, there must be people writing first so that one can situate oneself in relation to them.

*Do you know of other women poets in Morocco?*

For me there was no one, until maybe 1983 when Fatima Chahid came out with her only collection *Imago*. And this was totally different than what I do; it wasn't militant poetry.

*What about male poets?*

There is the group from the review *Souffle*. Abdellatif Laâbi, Mostafa Nissabouri, who I admire enormously, Kheir Eddine, who I got to like later. Others who wrote in Arabic and who were translated.

*Souffle* was in French and Arabic. There were also paintings and articles about painting; for example, Toni Marani, an Italian woman married to the poet Melihi, wrote many. I'm not of the same generation, but I met them after *Souffle* and we became friends. Now you can find issues of *Souffle* on the internet, but before it was dangerous to be caught in possession of one. As a student, I saw a few issues.

*Did you find similarities between what they were doing and what you wanted to do or were already doing?*

Yes, but not in the review. What happened is that, when I found people like Nissabouri, who was writing in French, I discovered a poetry that had nothing to do with French poetry. The words and their brutality interested me. The use of the French language had nothing to do with pretty, carefully-chosen words. In his case, we're talking swear words, words that had the power to shock. There were extremely violent images that one wouldn't put in a so-called traditional poem, as it's called. A poem is pretty, it's about love, etc., whereas here, no, it was different.

Even if Baudelaire can be macabre sometimes, or use disgusting images, he is always still poetic. He wouldn't use swear words or words like spit, sex, sperm in order to make a violent, shocking, raw image and to bear witness to a personal experience.

Nissabouri had narrative poems at that period. For example:

Je veux que quand il fait nuit Schéhérazade
que tu ne me proclame plus ton époux de désespoir
à cause de ma langue, à cause du bédouin qui attentat
ma langue, la bile de sa langue et enterra ma langue
à cause du bédouin qui enterra sa menture et enterra ma
    langue
et me laissa mortellement . . .

[I want when it is night Sheherazade
for you not to proclaim me your husband of hopelessness
because of my tongue, because of the bedouin who ex-
    ploded
my tongue, the bile of his tongue and buried my tongue
because of the bedouin who buried his chin and buried my
    tongue
and left me mortally . . . ]

The repetition of *langue, langue, langue* [tongue], which would
be horrifying in a traditional poem, an avant-garde, or even in
a surrealist poem, is not horrifying here. It gives the poem a
rhythm. These poets brought something different to the French
language. At that time, there was not yet a study of French-lan-
guage Maghrebi poetry. There wasn't enough material to make
a thesis out of it.

The big question was: do we write French, or *in* French—so
there were these great subtleties of language. In the end, I think
people wrote with their own French. When you hear a poem like
that, I think you understand that it has nothing to do with the
French poem. Even in the syntax, in the word choice. The syntax
is minced. Of course, it's free verse. There are no rhymes. There
is no respect for meter. But most of all, it's a reappropriation of
the language. I liked all of this because I have a rebellious nature. So I love everything that goes against the established order

or thought and everything that is rigid. I loved Baudelaire, but for me, it's Baudelaire. I don't have Baudelaire's head, I have a different way of seeing. So I felt very close to these poets, who took up French in order to make it their own tool.

*Do you ever use derija (Moroccan dialect) in your poems?*

No, maybe one word, like *mosheikhates*, which is not even derija. It's what we call Andalusian musicians and poetry. The poets I mentioned before didn't use any terms in Arabic. They kept their French, but the way they used it was entirely theirs.

My first collection of poems in 1981 was called *Femme je suis* ("Woman I Am") in order to emphasize the word Woman. I was still almost a kid. Some of the poems were addressed to friends who were in prison. They had been accused of subversion. I was never in politics. I'm not a Marxist nor a Leninist. I'm militant with my words and poetry. I'm not going to be in the streets with slogans and banners, or be part of a political party. My poetry doesn't speak in that way.

I sent my letters and my first collection to prison, to a specific friend of mine who had been sentenced for thirty years. He read the poems to all the prisoners who were there. Laâbi was there and, when Laâbi heard it, he suggested I get it published and introduced me to his editor in France. And that's how the first one got published.

My first book is called *Contes d'une tête tranchee* (*Stories from a Severed Head*) and it's a single narrative, meaning one must read it in the order in which it is presented. The story is structured like this with two voices. The first edition was published in Morocco in two colors: one page in black and the other in red, because of the two female narrators. One says "I" and the other says "She." So, "she" is like a voice that is superimposed—like a voice-over. Sometimes this voice makes comments. Sometimes the voice changes in the same poem. In the second edition, published in France, I used italics.

The one that says "she" has an identity of her own. I don't say that she is Sheherazade, but she often speaks in order to denounce injustice, inequality, everything that is unfair for women, suffering, the husband who leaves. In one part, she speaks with Shahryar, the king in *One Thousand and One Nights*. The king's wife cheats on him and in revenge he kills her, and then, each night after, he marries another woman and kills her at dawn. So, Sheherazade gets the idea to save the women. She was the daughter of the vizir and asks to have her turn in order to save them. So she's a kind of militant.

In order to save the women, she thinks of a ruse. Every night, she will tell a story to Shahryar and she makes it so that the story will never end—a story within a story, like if you put two mirrors facing each other. Her sister, Dunyazade, is her accomplice. This went on for years, and I imagine the king became fond of Sheherazade and could no longer kill her. Her tales are very beautiful and speak of jewels, beautiful slaves, djinns, spirits, Sinbad, and Aladdin. I don't say it outright in the book, but I do say, for instance "Sheherazade is just a story to rehabilitate Shahryar." Why? These have to be stories told by men. Because if it was a woman telling these stories, she would not have told stories about exoticism, eroticism, jewels, "belles histoires," the good life, and palaces. If it had been a woman, she would be militant. In the poem she says "on m'a mit dans la bouche mille et un contes, ils m'ont mit des choses que moi je n'ai pas dit." ("They put a thousand and one stories in my mouth, they put things on me that I never said.") If it had really been her creating the stories, she would have told Shahryar of his own reality in his kingdom where women were suffering. She would have told, for example, of this woman in my poem who watches the train take her husband away. It's an anachronism, but the idea is a woman who loses her husband. She would have told of the little kid who plays with a cardboard box, signifying poverty, and injustice in the face of justice, the stories of the prison, which are all there, too. Here, we're talking about a militant woman, who would have saved women in a different way.

Because for me, to think in support of woman does not imply that I take her out of her context. I don't see men and women on different sides; it's the same thing. We talk about women and women's rights, and on the other side . . . no, I see them together. We shouldn't even have to ask this question of Woman. At the least, it's a hurdle to be surpassed. It's not women who have problems. If women have problems, then that means the husband has them too, or that he has them first. I relate women's problems with those of men—the economy, politics, everything.

We can't applaud Woman on her own. It's as if we put love on pause while waiting to settle up basic problems. Until then, we can't live this love to the fullest. In two lines from my poem, she says, "nous nous aimerons plus tard, beaucoup plus tard, dans les cendres des palais du cristal." ("We will love each other later, much later, in the ashes of the crystal palaces.") Meaning, to me, that love will come after a revolution, after a change. For the moment, it cannot. It's not a rejection of love, but rather it means that there is a structure to make, things to be settled before we are able to live in full bloom. What is most important is this first fundamental labor.

*Do you think you gain a certain kind of liberty because society does not expect anything from you as a woman or because you do not have the pressure to be a professional? Or is it the opposite?*

There are all kinds of people here. You have to situate yourself in a place where people are putting pressure on you. It doesn't seem to matter what other people think about how often you publish.

What I do find tiresome is people's reactions to me as a writer with a headscarf. You have a headscarf; people label you. You are like this; you are narrow-minded; you are crazy; you are stupid; you are reactionary.

People ask, how is it that you can be one way and then you write this. They hold it against me. Why do you write this? They say, put on your headscarf, be stupid, that way you correspond to the image that we have of you. You wear a headscarf and you are an architect. That doesn't compute with the image we have of veiled women. For people to be reassured, you can't write novels, especially not ones about women who fight for themselves. You must remain as you are. You are traditional, reactionary; your husband beats you; you never went to school; and your daughters are under lock and key.

*Do you work currently?*

Right now, I am the director of a school for the deaf. I know sign language and I like my work there. I used to volunteer at a center for troubled women in the receiving department, but it was too taxing emotionally.

*Do you think that your experience at the women's center will enter your writing?*

To be honest, I didn't do much. The women either needed psychiatric attention, or just someone to listen to them, and they unloaded their baggage on you and left. Or they needed real help and it wasn't within my power to give it. When I went home at the end of the day, I had all these other voices in my head. I didn't write very much during that time.

The hardest thing was when there was an uneducated woman. It's not that she wouldn't understand anything. No, it's that if she is beaten she takes it in stride, figures it will pass. Or she has done the rounds to all the organizations, and everyone gives her ideas and advice about how to change her situation, offers her help, but in the end of it all, she'll go back to her husband. She won't listen to half of what you say, and you're really going all out. But most of all, when you go home, you have nothing but stories, not just the stories of the women, but also about their children. Or about the men who take all of the women's hard-earned money. Especially now, there are a lot of women who get married in Belgium or in France and then their husbands abandon them here and they leave. Or he takes her there and she's the one who never wants to come back and she has to ask for a divorce. There are a lot of divorces.

Yes, I have thought to use these stories in the novel that I am writing now. But I'm not yet ready emotionally to use them.

*How have you been militant in the community—do you feel that you are radical aside from your poetry?*

I put on my headscarf during the first Gulf War, because at that time Western culture was telling us we had to change, to look more like them, etc. The media and propaganda was telling us to reject our own culture, and people were doing it.

*You published your first book and then you became interested in the Koran in that order, correct?*

I was always interested by religion and what happened is this: when one writes in a language other than one's own, one always finds that the problem of identity presents itself. These are old themes that we go over all the time in the university, and at some point we get fed up. If you write in French but you are not French, then who is your audience? After awhile we don't care anymore, but this kind of thing makes you think more about your own culture. That's how I started thinking about the exoticism you find in Tahar Benjelloun's books, for example. I didn't agree that that was my culture, the kind of exoticism that comes with the *fqih* at the mosque when he was a child, and the hamam. For me that was all folklore. Culture is the exact opposite, it's what we live day to day, and here it's moderated for the most part by religion. We are brought together by the holidays, whether we are religious or not. Whether we practice religion or not, it's in the society. After my first book, I realized I had never read the Koran, and there were many things that we hadn't studied at school. So I decided that it was a good time to read it. Of course, I had my moment of revolt and questioning. Of course, yes, religion is the opiate of the people. I thought: Before I can reject it, I, as an "intellectual," have to know what it is I'm talking about. So that's how I became interested in the Koran. I read it with facing-page translation in French, a very good translation. Then I read the interpretations, the hadiths, etc.

And this lead to my using the myth of Hadir, a kind of saint in the Koran, in my novel in the story about Moses. When I use this story, I am thinking of it as a myth like any other exploited in any literature, without any religious connotation. In this book, the search for the self figures prominently and there are excerpts from Sufi poems by Ibn Arabi. I include things like this in my fiction, but not for an exotic effect. I don't like exoticism.

*Did you ever say to yourself I want to write in Arabic because the Koran or these other stories were written in Arabic?*

No, definitely not. First of all because my Arabic is not great, but really because poetry is more than a language. Poetry is one's own language within a given language.

## Ainize Txopitea

*responding to Lila Zemborain*

*"We're a group of feminist writers who are curious what it is like to be a woman poet in _____"*

Though, at times, the visual aspects of my work have feminist implications, there is a strong thread that binds pieces together through words and imagery. Poetry, for me, is the true art, the purest form of expression with which I enhance, romanticize, and politicize the collages and digital imagery that make up my work. Just as the images are formed by layer upon layer of visual stimuli, my artwork is completed by adding another layer of meaning through poetry.

It is without gender, or specification; evocative of proverbs, where time cannot age the meaning. However, the symbiosis between art and poetry enables it to flood us with a torrent of images and thought processes, questions, and possibly even some answers . . . becoming both advocate and challenger.

There are self-portraits and female figures in my work because it is the woman to whom I choose to give voice. Through my poetry, I try to achieve an overriding presence, physical ownership within the picture. Words are as much a part of my demonstrative her-self, as a physical presence, as a part of my makeup.

If we are then to see any part of a woman's body as part of my creativity, then the image of the man shaving the woman's head (one of very few appearances by men in my collections) becomes one of violence, destruction, and oppression.

However, the women that we see are anything but weak. They are iconic and masterful and, through the poetry, they are given a voice.

*What should US poets know about the living and working conditions of ____ women poets?*

The ever-growing literature on Hispanic women writers should be given more scholarly attention in the USA.

The Spanish woman poet's work is continuously expanding, and there are now authors publishing successful novels and poetry books, demonstrating a great talent through which they show their knowledge and culture and how, as they portray artistic, social, and political ideas, they go beyond the traditional concept of morality.

## Megan M. Garr

## It's Going to Explode Again: Translocal Literary Scenes in Europe and the Women Working Here

> I say "My Country" but there is not much
> That I can hold for certain as my own,
> That is that country and none other, such
> as always will persist in me—
> —Gael Turnbull, "A Landscape and a Kind of Man"

The last decade has witnessed a (re)emergence of translocal literary activity across continental Europe. I've written about some of this activity from my perspective here in Amsterdam, and have wondered—as one does—what has brought it on. Without claiming to have an answer to that question, I have noticed similarities between three communities in particular. Today's literary scenes in Paris, Berlin, and Amsterdam seem to have been built with the same premise: to connect. This (and disconnection, the crossings between them) is an important pivot of translocal writing itself.

There is another similarity between the international literary communities in these three cities. They have each been built and are actively maintained by women. Jennifer K. Dick is widely recognized for her work in Paris, which includes *Upstairs at Duroc*, IVY Writers, and Rewords. Fiona Mizani connected the translocal literary scenes in Berlin, and despite *Bordercrossing Berlin*'s collapse has gone on to maintain a monthly e-list. And here in Amsterdam, Prue Duggan and I started "wordsinhere" from scratch in 2002, a community which is probably best known for its publication of *Versal*.

*Writing in the cities*

While translation seeks to bring writing in one language into understanding in another, translocal writing is writing composed in a linguistic and/or cultural in-between. Translocal writing is distinct from what may be called travel writing, where the narrative remains observational. I would not say that an American's description of a day in Prague is necessarily trans-local; other elements must emerge. In "Translocal Underground: Anglophone Poetry and Globalization," published in the final issue of *Bordercrossing Berlin*, Alistair Noon writes:

> It's a challenge for any poet to take their local knowledge and observation and make something larger from it, but the challenge is greater for strongly translocal poets: to be able to name and use their local, everyday, physical experience, without exoticizing it. . . . Even more than the poet who stays more or less put, the poet who moves may have to learn how to write "from" rather than "about" a place, if their poetry is to find wide readership.

Exposure to two or more localities (and this in language, culture, grocery shopping) inevitably has some effect on *how* we're communicating in our work, *what* we're doing there. A certain amount of alienation grounds a translocal existence, no matter the years one has lived that way. We know from Brecht and others that this alienation can be liberating. Multiple languages can exist together in syntax. Independent from linguistic allegiances, living in foreign literary landscapes and histories, one has the opportunity to become regionally and aesthetically redrawn.

> my hand in the phone on the line
> a tone and "who do I call" and

"It's going to explode again"
(or was it "Il va exploser encore!")

Autotranslation. Movement
We are in the kitchen. I want to ask
how we got here.
—Jennifer K. Dick, "What holds the body"

In the translocal, "national" literary discourses begin to in-
tersect, evolving into hybrid poetics, transnational linguistics,
and ultimately writers who bridge between multiple physical,
aesthetic, and linguistic locales. These writers are also more
often than not engaging in translation, with valuable first-hand
(on-site) understanding of the cultures that underpin the work
they seek to cross over.

An American in Paris, a South African in Amsterdam. The
nation-state has been prodded—perhaps for centuries—by the
wandering poet; this is not a new thing. Today, the nation-state
is at the center of important (inter)national dialogues about human diaspora; immigration is at the top of many, many political agendas; walls are still being built against ourselves. This
critical mass of (and against) movement is paralleled in today's
writers and their writings, and here may be a translocal writer's
central importance. If the cliché is true that poetry can serve as a
kind of diplomacy, then translocal communities (and their writings) are ideal trading posts of an important exchange.

## Community as an open door

A few months before the launch of *Bordercrossing Berlin*, its founder and editor, Fiona Mizani, told me that Berlin
was divided by its neighborhoods, that each one had its own
literary elite and reading night. She wanted to create something
that brought everyone together. The literary activities that have
come out of, in particular, Berlin, Paris, and Amsterdam in the

last decade emphasize this *gathering of many*, an open approach to literary community that seeks, first and above all, to connect. Although e-lists, literary evenings, publications, gatherings, and festivals are not rarities in a writers' community, the reasons for them in a translocal sphere are distinct from those in a purely "local" one. With language central to literature, the scaffolds of a "native" literary scene may be harder to grasp if you're *not from here*. The creation and maintenance of translocal community in a city like Amsterdam can operate as a bridge, on or through which writers can continue to work and grow.

These communities are not necessarily more innovative than "home" communities, but the questions such outposts face are perhaps different from those faced *back home*. The very fact of our (dis)location engages us in a discourse of physical gathering in which aesthetic multivocality is embraced. One example of this gathering can be found in the publications that have come out of these cities, which span a range of aesthetic schools. In *Bordercrossing's* first editorial, Fiona praises the "extraordinarily broad range of writing being created in [Berlin]" and speaks about *Bordercrossing's* work to collect it. Some of the "locals" in its contributor list include Donna Stonecipher, Mark Terrill, and Emily Lundin—all very different writers. *Versal* has also been noted, on NewPages.com and elsewhere, for its aesthetic range. And in 2007, American poets Jennifer K. Dick and Sandy Florian began the blog Rewords, which invites poets and writers from around the world to participate in an online poetic conversation. In her opening post, Jennifer writes:

> I have always been a fan of the response poem . . . of seeing the spaces where someone else's voice meets or strikes against my own . . . in short, I adore the putting of voices into dialogue. Is this not really the history of all literature to date?

She calls it a "textual ping-pong": the gathering of over fifty known and unknown poets in direct exchange of words. Rewords and other publications from these cities seek to encapsulate the translocal: connective, open, and encompassing.

## The trouble with the numbers

The "numbers trouble," a discussion about discrepant ratios between men and women in literary America, may also apply to translocal communities and activities in Europe. A quick survey of recent happenings finds that Berlin's Poetry Hearings Festival has featured twenty-six men and only ten women since it started in 2006. *The Prague Revue*, newly revived in issue 8, published twenty-eight men and nine women. Rotterdam's Poetry International Festival brought eighteen men and six women in both 2008 and 2009. And though Alistair Noon sketches the translocal European landscape in "Translocal Underground," he names only two women: Elizabeth Bishop and Sylvia Plath. No living women writers are mentioned in the piece, much less as practitioners of modern translocality.

I have singled out Paris, Berlin, and Amsterdam because these are cities which have been (re)animated by the leadership of women. That gender has nothing to do with the successes of these communities may be true, and by pointing out this fact I do not mean to engage in essentialist rhetoric. My agenda, if anything, is one of a visibility politic: in that I think it is important that women are organizing communities, just as it is important that we are editors of journals and presidents of nations. As such, it is significant that three literary capitals in Europe are home to translocal literary communities organized by women.

Just because we're working here doesn't mean our publications level gender discrepancies. Even *Bordercrossing* only published half as many women as men in its three-issue run. But

I am reminded of Shari Benstock's corrective history, *Women of the Left Bank*, in which she describes a Paris more expansive than Pound and Eliot and a legacy greater than the Hemingway novel that tourists buy en masse from the "new" Shakespeare & Company. To document the efforts of women in today's communities is to counteract precedences—so that later histories may not easily marginalize them. If Paris, Berlin, and Amsterdam are contemporary locations of translocal literature, as these pages suggest, then they are asking how wide inclusion can be, how far it can go. And in so doing, they seek—however implicitly—a translocality that lives up to its name.

# Maria Attanasio

*responding to and translated from Italian by Jennifer Scappettone*

*Is there an expressive distinctiveness within women's poetry?*

Not in the 1970s, & not now: I do not believe in the distinctiveness of women's writing. It has therefore always irked and embarrassed me to be defined as a "poetess" due to the confines and the fences that this definition suggests: the delimiting of an ambit—the feminine ambit—within the one that defines *poets.*

There is no poetry reserved only to men, to women, to gay people. Just as, in my estimation, there are not—nor should there ever be—particular evaluative connotations, or particular expressive ranges reserved to feminine poetry.

Metaphorical or experimental, narrative or lyric, writing either is, or isn't poetry; whatever one's sexual, historical, or geographical affiliation may be: otherwise, women are reduced, once again scraps, exile, marginality. That is, literarily speaking to inexistence.

Anyone who writes is equally implicated in the unrepeatable singularity of creative experience: a silent and implosive interior cadence, which, *then,* can become voice, scream, communication, figure, differentiation, and definition of gender, of genres, of languages. But all this always comes *afterward,* and has nothing to do with poetry. "Alone: you with words / and this true solitude," wrote Gottfried Benn in a text from *Apreslude.*

It is also true, however, that artistic representation finds concreteness and specificity in gender identity, as it does in historical, geographical, and racial identity, & etc.; not as evaluative, but as connotative elements of writing.

As far as women's poetry is concerned—and therefore my own as well—such connotations lead a number of themes, points of view, and unpublished readings of reality to become visible after millennia of silence.

The body, for example: central and unavoidable—today—

in the writing of women. Eluding the false and sugary images of millennia of masculine literature, we women often restore it from the inside: in the vibrant materiality of an ignored, repressed, negated viscerality that has been passed over in silence in Western culture.

To write with the whole body, sex and intellect included: this is my *poetic;* and it includes as well the awareness of living in a dramatic contemporaneity of migrants, wars, mutilations, of a rabid liberalism that globalizes and starves; and in the midst of tools of information—and mental coercion—more invasive and pervasive than human history has ever produced.

Because, for me, poetry has been, and still remains, the singular form of expression in which everything finds itself indivisibly wed: my history, and history at large.

# Laura Cingolani

responding to and translated from Italian by Jennifer Scappettone

It is the word that no longer functions, but it has helped us to combat frigidity and violence. It has been primordial and often ridiculous, this dynamic fossil, that leaping and joyous feasting, depressing mourning ritual of a crone, outrageous screaming of a little nun. Disruptive, it has cracked the upper lip, has unearthed the black mirror clash and the dark fissure, has drunk the blood of your blood, has dug into history, has uttered the names of matter and of the body, and as the furrow became more visible its skin struck the paths of man. It became banal man, then returned as a keyword, self-conscious culture can create and then destroy. It is characteristic of her stock to disavow what she writes, but now, finally, now, she writes, reinforces her lipstick, sex more turgid and compact, a little feline and always ancient Egyptian. Adored, revered, craved, contemplated, fantasized, respected, denigrated, insulted, destroyed, decapitated. Every idealism of a certain importance is like a deceased womb and we know it, but even this is a breast still grave and startled, a threadbare old man still alive who watches us, and as you know, he has polished the fruit in the family album: the photos and various protests fill our mouths and we eat on top of them, because one mustn't throw wholesome food away, and this type of thing is difference, and like a pure red wine it is a ruby ruby red, a red sacred yet never divine. Ah feminism, ugly slut, you were even right, but you have made me so angry, you have made me argue with everyone, and I have split my skull in making in making you reason, but it's just that you were an account that can't be balanced, yet you have made me change so so much, and good or bad, you are part of every very strange design of mine and you are a pressing memory, a distracted motion, a precipitous stage; you are a powerful Popess, a spinster that smokes, a missing sister, you are a woman like many others: you are a sapphic

and clitoral mother, a pelvic and transvaginal daughter, you are
virgin, are anal, are a vertiginous, collective, avenging, pastoral
energy, the sleuth of a very deadly dull,

    but fundamental truth.

# Milli Graffi

responding to Jennifer Scappettone, translated from Italian by Milli Graffi and Jennifer Scappettone

In 1980, a big exhibition of women painters of the avant garde was held at the Palazzo Reale in Milan: *The Other Half of the Avant-Garde, 1910-1940,* curated by Lea Vergine. I remember only Meret Oppenheim's blunt refusal to participate, her letter pinned to the wall in the spot where one of her works would have hung. I remember her great pride, even her arrogance in refusing to be placed in a ghetto; I remember the exact vision of her own power, of her own stature as an artist, and the precision one could intuit in her vision of the complex life of twentieth century culture.

For me it has been a model of passion and intellect.

Feminism is the changing of all female attributes.

Sweetness is a pliant iron fist.

Beauty is tearing up ambiguous invitations.

Gracefulness is saying no over the telephone.

One's modest daily tactic is a never-ending act of bargaining and retracting and challenging—just like that of all my working-class and peasant grandmothers.

They constructed their determination day after day while fighting for bread, so that now we can construct the bread of our image.

Blow on the fire of inventivity deep inside the oven of a becoming  that is continuously changing: that should be our basic strategy. Tackle transformation with the most unexpected renewals of invention.

As a young girl, I thought I could change the world; I was very sure I could do it. I wanted to make it more human, and imagined that it would be enough to abolish the violence of men—and I mean men as male beings, the male gender, the violence of the ruling powers in the world, of the dominators, the presidents, of right-wing policy with all of its detestable forms of lies and exploitation.

Nowadays, I cannot help but realize that the world has not changed, that the dominant male gender is more odious than ever (and here in Italy there are too many women that adore or pretend to adore him).

Female attributes are a business. If you have money, you can buy them. And so, we can specify our tactics: never buy a single stupid thing. Ah, the marvelous network of a thousand wrinkles on Jeanne Moreau's enigmatic, solid, self-confident, silent face!

Our strategy must be to live the future immediately, not to let it be stored away in waiting, not to let it become a mere object of faith and enthusiasm. To chew on, taste, devour, delectate in parity, equality, independence—immediately. To enjoy the surprise and the panic and the wrath of those who don't approve.

Futurity is looking well into the eyes of every person you meet, intercepting him or her, and understanding immediately without wasting any time and energy if he or she is willing and available for direct contact with the future.

If I stop to describe the present, this present is already gone; I have already drowned in archaeology.

I push the needle of the present just a little bit further, and find myself exactly where my desire, my smile, my certitude are. And I live my future immediately.

Feminism is a different way of writing the present.

# Eleonora Pinzuti

responding to Jennifer Scappettone, translated from Italian by Fabrizio Ungaro and Jennifer Scappettone

## Italy: From the Margins

*Physicality of the speakable (Theory)*

If writing *with the body* has long been a modality of female speech aimed at subverting the male word, nowadays, as poetesses and as Italian poetesses (therefore tied to a specific place, which is still affected by traditional male chauvinism in attempting to access the "canon") we must write of the body, and more specifically of the lesbian body, with the intention of subverting a continuous form of silencing, of giving speech to the unspoken, to what has been silenced and what, even today, in Italy, exists in a shadow, zone of a substantial subculture. We have to turn our desire (sexual desire, insofar as sexuality is a modality of expressing the self) into the compass guiding our steps, the breath escaping from our lips, the act affecting an expression that has to become "common," "acknowledged," "familiar," existent, *without becoming domestic*. We need to be "wild" and propose an "irreverent" wording that is not tameable. In this sense, the poetic word must become meta-morphosis of the very act of being, and existing everywhere: existing thus in language as an unlimited space. We have to place ourselves at the center of the poetic act so that this becomes a "usual" and recreative act, in a continuous inequality with the Self and with the word, which is not a metaphysics of being, but a physics of being. I want a word that is "fi-si-ca," a word that is "fica," which writes me, and which I write.[1]

*Cartography of the un (in)-speakable (praxis)*

Being and existing in the unspeakable as an act of resistance and observation that, from the margin, becomes the center of the margin. It's necessary, especially in Italy, for lesbian women to gain access to academic institutions (still closed, for example, to gay and lesbian studies: in Italy there is no chair or department dedicated to this), producing knowledge, affecting the culture-making process against any culture-shaping "ism" of academic knowledge as institutional power acting upon a minority subject. Women, poets, Italian feminist scholars, and lesbian-feminists must look up and beyond the perimeters of a professional precariousness that leads to the fragmentation of forces. We need a plan that creates synapses, and that continually collapses upon its own meanings, taking, retaining, and releasing. A web-zone that establishes nodes. We need a particularity that is not part of, but that moves between the inside and the outside of, the self and the other. That is not "personalization," but a clear act of incidence/occurrence. If I recognize you, I recognize my-self. And the poetic word must be lava, spit, trama (woof/story). To bring toward speech the un-speakable, the feminine sex, which by tradition (especially in Italy) has not spoken with the language of desire's physicality, fearing an ostracism exerted a priori, which relegated Eros to pornography. We must become "obvious," in anti-canonical acts of tradition. *We must create text out of our sex.*

*Text*

I quivered still.
Enough, the sound:
the peal of your voice
by phone
became rumble, thunder.
And in the deep cavities the blood,
and the lava
     of the pussy gushing and
howling at you. Eating herself.

I have never had you:
not even a caress
to blow a little breath
        over the fire.


1. Translator's note: "fica" is a common slang term for female genitals
and therefore in chauvinist language, in a derogatory sense that yokes
woman to her biological sex, it has come to stand for a female in general.
Early on in this text the author uses the term "poete" rather than the male
plural form "poeti," declining as well to recur to the traditional feminine
term "poetesse." We have chosen to translate this using the uncommon
term "poetesses" to mark the difference.

# Etela Farkašová

*What does it mean to be a woman writer, poet, playwright in Slovakia? In general, what are the working and living conditions of women authors in your country?*

I believe that the material circumstances of women writers in Slovakia are comparable to those of their male colleagues. There is a lack of adequate institutional support on the part of the state (subsidies are restricted). We have no tradition of financial sponsorship for the publication of original fiction. All of this is further aggravated by the prevailing attitude towards books and cultural production in general as commodities, even though the number of copies sold rarely coincides with the quality of the book on sale. Unfortunately, social circumstances offer few incentives for the possibility of men or women to work as freelancers so that they could devote themselves to creative work. However, women authors are de-privileged in other ways, such as with their double or even triple workload. Women work, take care of the family, are socially committed. They have less "free" time in comparison to their male colleagues. Furthermore, there are fewer informal (literary) "women's networks." The lack of awareness about gender among critics and writers (usually men in places of power, different committees, etc.) affects, for instance, the creation of anthologies (there tends to be an over-representation of male authors in relation to women authors, which—at least in my opinion—bears no relation to any criteria of quality), the distribution of awards, the creation of various comprehensive overviews of the literary scene, and also the writing of school textbooks and scholarly monographs that deal with Slovak literature. In comparison to their male colleagues, women get less attention (regardless of the quality or extent of their work) and the evaluating criteria tend to be often implicitly masculine, based on male experience and world-view.

responding to Stanislava Chrobáková Repar, translated from Slovak into Slovene by Stanislava Chrobáková Repar, from Slovene into English by Iva Jevtić

This leads to certain themes being prized as more literary than others. I find it absurd that among the ten works chosen to be translated within the international project "One hundred Slavic novels," not a single one was written by a woman. This is bound to be an infamous Slovak peculiarity within the international context of the project. However, despite everything I have written above, there has been some progress made, both on individual—a move towards more gender sensitive criticism—as well as institutional levels. I find the foundation of the Biblioteka book fair award for best female author a positive achievement. Even though it is questioned by those who understand it as positive discrimination, I believe it is, seen in a larger context, a definite move towards a greater equilibrium between the sexes and a contribution towards greater equality/justice in our literary scene.

*What is the role of the relevant institutions in this field (societies, organizations, civil initiative, media etc.)?*

Due to limited space, I would just like to mention the role of special interest groups and societies. We have two such feminist societies: the feminist cultural society, Aspekt, that, among other things, provides support for women authors, and the club of Slovak women writers, Femina, which I co-founded, and whose main goal it is to organize readings and stimulate discussion of the work of Slovak women writers and the publication of anthologies of their work (so far we have managed to successfully publish two Austrian-Slovak anthologies, one Norwegian-Slovak anthology, and five Slovak anthologies).

*What, in your opinion, is the relation among the writing of women, women's writing, and feminism (or feminisms)? Does feminism have an influence on the situation in your country? If so, please define this influence and the level on which it manifests (in theory, in practice)?*

I do not think that writing done by women is the equivalent of feminist writing. There are many women authors that reproduce faithfully the "gender neutral" literary canon (along with its stereotypes). Moreover, in Slovakia, there are many women writers who adamantly refuse to be characterized as feminist, even as they write mainly about female experience and even critically address the issue of gender inequality. I suppose they are worried about being excluded from the literary community, which refuses to see feminism as a serious political and reflective activity. And yet the influence of feminism continues to grow both on theoretical and practical levels, which affects the understanding and the possible resolution of the already mentioned problematic (just by addressing it). I am convinced that initiatives such as these will change things for the better.

# Anna Grusková

responding to Stanislava Chrobáková Repar, translated from Slovak into Slovene by Alenka Šalej, from Slovene into English by Iva Jevtić

*What does it mean to be a woman writer, poet, playwright in Slovakia? In general, what are the working and living conditions of women authors in your country?*

I am primarily a playwright and have been trying to do art as a "full-time job" for the past four years. My background is in theater studies and I also have some practical experience in theater, so apart from my own writing I also translate academic texts and foreign plays, write for newspapers and journals, and I have also begun to direct. All of these are non-commercial activities. On top of this, I also share household responsibilities with my nearly grown-up son and a rather busy husband, which I also count as work. I am currently waiting for the reply to my application for a year-long writing stipend. If I get it, I will be able to write a novel that I have been working on and whose fragments I have been sporadically writing into my computer over a long period of time; if not, I will have to stop "freelancing" since I cannot make a living this way. Many authors, both male and female, are in a similar situation, probably not only in Slovakia but also in those countries with bigger markets, unless, of course, they decide to write commercial literature.

*What is the role of the relevant institutions in this field (societies, organizations, civil initiative, media etc.)?*

Literature produced by women has been supported by the strong publishing activities of the women's interest group Aspekt. Contemporary Slovak playwrights have been taken active care of by the Theater Institute of the Slovak Academy of Sciences. It organizes an open competition for best play, publishes texts, organizes the festival New Drama, theatre workshops, and readings. Compared to the past, this has been a huge step forward. However, there is no adequate system of support for original Slovak productions; there are very few stipends and they are meager and often awarded in a non-transparent way.

*What, in your opinion, is the relation among the writing of women, women's writing, and feminism (or feminisms)? Does feminism have an influence on the situation in your country? If so, please define this influence and the level on which it manifests (in theory, in practice)?*

Many good women authors have gravitated towards the interest group Aspekt in the years since its establishment. By providing a clear and respected space for publication, Aspekt encourages their contributors' growth, opens up new subjects and literary methods, and has both a theoretical and practical influence on women's lives. Aspekt's press, which has been active for over a decade, is well respected and recognized. I cannot think of a single female Slovak author of interest who is not in one way or another connected to Aspekt, and this is also true of those authors living abroad. All of them, however, do not declare themselves feminist, especially because, in Slovakia, feminists are still seen as problematic women who dislike men.

# Derek Rebro

responding to Stanislava Chrobáková Repar, translated from Slovak into Slovene by Alenka Šalej, from Slovene into English by Iva Jevtić

*What does it mean to be a woman writer, poet, playwright in Slovakia? In general, what are the working and living conditions of women authors in your country?*

I am not a woman author and therefore not directly addressed by this question, but because I have been researching this topic for a long time and have an interest in women's writing (and art in general), I will try and answer these questions. (I shall limit my answers particularly to the field of literature.) There is an abundance of women poets in Slovakia. However, on the surface, there are few authors (not only poets), who reflect the issue of their gender in their work. It might seem that this is not needed. I believe the opposite to be true, since those few texts that do address the cliché of the "feminine" (i.e. "feminine" as sentimental, emotional) are regularly labeled as "pre-intellectual" at best. At the same time, there is a general feeling that women have always been (adequately) represented in the history of literature. Thus, new readings that would place women authors in different (more "precise") contexts are still waiting for a change in the social climate, in which those of us who refuse androcentric readings would not be considered "stinkers." The working and living conditions of our authors, both male and female, are such that a person simply cannot make a living as an author. As far as the academic milieu is concerned, there is a "glass ceiling" still in effect. Of course, a restructuring of the family would also help, in the sense of sharing household responsibilities between men and women, as well as in the sense of loosening strict gender polarizations. We could show our children early on that life can also be different from the one that we ourselves are living. Education and personal influence can gently (and in this way more effectively) establish new conditions for men and women of the future.

*What is the role of the relevant institutions in this field (societies, organizations, civil initiative, media etc.)?*

In Slovakia, we have greatly benefited from the feminist educational and publishing project Aspekt which has distributed a wide spectrum of feminist ideas and has enriched Slovak ideas of "women's" art, "women's" thought, and feminism. Of course, it only enriched those who wanted to be enriched. Another hub of positive activity is the Centre for Gender Studies at the Faculty of Arts in the UK which has succeeded in bringing new perspectives into academic thought, especially with the help of its pedagogues and visiting professors. They are challenging the still prevailing stereotype of what it means to be a "woman."

*What, in your opinion, is the relation among the writing of women, women's writing, and feminism (or feminisms)? Does feminism have an influence on the situation in your country? If so, please define this influence and the level on which it manifests (in theory, in practice)?*

To be a woman author in our country fundamentally implies not wanting to reflect on one's own gender. Many authors, even those who do address gender issues (subconsciously?) in their works are treated as gender neutral "authors." Much of this has to do with the ignorance and fear of being labeled a "woman's author"—the term "women's writing" has so far been generally applied to the sentimental work of authors like T. K. Vasilková. Another effective deterrent is the fear of the label "feminist," since it is associated with a vulgar and distorted view of feminism. There are exceptions both on the side of authors (E. Farkašová, U. Kovalyk, I. Hrubaničová, and S. Repar) as well as theoreticians (S. Repar, E. Farkašová). As seen from the examples above, those not afraid of being "women" are those who have already looked beyond the "stale curtain" of our intellectual and cultural milieu and have dared to reveal the head of the

Medusa, which we have all—needlessly—feared for all these years. Despite gynocritics, feminist critique, and gender studies being established for decades abroad, in Slovakia there remains a fear of re-evaluating traditional thought patterns. I experienced this first hand when I applied for my PhD. Despite being familiar with feminism and holding an interest in poetry written by women, I was forced to turn my attention to a different field—in case I wished to pursue my studies not only personally but also institutionally. Our book market is positively influenced by the presence of Aspekt, which is publishing academic and fictional work, and is widening the horizons of women's production and our ideas of what it means to be a woman.

# Stanislava Chrobáková Repar

*translated from Slovak into Slovene by Stanislava Chrobáková Repar, from Slovene into English by Iva Jevtić*

*What does it mean to be a woman writer, poet, playwright in Slovenia and Slovakia? In general, what are the working and living conditions of women authors in your country?*

Being a woman writer is a continuous act of balancing on the edge. At least it is for me. Balancing between the need to make a living, to be independent, and the need to create, read, and write. Balancing between certainty and uncertainty, responsibility and pleasure. Because I chose science and editorial work as my field of activity (especially in the existential sense), it is also a balancing between research, writing of academic texts (essays, reviews), editorial work, translation, and finally, literary creation itself. I have learned to live with that, and through the combination of my interests and needs, I have in many ways enriched myself—but I am also aware of the other side of the story. I am aware that our energy is not limitless, that the authorial impulses limited to the level of intent reveal a certain weakness.

At the beginning of my professional and life path, I was naturally engaged, but also gender blind. This, unfortunately, also meant that I let myself be used for other people's goals and intentions, and I never even noticed it. It was only my life experience that prepared me for feminism. Sensitivity to gender issues is, to me, a test of social intelligence, for men and women alike. I do not see feminism as the domain of dissatisfied women. However, even if life were kind to me, there'd still be so many cruel fates out there that it would be impossible to remain untouched. The true cause of such suffering often remains hidden, since we do not understand the structures of gender dependence and asymmetries. We could say that in a patriarchal world women still merely "save their own skins," forming more or less resourceful communities on the basis of solidarity. We are faced with a paradoxical situation: the antidiscrimination legislation in Slovakia and Slovenia is, in many ways, far ahead of our social consciousness—by this I mean the awareness of gender issues. It is usually the other way around: the legislation trying to catch up with an already established societal need.

*What is the role of the relevant institutions in this field (societies, organizations, civil initiative, media etc.)?*

Minimal. The media barely even reflect on the gender issues or dimensions of life—in Slovakia and in Slovenia. It is the same with writers' associations, with ministries of culture, academies of science. They all support and groom the literary canon as a gender monolith, i.e. an almost exclusively male category. This affects the distribution of literary prizes and awards, the presentations of work abroad, the creation of anthologies and textbooks and so forth. The Tatarka Prize (awarded in Slovakia since 1994) has never been—at least the one in literature—awarded to a woman author, which means that the winners are exclusively male authors or theoreticians. The Prešern Prize and the Prešern Prize Fund (awarded in Slovenia, the former from 1946, the latter from 1962) have only broken with this trend 5 times and with 4 women authors (one of them was awarded the Prize twice). The system of distribution of stipends (in Slovenia) is equally discriminatory. Under the aegis of formal equality (with ostensibly strict criteria in place) the incomparable is being compared—disregarding the double, almost triple workload of women, the system is patriarchal and rigid and primarily a good alibi—basing its criteria, for instance, on the awards of national significance (see above) or the publication of texts in anthologies (!!!). This situation is duplicated on other levels also, for instance, on the level of authorial language or national identity. Personally, as an author living in Slovenia since 2001 and a Slovene citizen but also as an author who has so far written all of her works in Slovak, I am being (even without the gender aspect) discriminated against and marginalized precisely on the basis of my national and language identity, of course, in formal accordance with the rules. However, what infuriates me most is the coalition of rigid institutions and chauvinist individuals that legitimize each other's conservative tendencies and limitations—in editorial boards, various committees and panels, organizations and boards, etc. Since similar gender chauvinists also exist among publishers and translators, this helps create and determine both Slovak and Slovene literary production and the publication of translations for years ahead. As you can imagine this does not benefit women and their creative achievements (I do not mention literary quality here, since I take this to be a given, something already present). This can only be changed by enlightened individuals. And there are a few; however, not nearly enough to tip the balance or reach the necessary critical mass.

*What, in your opinion, is the relation among the writing of women, women's writing, and feminism (or feminisms)? Does feminism have an influence on the situation in your country? If so, please define this influence and the level on which it manifests (in theory, in practice)?*

This is a complicated question that should be given more space. I believe that feminism proved itself to be an incredible incentive to women's writing, and it has definitely encouraged the writing of a liberated "women's writing" [écriture féminine], as defined by the French feminists in the seventies and then further developed by American theorists working in the fields of gender, intercultural, and queer studies. Those who still believe today that women's writing equals the writing of sentimental soaps (whether they reject them or not) are hurting their own cause and reveal their lack of education. But, of course, there should always be space for discussion.

Aspekt—a publishing house, web-zine, and a women's interest group—played one of the key roles in this area in Slovakia; however, even with Aspekt, I find certain problems, i.e. various kinds of hegemonist tendencies. Personally, I would like Aspekt to be more open to projects of a similar or compatible nature; I would like its self-defense mechanisms to loosen a bit. However, I might be misreading the social status of Aspekt and its initiatives, and may be expecting the impossible: a greater openness and lesser degree of competitiveness in our own ranks. In Slovenia, feminist initiatives remain cemented either in academic exclusivity or in pragmatic (European) operationalism. I greatly value the contributions of the City of Women festival and the LGBT community in this area, but I still notice a lack of willingness to connect and join efforts—at least I see it that way. In our publishing house and our journal, *Apokalipsa*, we try to map the terrain, to distribute feminist knowledge as widely as possible within the social space, and also to cover the field of literature. All this from pure conviction and enthusiasm, without adequate financial backing or the necessary infrastructure. However, these remain only morsels of what is actually needed, more so because of their unsystematic and sporadic nature. And here we come full circle to our balancing act on the edge, the practical capacities of individuals—their energy capacity, the economy of life, and their priorities.

# Jana Kolarič

responding to Stanislava Chrobáková Repar, translated from Slovene by Iva Jevtić

*What does it mean to be a woman writer, poet, playwright in Slovenia? In general, what are the working and living conditions of women authors in your country?*

I work as a freelance poet, writer, and playwright. Based on my experience, I can say that in our country (probably due to a small market) it is impossible to make a living by writing books. As an author who, together with her husband, supports a family, I have to do a lot more on top of my basic work for us to survive. So I proofread, translate, write essays, do editorial work, every now and then I direct (I am a theater director by education). I depend on authors' fees, but here they are not paid regularly. Sometimes they are months late, if they come at all. This is why my female writing colleagues are generally not independent, but hold on to regular jobs (mostly in education) and create alongside their day jobs, when time permits. There are more freelancers among men.

*What is the role of the relevant institutions in this field (societies, organizations, civil initiative, media etc.)?*

I believe (and this, of course, is my personal opinion not based on any research) that the media has been going too far over the past few years in the glorification of the ideal of a fully active woman, a super-woman capable and perfect in anything she does. For instance, an artist who is also an ideal housekeeper, mother, wife, daughter (helping her elderly parents), and at the same time financially successful, while all of her life (from her apartment to her cooking) is adequately designed, above reproach, not to mention her looks. On top of everything, such a woman author should also be versed in the art of promotion and book sales. No wonder, then, that she is left with no creative energy for her basic work. Women artists who do not wish to succumb to such pressure and move away from the mainstream are marginalized and overlooked, as if they did not exist. They do not have a media existence, no matter how much or how well they write.

# Breda Smolnikar

*responding to Stanislava Chrobáková Repar, translated from Slovene by Iva Jevtić*

*What does it mean to be a woman writer, poet, playwright in Slovenia? In general, what are the working and living conditions of women authors in your country?*

I cannot say that I am not a well recognized and respected author among readers, experts, and literary connoisseurs in Slovenia, but ever since my book, *Ko se tam gori olistajo breze*, was a subject of a court trial, I have noticed that I have become interesting mainly as an example of a shocking miscarriage of justice. I have been both awarded prizes and persecuted for my books. In the eighties, during the previous regime, I was given a three-month suspended sentence for books that described the war. And then, in 1999, in a newly independent Slovenia, I was sued by five women I had never before met (two from the US and three from Slovenia). In a trial closed to the public, they accused me of describing their parents' romance in my work *Ko se tam gori olistajo breze*. Consequently, I had to pull all copies of my book from the market and settle all legal fees. The publication of my book was banned forever (in perpetuity) and I was sentenced to pay a huge fine for any copies of the book that might have been left in the stores (on one copy I would have owed 160,000 Euros). I was about to declare bankruptcy, since, because of these women, my assets were frozen. I fought my sentence for eight years in many ways: I burned my books publicly; I locked them; I translated them; I made CDs instead of the books I was forbidden to produce; I published stuttering and coded works. After eight years, the Slovene Constitutional Court declared all of the previous sentences void. Now anyone who wishes to do so is free to read my book, which has been described as a "masterpiece" by the experts (Slovene Comparative Literature Association).

I'm used to presenting my work autonomously, and therefore confidently, and throughout these years I have reached my readers and lovers of literature by publishing my books privately, at my own expense. And, of course, this takes money. I can only publish a book once I finish my day job, the difficult manual labor of a cleaning woman. I write during the weekends, at night, during holidays. Over the past few years, it has been a little less difficult: I was invited to Switzerland, where I am supported by some Swiss authors to write and create at the local convent in Ittingen. The Slovene Ministry of Culture refused to subsidize my new book, since I had not published five new books during the previous two years. Of course, I did have five books, but reprints and translations published privately do not count. Even the previous regime wanted independent publishing to disappear—an impossible task if your opponent is implacable, even with the measures currently imposed by the current regime. In the end, there is always the manuscript, and if nothing else works, you can still distribute it. No system can quash a person's dream. Of course, I make no distinctions here between men's and women's writing; as far as I can see, the men authors have it equally hard.

*What is the role of the relevant institutions in this field (societies, organizations, civil initiative, media etc.)?*

I have always been walking a path of my own and almost never deal with institutions that would only try to manipulate me. The media has been on my side throughout, especially during the years of the trial. It is true, though, that many books get published these days, and even the media have problems keeping up with this production and figuring out what is good and excellent. The state institutions, on the other hand, are far behind, not only in terms of literature but other arts also. They have no interest in real art. They function as power does and are only interested in distributing and dividing, instead of adoring art.

*What, in your opinion, is the relation between the writing of women, women's writing and feminism (or feminisms)? Does feminism have an influence on the situation in your country? If so, please define this influence and the level on which it manifests (in theory, in practice)?*

As you can imagine, my work days are spent far away from art, and the system in which we live obliges me, first and foremost, to support my family. There is barely time for discussions of art, for seeing a play, presenting a book. I have to do it all alone. Given this, women's literature and feminism are not significant questions for me. I do not separate art into male and female; there is only one art. And come to think of it, art has always had a hard time. There are many male authors in Slovenia who seldom, if ever, make it into the newspapers or TV, no matter how much they deserve it. They are not recognized, given awards or reviews.

# Nataša Sukić

*responding to Stanislava Chrobáková Repar, translated from Slovene by Iva Jevtić*

*What does it mean to be a woman writer, poet, playwright in Slovenia? In general, what are the working and living conditions of women authors in your country?*

I started working as a freelancer after the publication of my first work; I have the status of a person "self-employed in the field of culture," a status that brings some benefits when it comes to taxes; however, I have to pay for everything else (insurance, pension) myself. On the level of everyday life, this means I have to survive by working on various projects and get by the best I can. I write in the evenings or on my days off. In this way, writing literature is a sort of privilege which I can only afford when I steal myself from other work.

Another comment on the status of a "self-employed [free-lancer] in the field of culture": I would like to remind here of the problems that two of our best authors had obtaining a similar status (the only difference being that their insurance would be paid for by the state). For Nataša Velikonja and Suzana Tratnik, some of their more established male colleagues and the Ministry of Culture itself were put off by the fact that they both write so-called women's literature.

*What is the role of the relevant institutions in this field (societies, organizations, civil initiative, media etc.)?*

My book appeared as part of the Vizibilija series at ŠKUC publishing house (an NGO), which publishes works in feminist and lesbian studies and lesbian-themed fiction; this series struggles against mainstream production of books that are too expensive and generally do not deal with "marginal" topics.

As far as the media is concerned: there's the interesting example of a literary journal with the ostensible aim of promoting new Slovene titles; they rejected the proposal of the Vizibilija editor to feature new ŠKUC-Vizibilija titles in their journal. Their argument was that these books are of no interest to the general public. One of the more beloved arguments of homophobe literary experts is that homoerotic literature is too hermetic. An implausible argument not worthy of serious discussion.

*What, in your opinion, is the relation among the writing of women, women's writing, and feminism (or feminisms)? Does feminism have an influence on the situation in your country? If so, please define this influence and the level on which it manifests (in theory, in practice)?*

In relation to women's writing, I have to agree with Hélène Cixous, who claims that writing is a bodily process. I believe women should write about sexuality, about these infinite dynamics within us, about our eroticization. I see the need for women to oppose different forms of censorship through their writing, the need to write through our bodies and invent always new nuances of language. The more that we are bodies, the more we wish to break the silence about our bodies, the more we become writing. This is how we break the monolithic discourse of men and leave behind us a public trace. In this lies liberation. However, a woman's body is not a single body. It is not homogenous. The body of a lesbian is different from a body of a heterosexual woman. And yet there are many crossing points. Just as there are crossing points with other bodies: male, female, and transgender. I cannot truly define what women's writing is. I only know that it is important for women to write. I leave it to others to try and categorize it away into the narrow confines of a definition. One needs to be careful when forming this type of definition, since many questions arise here: Can we also speak of women's writing when talking about the writing of woman caught in the body of a man? Is this still women's writing? We should ask ourselves what "femininity" and "masculinity" mean in the first place. In what way is the sexual subject represented in contemporary literature? I find all of these questions very relevant to our situation. Anyway to me, all writing is bodily. And in the liberation of women's bodies, feminism plays a key role. This is why it is also important for the development of women's writing. It is important that there should be both feminist theory and practice that analyze and deconstruct the self-evident givens rooted in the heteronormative matrix and that also boost women's self-confidence and, in this way, nurture their creativity.

# Iva Jevtić

*responding to Stanislava Chrobáková Repar, translated from Slovene by Iva Jevtić*

*What does it mean to be a woman writer, poet, playwright in Slovenia? In general, what are the working and living conditions of women authors in your country?*

Dear Stanka, I find it difficult to answer your first question, probably because it is difficult for me to identify with the label writer, poet, etc. I dedicate most of my time to my academic work, even though, at best, academic work and writing co-exist with and enrich each other. I cannot, therefore, write about the "working conditions" of authors, since I believe there is a great difference between those of us not primarily dependent on our writing for our living and other women authors who work as freelance artists. The livelihood of freelancers is indecently precarious. I imagine that the decision of many not to become freelancers is, to a great extent, based on the unfreedom of the "free life," since, at least judging by the experience of some of my colleagues, most of the freelancer's time is spent in anything else but writing (securing basic livelihood, demanding fees). Given space limitations, I would like to conclude by saying that the situation of women is somewhat different from that of their male colleagues, since I am familiar with cases in which women get paid less for the same work, etc. Of course, male authors and, to a slightly lesser degree, with women authors, much depends on where they publish and what social and cultural networks they choose to move in.

*What is the role of the relevant institutions in this field (societies, organizations, civil initiative, media, etc.)?*

Both the state and media (with a few bright exceptions) ostensibly support art and the work of women, but in reality women's work within art is devalued and only tolerated if it limits itself to providing service. The situation is more varied on the level of NGOs and civil initiatives, since we do have organizations that continuously strive for the promotion of a "different," more inclusive image of culture. What they all have in common is, I believe, their firm theoretical groundedness and the fact that they cannot be separated from relevant social movements and activism (as an example, I would like to mention the yearly LGBT reading that succeeded in forming a readership/public of its own and has grown from a relatively small event to an almost carnivalesque celebration of "alternative" literature). The problem is that organizations of this kind cannot always count on the support of the state and, in this way, are often subject to control (for example, the journal *Lesbo* published quality articles in the field of queer studies, but was denied additional funds some years ago).

*What, in your opinion, is the relation among the writing of women, women's writing, and feminism (or feminisms)? Does feminism have an influence on the situation in your country? If so, please define this influence and the level on which it manifests (in theory, in practice)?*

I have partly addressed this question above. First, we should try to define what women's writing is, since the basic meaning of women's writing, or écriture féminine, differs in many ways from the writing of or by women. I believe most initiatives in Slovenia aim primarily at the latter, at writing by women, which is a good indicator of the social devaluation of feminism in our country. We still mostly limit ourselves to a species of cultural feminism: the emphasis on the relative differences between women and men, the emphasis on the positive aspects of femininity. This is also a sign of the depoliticization of feminism, since, in Slovenia, feminism prospers in theory but not in practice. The term écriture féminine originally refers to a specific use of language that breaks away from phallocentric discourse; we do not necessarily have in mind writing by women, since Cixous, for instance, sees Joyce's work as feminine writing. Joyce, of course, was an egomaniacal self-promoter, for most of his life serviced precisely by women (Harriet Weaver as his patron, Sylvia Beach as his publisher). This does not in the least diminish the legitimacy of écriture féminine as a feminist literary theory; it does point towards its political limitations, though. I believe the contribution of queer studies to be more fruitful, since they set out by examining the way in which concepts of "femininity" or "masculinity" get formed in the first place. One of the more productive segments of Slovene culture is the LGBT community, in part because of the close interrelation between theory, literature, and activism. I find there is no feminist "counter-sphere" (to borrow Rita Felski's term) of this kind in Slovenia, and we are fated to an unbridgeable gap between theory and practice, and the relative powerlessness of theory. But it is definitely high time, as is already evident in the question, for us to begin to speak about feminisms in the plural.

# Veronika Czapáry

## I Am a Woman in Hungary

responding to Zsófia Bán, translated from Hungarian by Eszter Orbán

I am a woman in Hungary, and the way I experience it is like this: it is hard being a woman in Hungary, if you reveal yourself. They'll call you a whore, but sooner or later they'll call you a whore anyhow.

The way I experience it, I exist alone and I alone exist as a woman in this world. Within the realm of literature, women are not any more gracious to me than men are. The ground rule is: kill or be killed, strike or you'll be thrown out of the ring. That is what it's like being a woman here.

I cannot differentiate between the relations of males and females towards me. Or maybe in one respect I can: so many editors, professors, and what-not tried to fuck me and took their petty vengeance on me PROFESSIONALLY because they could not. Women don't want to fuck me, although I'm bisexual, but they are envious, jealous, just like me. And there is no one to help me in this unsparing world, in the great fight.

I am forlorn.

Being a woman in Hungary is being excluded from something that the great drinking buddies, men, are not. I could give a long detailed list of this *something*, which can range from workplaces to the restriction of the freedom of speech. Here, women cannot actually have their say in things that concern serious games of money and power. Out of the 240 literary periodicals in Hungary, only about ten have female editors-in-chief. That's pitiful. And it is frequently the women themselves who are the most jealous of each others' success. Although there are steps that can be taken to ease this tension, it all goes very slowly.

Living in Central Europe is not a good thing, but I don't want to leave, because I was born here and this is where I have to fulfill my fate. I don't know how many thousands of years I've been single and for how many thousands of years I'll remain so, just because men consider me a crazy woman artist and are afraid of me or consider me too strong. In any case, they get scared. And the position of the peculiar oddball is not suited for a marriage proposal. And the women . . . I don't even remember when I last had a girlfriend, as they are as rare as a blue diamond; you have to particularly hunt for them, go to the clubs, and I don't feel like doing that. I want to find love the natural way.

Being a woman in Hungary means it is part of my everyday existential situation that, no matter what I put on, men will shamelessly give me the once-over and will examine whether my skin is supple from my ass to my tits and whether my bone structure is all right. Which means a pretty thorough look. A look a woman would never give a man. You look back and he still stares at the accidentally visible strap of your bra on your shoulder. They look at me on the street because they think I put on the skirt for them and they whoop at me if I ride my bicycle. And I have to watch those commercials and posters on which they sell female bodies, day after day. The whole city is full of them. Take it; buy it; here you go. It's more than food. Everything from razor blades to shopping baskets to shower cabins is advertised by female bodies in Hungary. Not to mention the innumerable adult shop and adult bar ads. On a basic level we see such huge posters everywhere around the country, inviting us to go to Tesco for our shopping, but how? Well, there is a female body wearing a bikini lying next to the food. Come, buy me, eat me: she is placed desirably on the center of the platter, beside the fruit and meat, all kinds of products, and there's a discount at Tesco. Abroad, the advertiser would have been sued long ago, or not even sued, as the ad would not have been allowed—because what is this if not open prostitution?!

But what is banned elsewhere is allowed here.

It's no accident that the average life expectancy is the lowest here in the whole of Europe. Who can bear this and stay sane?

# Ágnes Rapai

responding to Zsófia Bán, translated from Hungarian by Eszter Orbán

*Dear Diary,*

The way things are, you can't write a poem or a piece of prose about a contemporary writer because he'd get mad at you or jump out the window, his wife would divorce him, he wouldn't recommend you for any prizes and would make things difficult for you wherever he possibly can. He'd spread the news around that you are a habitual liar, a kleptomaniac, having men by the dozen, a rube, etc., etc. However, if you still had the audacity to do something so condemnable, you can be sure you will never be invited to another reading, they will not publish your poems, you will not travel abroad as part of a writers' delegation, no reviews will be written about your work, and you'll soon fall out of favor, just watch! As far as I'm concerned, I still consider G. B. Shaw's words the benchmark. Shaw sent a message to Sartre when the latter rejected the Nobel Prize: "A prize should not be rejected, on the other hand, one should behave in such a way that it cannot be awarded to one."

But before I depict the exciting, bittersweet scene between me and the already well-known writer—beware!—on November 22, 1985, I'd like to tell you what a naïve creature I was at the time. I imagined that the value of a female poet's poem is no different from that of a male poet's.

At that time, I still believed Virginia Woolf who in *A Room of One's Own* explained that we will become equal to men if and when we create our own livelihood.

Tralala, tralala, well, I thought, I have a nice little job in the editorial office at the magazine *Ország-Világ* (*World and Country*), so judge my work as you'd judge a man's! Foolish as I was, I thought they, too, agreed with Virginia and took the beautiful principle of Liberté, Égalité, Fraternité seriously, but I had to suffer disappointment in this case, as in so many others. The bleak experiences of recent years have proven me wrong.

So. This is one thing for which both regional and urban writers could always find a common denominator. As far as women are concerned, there is no difference between the two camps. Both of them turn towards us full of prejudice, with centuries-old condescension. They pat our heads and give us a kiss on the cheek if we behave ourselves.

*What is a poetess like?*

1. Frivolous, as depicted in Sándor Weöres' *Psyche*, but never as talented as her;

2. A little mouse wearing glasses, Hegel under one arm and Hölderlin under the other, her heart is a man's heart;

3. A depressed, alcoholic whore.

I tried to fight these prejudices. "I'll show you!" I said and, with murderous passion in my young heart, I renamed myself Láng Olivér (Oliver Flame) and there I was, shining on the pages of the most elite literary magazines in my male disguise.

Can you imagine, my dears, what an ecstatic feeling overcomes a girl when she receives a letter from, for example, Szabolcs Várady (a well known poet and editor), being addressed as "Dear Sir"? Or when Gáspár Miklós Tamás (essayist) criticizes her ("his") taste with biting irony in the literary monthly *Beszélő*: "How can our poet like a woman who wears blue shoes with a beige plisséed skirt? I think that would stir up a scandal even in the local bank of an obscure village in the countryside!"

I relished to the full those two, short months when nobody knew who Oliver Flame might be! But I had to realize that this was all nonsense, and that I had to become their equal as a woman.

The other day, I read that Ágnes Nemes Nagy (an important Hungarian poet) was a good poet because she wasn't like a woman poet. Brrrr. So should I deny my sex?! Is that what you want? Will I then meet your high aesthetic requirements?

Notsofast! And grumble, grumble!

A noted critic went on to declare the following rubbish—oh, I am not going to say his name, as my diary may be stolen and then I'm done for!—"unfortunately if a woman poet writes prose, she cannot write simply. She can only write things like 'The yellow puddle of light spread over the parquet,' instead of simply writing: 'The sun shined into the room.'"

So here it is:

THE SUN SHINED INTO THE ROOM at 5 PM on November 22, 1985. The snow started falling outside, which I found a little kitschy, when the famous writer leaned over to me . . .

You know Dear Diary, at the beginning I wrote that I consider G.B. Shaw's words as my benchmark. What I didn't add then was: I would if I was stupid.

# Aida Bagić

## To Dear L, about Who is a Woman Poet

responding to and translated from Croatian by Ana Božičević

> *the gal came along*
> *carrying water*
> *singing a song*
> *la la la*
>
> *the water spilled*
> *but the song's*
> *still here*
> *la la la*
> —*Sve pasiva,* Tamara Obrovac and the Transhistria Ensemble

Dear L,

Again, I'd like to start this letter with an apology: I'm sorry, I haven't been in touch because . . . but you already know I don't have a good reason. Except the one you're not willing to accept: that the time when writing long letters was polite is long gone! It would be simpler if you'd finally agree to get a computer, get on e-mail, and stop playing at "simple life." We haven't seen each other for months! I really don't understand how you manage to live without electricity, TV, or the paper . . . what if something happens and you don't have a phone or a cell? And why do you care so much that I write by hand? Your "simplicity movement" doesn't strike me as very simple at all.

Still, I'm writing you today because I need your help. I thought that, by writing you, I might finally be able to put together " . . . two pages on the position of the Croatian woman poet. Any aspect." That's what D. wrote in her call. I don't know who else I could talk to about this. At first, it all looked simple. (And it would be simple if you were here with me!) Two pages,

I thought, are a piece of cake. One morning will suffice. Or one afternoon. Fine, before noon I'll write, after noon I'll read it over, I'm sure to be done by tomorrow, Friday at the latest . . . and another month has passed in this way.

Maybe I haven't properly understood what it is I should be writing about. About the position of the Croatian woman poet? Any aspect? Should I approach the subject from my own experience or the history of literature? There's no one else to blame: I should have asked for clarification while I still had time.

If I choose to write from experience, the basis of the entire text will be very shaky. It's not certain that I can call myself a *Croatian* woman poet; it's uncertain I can call myself a woman *poet*. You know that I've only recently summoned up the courage for my poetic *coming out*. OK, it's true I'd published here and there, so I wasn't entirely in the closet, but I only decided about a year ago that it was time to stand in front of a crowd of strangers and speak my own verse. It was a very precious experience. (Which I would wish on you as well, because reading one's verse at the Queer Festival is something quite different from "fraternizing with the birds of the sky!" Sorry, I'll say it again, I really don't understand why you left and why you need all this.)

I still find it quite incredible that these very private *objects* of mine (remember, like in Slamnig: linguistic objects, toys made of linguistic material) could be understood by another, and through that understanding be made their own. You know my position in Croatian poetry is quite marginal. How many people, yourself included, even know that I write poetry? It is only thanks to Dubravka Djurić, the poet, critic, and editor of the Belgrade journal *ProFemina,* who had encouraged me to publish again after a pause of many years, that I even had the insight that what I had written belonged to Croatian poetry, though not altogether *visibly*. You read her text, but for that sense of belonging this paragraph is most crucial: "Although we could say that the poems of Aida Bagić are created outside of the context of the so-called 'Croatian poetry of the 90s,' they are, in many stylistic aspects, its invisible part and parcel. The author practices a highly aestheticized poetic form. This form is a recognizable constant in Croatian culture, established since the 50s as its mainstream."[1] Isn't that unusual? It took a critic whose point of reference is primarily Serbian poetry to notice that my text belonged to the Croatian poetic corpus. (As if I could only be a "woman poet" from somewhere else? Is that why you left?)

You know that, today, poetry, or at the very least verse, is written by many people. Children, young people, and adults. In their middle and late middle age. Women and men. Transsexual and transgendered. Writing poetry is a fairly cheap activity. It doesn't require much in the material sense, a pen and paper are enough, and a computer is not too hard to come by. (Unless we're dealing with someone like you, who "dislikes spending time with mechanical beings"!) Finding a publisher is a little more difficult. But a man or a woman poet can always publish their verse free of charge in the classifieds. Especially if they want to attract a wider readership. (I still don't believe you burned all your early manuscripts. One day you'll tell me where you've hidden them!)

I think I find it so difficult to write about the position of the woman poet (I know, you'd say this was really about the "power of women in poetry") because I don't really know what or who a woman poet *is*. Is it enough for a woman to write a poem or must she publish it? Where would publishing her poem count? On her blog, in the local papers, or is the real poet only one who is published in a nationally acclaimed literary journal? Is one poem enough or must it be a whole collection? Several? Are readers important? Or are critics, and where they speak about her work, more important? (You, for example, most certainly *are* a poet, even if I am the only one aware of that.)

Instead of all this guesswork about what a woman poet might be, and whether I have the right to speak about women poets, perhaps I should have sketched, in a page or two, a blueprint of a socio-politico-cultural-etc. investigation into the position of women poets in contemporary Croatian society. The goal of such research would be to clarify the social position of female persons publishing poetry in the Croatian language. Its purpose would be to develop a set of recommendations towards the improvement of the social position of all women, but especially those with poetic inclinations, in accordance with the national policy for gender equality in the Republic of Croatia in the period of . . . but don't you think this would be pretty boring?

Still, such an investigation could unearth interesting insights about women poets in Croatia. For example, the woman poet could empirically be defined as the winner of the "Goran's Spring" award.[2] A simple count would then be enough to arrive at an astonishing discovery: after the age of thirty, women poets disappear!

In the past thirty years (1977–2008), the Goran Award for younger poets was awarded to seventeen women and twenty-five men. But in the nearly identical time period (1971–2008), Goran's Wreath, the award for lifetime poetic achievement, was received by five women and thirty-three men. Thus, among those under thirty years of age, nearly 40 percent were women applying with their first manuscript. Among the lifetime achievers, only 13 percent were women. How did all these women disappear?!? Where should we look for them? We must certainly discuss this when we meet! (By the way, how come you never sent anything to Goran's Spring?)

How could we find out where the women poets have disappeared? (Except, of course, those who, like you, I know to be a little nuts.)

Only, this might be yet another poorly formulated question. Right now, I'm listening to Tamara Obrovac, who most certainly is a woman poet, though not one of the vanished Goran winners. She sings about a *gal* carrying water and singing—must be the *gal* is a poet too. (Too bad you can't even listen to a CD, as I listen to her I can almost see you carrying and spilling water on those rocks, on purpose!) Perhaps the real question is: how are women poets made? When they write a poem? When they publish it? Or not until someone says: "look, a poet!"?

We can talk about all this when we see each other. (I hope you won't hold out there for too much longer!)

Until then,

love from

Aida

February 18, 2008

1. Dubravka Djurić, "The Construction of Heterosexual and Lesbian Identities in Katalin Ladik, Radmila Lazić and Aida Bagić" in Blagojević, Jelisaveta, Katerina Kolozova and Svetlana Slapšak (eds.) *Gender and Identity: Theories from and/or Southeastern Europe*, Belgrade Women's Studies and Gender Research Center, Belgrade 2006.
2. Translator's Note: "Goran's Spring" is the preeminent award for younger poets in Croatia.

# Asja Bakić

## Being Small in a Small Country's Literature

responding to Dubravka Djurić

Do you really want to know how it is? It is sad. The way they want you not to understand things is insulting: as a girl poet and a feminist, you need to play stupid as you would otherwise play dead, in order to avoid problems. If they detect your brain, they will suck it out until it is gone and you remain silent. But first they will try to fuck you. I guess Bosnia and Herzegovina is not that different from the rest of the world. The problem is that it is smaller, which makes it harder to succeed if you tend to think outside the box.

If one is to believe the media, Bosnia is going to be the center of American attention in the coming years because Bosnian citizens may become possible terrorists. What about poetry? I sincerely doubt that anyone cares about Bosnian poetry, even if it has some intriguing political context. Even the people around here do not seem to care. And why should they? The mainstream literature in Bosnia includes some really bad and boring books, and it is evident (that is why I am writing this text in the first place) that it ignores and undermines everything that could shake things up and shape them differently, just like in politics. Bosnian female/feminist poets (all four of them) have always been the underdogs, and it is easy to imagine why they are not welcome in the traditional literary milieu. The female poets who share the same values as their male colleagues, on the other hand, are well received because they're likely to give interviews saying how much they hate feminism. Some of the female poets are ambivalent: they are too ambitious to fight for a women's cause, but they understand the problem that chauvinism represents. Others are just too bad to even try to write without an older, influential literary critic or college professor as a supporter. I could give you some names, but I do not see a point in that: the list is short, the names are mostly insignificant, as is the entirety of Bosnian literature. That is why this text is short and simple: it illustrates the poverty of our literary production in the best possible way.

# Aleksandra Čvorović and Tatjana Bijelić

Due to a rather negative attitude towards feminism in Bosnia and Herzegovina, only a small number of Bosnian women poets publicly declare themselves as feminists. However, this negative general picture started changing recently, thanks to larger public exposure to contemporary women's literature and feminist issues in the media. Also, many international and humanitarian organizations are increasingly contributing to a better understanding of feminist concepts through organizing relevant lectures, seminars, and workshops. On the other side, although women poets are nowadays present on the Bosnian literary scene much more than they were in the past, there is an evident lack of critical studies and anthologies of women's writing. The main reason for this is that the state invests very little money in culture and literature in general, so that the Bosnian literary scene seems almost invisible in comparison to literary scenes in other countries. The things that would greatly help to improve the unenviable position of Bosnian poets, especially women poets, are better financial support, an insistence on educating the public, and cultural exchange programs.

# Vesna Biga

responding to and translated from Croatian by Ana Božičević

When I received your invitation to write something about the position of the woman poet today, another word immediately came to me: *condition*. "Position" in a way presupposes a somewhat fixed point in relation to . . . what? And what not? *Condition* allows for the possibility of an entirely fluid shape, connected by tenuous threads to a narrow circle of readers, tailored almost to the specifications of some old-school romantic. We've nearly reached such a retrograde position, one that results in questioning the meaning and purpose of literature, and especially of poetry today. A position in which the dilemma of whether to publish or not (the impossibility of publishing is a separate issue), or rather of whether to write or not, occurs naturally. This "position" doesn't appear to me sufficiently grounded in reality, it's nearly virtual in regard to what we call subsistence, monetary reward for work performed, the space of resonance intrinsic to the act of publishing, etc. Given that the very act of writing and the need for it persist, we must conclude there is a certain sinewy "self-reliance" to what we call poetry today. Or, to be optimistic, the "indestructibility" of poetry as a need, regardless of all the aforementioned external circumstances that I will not linger on here, which gives me the freedom of continuing on an entirely individual level.

Here, I'm again faced with the uncertainty of where to place the "fluid," materially almost superfluous body of the woman poet into a more or less confined space, or a life in the "spotlight," whatever that may be. As concerns myself, I could certainly inhabit the former, and that would direct our subject or, if you will, my approach to the subject, somewhere between the four walls of consciousness and individual fate.

Taking into account my frequent travels, the walls of the room could easily be replaced by the train car I sit in between two cities, in a space fleeting or motionless like the headrest of the seat in front of me. This space can, like a bargain with time, either move or to all appearances stand still, depending on which point is fixed by the gaze. The journey between Zagreb-Belgrade and back, "and back again," seems to me akin to walking a line that connects two essences, two levels of consciousness—positioned between two cultures where writing interacts with the Other (depending on whether the familiar landscape beyond the window is visible, or becomes just a monochrome curtain the gaze can't push away to the left or right). This shift from one culture to another certainly leaves its trace in writing. Especially if neither of those spaces is experienced as linguistically foreign or different. Certainly, one nests more strongly into one of the languages, but countless bonds persist that bring the two together . . . I wouldn't say I sufficiently respect the pressures national bureaucracies exert on language, from this or that side, thus deadening it by excessive caution, rendering it artificial—at least not enough to allow them to walk into my writing space and perform their roll calls. I allow myself, or at least I hope I do, freedom in the use of words, although, of course, one is always conscious of choice, and rightfully so, so that defying the wardens wouldn't overwhelm and take its toll, quite similarly to their enforced "choice." I think one should not yield to pressure and intentionally nurture the differences specially, "work" on them, or insist on the similarities and affinities, but rather try to move freely between languages and take in only what finds its "natural" place.

I could add to this that the difference between Croatian and Serbian always brings me joy; in other words, words or phrases I discover as "new," primarily, of course, in Serbian, are often the most interesting or, to use "too strong a word,"[1] they're what's most exciting to extract from a differing clamor.

1. Translator's Note: "I was killed by too strong a word"—epitaph of the Serbian poet Branko Miljković.

# Elfrida Matuč-Mahulja

## Being a Woman Poet in Croatia

responding to and translated from Croatian by Ana Božičević

What to tell American poets about the work and lives of Croatian women poets? The question is more complex than it would seem at first glance. Not long after I received an e-mail with the invitation to write this essay, I also read about the project on the web, on the daily updated blog of a literary critic. One of the comments on the blog announcement claimed that an internet invitation could only reach less-established poets, rendering all responses irrelevant, unimportant, and thus beside the point.

This comment, in my opinion, contains the answer to the question of what it's like to be a woman poet in Croatia.

My opinion (which should be read as such) is based on the fact that I, too, am a so-called less-established poet in Croatia. Despite the fact that I've published three collections of poetry, one book of short stories, and a novel written in collaboration with a Belgrade writer, which won a literary contest. Despite translations, publishing at home and abroad, appearing as a guest on radio shows . . . Not many people know of these things and they are entirely irrelevant to the perception of someone's stature in our parts. Most people here would say that these are the kinds of facts less-established poets use to feed their vanity . . . although it's hard to define a majority qualified to pass judgment in a country of four million inhabitants, as many as would fit in one of the world's capitals.

Still, it's possible such a qualification is partly correct. I'll allow it because, as an individual, a person writing poetry in the Croatian language, I'm not terribly affected by whether someone imagines me to be an established poet or not. In Croatia, it's impossible to make a living writing, poetry especially. And that's a fact.

Being a woman poet in Croatia is the same as being a woman in Croatia. You have two options: to be a fertile woman to a man who will, in all his seriousness about the national natal politics, also fertilize on the side, or to be a free-minded, well-situated "babe" playing a sexually liberated dominatrix as long as age will allow.

Being a real, normal woman, with normal sexual needs (though in these circumstances we often wonder what those might be), a woman with a family founded on egalitarian, harmonious relations, with a job where she's treated as an equal . . . and with a venue for expressing her talent, or need, or affinity—for poetry, for example . . . is simply out of fashion, unwanted and unacknowledged. That is not likely to change.

Thus, being a women poet in Croatia is a fairly difficult, frustrating choice. Your psychological make-up is crucial. How strong you are, how tolerant, how well you can deal with lack of success, ignorance, and above all, how conscious you are of the role of the woman poet in the social life of the country and people you belong to. Those are, simultaneously, the things we can always work on, where we have leeway to improve how we express what we see and must say through words, through poems. Because poetry isn't just a love song. Poetry is the all-encompassing expression of a wholly conscious being in the body of (in this case) a woman.

# Darija Žilić

*responding to Rade Jarak, translated from Croatian by Ana Božičević*

*How would you define women's poetry in Croatia, today?*

Instead of the term *women's poetry*, I'd rather use the term employed by the critic Tea Benčić Rimay: poetry written by women. I would say that contemporary Croatian women poets write about the body, the relationship between body and language, word and thing, the quotidian, etc. I'd like to point out that they avoid politics, preferring to write about their "I" and about a somewhat autistic dream-world. They use differing poetic strategies: everything from narration, language poetry, utter disregard for the poetic tradition, to the need to integrate intertextual elements into their expression. In other words, the poetic practice of contemporary women poets is diverse. I should also emphasize that there is a strong push to establish a women's poetic tradition, with research into the collected works of poets like Vesna Parun, but also Marija Čudina and Dora Pfanova. This includes not only their poetry, but critical and theoretical texts about these poets, which influence how we view their work. As I am involved with feminist critical theory, I'm interested in exploring how women write about body/sexuality, motherhood, etc.

*The style makes the man, as the saying goes. But it appears there aren't very many people in our parts; are there any women? Or: has the poetry written by women brought a new sensitivity, in the form of literary experience, to our everyday lives?*

You put that very well—the need for a new "sensitivity." Recently, Kemo Mujičić Artnam made an interesting comment in the magazine *Tema*. As he read an anthology of poetry from the former Yugoslavia in the *Sarajevo Notebooks*, he noticed that 70 percent of the poems spoke about blood, knife, nationhood. That tells us all we need to know about the current zeitgeist. I think women authors much more significantly undermine the national(ist) discourse, they are more sensitive to "difference," and the themes they investigate are closer to the everyday. Generally, they don't crow about the spirit of the nation, writing instead about the body, motherhood, etc. For example, Tanja Gromača has exceptional social sensitivity, and her novel *Black* entwines in an incredibly poetic manner both race and class issues. Radenko Vadanjel, a somewhat neglected author, offers in his *Diary of a Deadbeat* an exquisite poetry of the quotidian, in contrast with the depthless narrative so endemic to our writers. Those are just some examples. I should also say that his lyrical "I" is extremely sensitive, so I certainly can't accept some feminists' claim that female authorship is sufficient to establish "sensitivity." That fact alone doesn't guarantee literary quality. It's interesting to note that Belgrade's AŽIN collective, moderated by the distinguished theorist Dubravka Djurić, attracts young women poets who are not interested in poetry as an autistic act; rather, they are interested in collaborating, encouraging one another, learning. In this way, they deepen their sensitivity, work on the quality of their writing, learn theory. That should be a significant incentive to our local poets.

Originally published in *Knjigomat*, October 18, 2007.

# Dubravka Djurić

# Notes about Feminism, Poetry, and Transition in Serbia

*translated from Serbian by Nada Harbaš*

*The marginalization of poetry and the disintegration of SFRY*

Poetry was for a long time a marginalized genre in Serbia. But this was not specific to Serbia. Who reads poetry today? Who buys poetry collections? Yet in Serbia this marginalization occurred in specific social circumstances, particularly after 1991 and the disintegration of the multicultural Socialist Federal Republic of Yugoslavia (SFRY), a dissolution carried out in bloody wars in which Serbia, of course, "did not take part," as leading politicians of Milosevic's Serbia of the 1990s used to repeat. Wars were waged so that one stratum of the old-new political elite could preserve power and gain economic wealth, which would have been impossible in peacetime conditions. Parallel and tightly conjoined with these events was the homogenization of former Yugoslav nations. New states emerged in which the notion of nation came to be redefined. From the linguistic community of the former "Serbo-Croatian language," lines of demarcation were drawn around newly emerged (and still emerging) languages (Serbian, Croatian, Bosnian, and, the latest, Montenegrin). Language and literature became important in defining national literatures, as literature had power to represent relevant identificational matrices in the new political-economic-cultural conditions of transition. Prior to these transitions, the national identities of Yugoslav cultures were defined in the frameworks of a common multicultural socialist state, i.e. in the state-political framework of a Yugoslav community of "nations and nationalities," as it was spoken of at that time. As this multicultural community, or communities, disintegrated, national post-socialist states emerged.

*A look back: autonomy of literature in socialism*

At the end of the 1940s, political turnover—away from the Soviet Union's influence, and towards the West—also marked a new way of defining the sphere of literature within the framework of Yugoslav socialism. Literature became increasingly defined as an autonomous and unique sphere, in which only artistic values mattered. This universalism privileged the discursive positions of the male subject. To the degree women successfully adopted this discursive position in their writing, they were present on the poetic scene, but always marginally.

*Poetry in socialism and women poets*

During Yugoslav socialism, especially during the increasingly liberal 1970s and 1980s, there was a large poetic scene. The sphere of poetry was traditionally defined as that of an expressive male subject and being a poet was a socially respectable activity. Literature and poetry were important to socialist society. While literature was, on the one hand, defined as a space of artistic freedom, it was still supervised and controlled because it was thought to have an important role in the construction of socialist subjects. This control was not always visible and direct. For instance, poetry in socialism was to deal with the concerns of the Yugoslav nations, of a working class (socialist) society. But later, the notion of the nation slid easily into the nationalist discourse that celebrates and constructs national fundamentalism (Serbs, Croats, Slovenes, or Muslims). The politicians knew this. So, at moments they would encourage nationalism in literature. And at other moments, they would punish writers and might put them in prison.

Although socialism proclaimed equality of sexes, and there were more women poets on the scene than before the Second World War, especially after 1970, their status was still marginal. In Serbia, the 1980s were the most plural in terms of actual poetic models and in the number of active urban women poets. However, anthologies published at that time show that anthologists (men, of course) always put them on the margins of dominant groups, or included them very selectively, if at all. Because, of course, although nobody ever spoke about it, it was understood, and is still understood, that women poets can never create top-notch artistic value.

*Feminism in socialism*

During the 1970s, SFRY, as a relatively emancipated and open socialist society, allowed the formation of feminist groups. Feminist groups were strong, especially in Zagreb (Croatia.) My friend, a feminist from Belgrade who remembers that time, says: "They were theoretically stronger; we learned from them." These groups were both elite and marginal, similar to other new artistic practices such as conceptual art, new media, and performance, practices that were possible only in the controlled space of student cultural centers, established during the 1970s after the 1968 student upheavals.

*From late socialism toward post-socialism*

In Yugoslav poetries in the late 1980s, melancholic retro postmodernism became dominant. (When I write "Yugoslav poetries," I remember how I laughed, when, in the late 1980s or early 1990s, I watched an episode of an American criminal series in which one policeman explains to another that their case is as complicated as "Yugoslav literatures.") This dominant retro style was a return to premodern and early modernist forms and topics. During the 1990s in Serbia, this dominant style rejected urban poetics and almost exterminated them. Since the 1990s, urban culture, with its (mostly, although not always) political, antiwar connotations has been revitalized.

*Feminism, literature, and postsocialism*

In the early 1990s, numerous feminist organizations were established in Serbia. These organizations were financially enabled by western foundations. In the mid-1990s, a number of women poets, many born around the year 1960, from Belgrade, Novi Sad, and Vršac, participated in and formed their own feminist groups. They wrote urban, emancipated poetry and educated themselves in feminism. But the dominant literary scene still remained saturated with misogyny and was distinctly antifeminist.

The most important NGO institutions for theoretical feminist discourse and the feminist writing scene were the magazine *ProFemina*, the Center for Women's Studies and Communications, and the feminist theoretical magazine *Ženske studije*, later renamed *Genero*. Female literary critics associated with the Center for Women's Studies dealt mostly with prose written by women and discussed the reasons why women writers were marginal to the contemporary literary canon. Women prose authors had an ambivalent attitude towards this critical attention. To declare that one is a feminist, or to be declared so by someone else, makes it more difficult to have a place in dominant national literature scenes. And yet, the attention of critics associated with the Center and *ProFemina* spoke to the relevance of feminism in these writer's work, a relevance that was not easy for them to renounce.

*Feminism and poetry*

The position of mainstream women poets towards feminism is interesting. Many entirely reject feminism, although they often write in a female first person voice and explore topics seen as female or feminine. Still, theoretical discussions about women's writing and literature have been so ubiquitous since the 1990s that they are impossible to avoid, and it has become necessary to at least be in conversation with these ideas. Some women writers will advocate feminist ideas for a short time, particularly when they have institutional support, but when institutional support wanes, they abandon their feminist positions. Feminist poetry critics almost do not even exist in Serbia, although there are female critics who discuss feminism.

Since 2000, feminist organizations have been primarily concerned with strengthening women's economic situation. This has been accompanied by an interest in exploring the ways in which literature may raise awareness of particular issues, whether economic issues or those related to feminist or gay and lesbian writers. At the same time, women's studies has been transformed from an activist project into a project exclusively associated with university discourse. This has meant that feminist studies of literature in Belgrade, very important during the 1990s, have become marginal again. Mainstream culture remains intolerant towards feminist opuses, if and when there are any. Currently, feminist approaches do still enter the university, although it requires a lot of hard work, especially in Serbian Language and Comparative Literature departments. More considerable breakthroughs have been made in the English and American Language and Literature departments, especially in the town of Novi Sad, in the north of Serbia.

It is a field of compromise, the field of critical response to women's writing, and one encounters both mainstream (antifeminist, mostly male) critics and feminist women critics. Feminist women critics, as I have already mentioned, gave necessary support to women prose writers, whose work was also already visible in the mainstream. And yet, feminist prose writing as a category almost does not exist, except in the practice of a single feminist prose author, whose work remains, inexplicably, beyond the interest of feminist women critics. It should also be said that feminist institutions (all of which were NGOs) were not capable of getting feminist prose writing to be a part of the dominant literary scene. And *ProFemina* magazine, which played such an important role in articulating female literary scenes, has barely survived since 2000, when financial support from international foundations vanished. This says a lot about the attitude of Serbian society toward such a project.

*New generation of women poets*

The end of the twentieth and beginning of the twenty-first century has been marked in Serbia by the appearance of a new generation of poets born after the year 1974, in which women poets dominate. This generation remains invisible, since for the first time in history, women poets are numerically dominant. Simultaneously, and unfortunately, urban women poets of former generations are almost disappearing from the scene. They either stop writing altogether or begin writing prose. Poetry writing has turned into an impossible activity, work done in vain, of interest to no one.

It often seems as if women poets have three choices in their work, all of which carry political connotations. There is the folk and/or Orthodox tradition, in which the female voice is that of the shepherdess, mother, fairy, holy bride, and sometimes that of the holy virago. This tradition is antimodern and writing in Serbia is more or less consistently steeped in this tradition. The second tendency is more dominant/mainstream and somewhat more emancipated. It reemerged around 2000 and is an urban, colloquial poetry in narrative form. This type of poetry uses "transparent language" and features a (pseudo) confessional female voice. The third tendency is represented by the women authors gathered around the AWIN (Association for Women's Initiative) School of Poetry and Theory. While urban poetry mainly excludes radical (experimental) poetic practices, this group includes them. When this educational project began in 1997, it began as a fusion of lyric and radical impulses. After 2000, many writers in this group developed complicated textual practices as they came under the influence of American language poetry, Russian Cubo-Futurism, Italian Futurism, Yugoslav Zenitism, and French ecriture feminine.

The group of younger poets in AWIN, who gathered on my initiative in 1997, started their educational project within the Center for Women's Studies and Communication. The Center for Women's Studies and Communication was an educational project that included feminist activists as lecturers, such as feminists from Belgrade University, a few critics interested in feminism, and also a few writers. At a certain moment, most of the lecturers wanted to concentrate more on university discourse and work more specifically with students, instead of with women of many different generations and levels of education. So the activists separated and formed their own organization: The Association for Women's Initiative. At the same time, we created the poetic feminist project known today as AWIN School of Poetry and Theory. This school, however, is considered to be of marginal importance to many feminist groups. The problem probably lies in, among other things, the radicality of poetic procedures practiced, which remain unacceptable to the larger feminist project. The School survives thanks to the persistence of its contributors, who have continued their work despite difficult group dynamics, minimal and sometimes no financial support, and a general hostility from mainstream culture towards experimental practices.

It is from this context that one of the most relevant contemporary poetic formations in Serbia for the generation of poets born after 1974 appeared. The paradox is that, although AWIN's poetic formation unexpectedly became immediately visible and relevant to the dominant culture (most poets got their first books of poetry, and sometimes their second, published by state publishers), it remains invisible on the feminist scene. My guess is that feminist poetry was possible in Serbia precisely because poetry is a marginal genre. And there is not much feminist prose precisely because prose is an important genre that constructs postsocialist national identities and their narratives.

*Anthologies*

Several anthologies have been published since 2000. Anthologies edited by men within the dominant culture primarily construct and display the poetic scene as exclusively or dominantly male and reflect conservative impulses both poetic and political. The dominant scene nurtures poetry that questions nothing, that is moderate, refined: a postsocialist academicism. In this work, machismo is allowed and feminism is scorned. If a woman writer in these anthologies has at one point defined herself as feminist, this feminism is considered by the mainstream culture as secondary, or ancillary, to her poetry—since the anthology is, of course, about "good poetry" (we all know what good poetry is!) and has nothing to do with feminism.

But at the same time, there are several female poetry anthologies. These are edited by women and collect urban and experimental poetry by women. Feminist frameworks made such anthologies possible, although they are conceptually quite different. *ProFemina* is again a relevant reference, as the magazine and institution that enabled articulation of a female poetry scene, and at the same time raised consciousness about female writers' problems in a male-dominated culture. The first anthology, *Mačke ne idu u raj* (*Cats Don't Go to Heaven*; 2000), edited by the poet and former editor of *ProFemina*, Radmila Lazić, collects urban women poets born between the 1930s and early 1970s. This project includes not only writers who are part of the dominant tradition of urban Serbian poetry but also a Yugoslav Hungarian poet and those who have, for various reasons, been on the margins, such as those who were part of the Vojvodina radical literary scene and those whose poetry was too subtle, refined, and obviously female. The second anthology, *Diskurzivna tela poezije—Poezija i autopoetike pesnikinja nove generacije* (*Discursive Bodies of Poetry—Poetry and Poetics of the Women Poets of the New Generation*; 2004) is an editorial project of the AWIN School. Most of the poets included are multicultural. And for the first time since the Second World War, this anthology introduces poetics as a genre, since all the poets included also write texts about their poetry. The third anthology, *Tragom roda, smisao angažovanja—Antologija savremene poezije* (*Tracing Gender, Sense of Engagement—Anthology of Contemporary Poetry*; 2006), was edited by Jelena Kerkez, a writer who has been actively involved in the queer and transgender scene. She includes not only writers from this scene but also writers who are more mainstream and writers from the AWIN School, and even a few poets who work with an educational theater group. This anthology is also notable because it refuses to limit itself to just one nation, and includes a poet from Croatia who writes in English.

# Danica Pavlović

## Serbia 2008: What Does It Mean to Be a Woman Who Writes?

*Weekend poet*

To be out of official literature circles and to not want to be isolated means being inside the feminist literature circle, which in turn means being out of the educational institutions, out of magazines and publishers.

To publish in magazines means being recommended by a friend who is a writer.

Sometimes, it means to receive an invitation to send in work that comes from the editor–acquaintance, but never to take part in editing anything.

To be a woman who writes in Serbia means creating your own writing strategies, ones that are different from the retrograde tendencies in contemporary Serbian literature. This is usually met with incomprehension, concealment, or sometimes loud critiques.

Nevertheless, there are moments when your work influences others, even if it is followed by silence or even if it is excluded from critical and theoretical discourse.

To be a woman who writes in Serbia also means not being a professional writer. It means being an amateur writer. It means to write in your free time and it means that writing is your hobby.

To be a woman who writes in Serbia means working in the office from nine to five and reading in the evenings before sleep. It means meeting other writers on weekends so as to share information and write together or by yourself.

To be a female writer in Serbia and to work with other female writers means little opportunity to finish your work and lots of difficulties.

To be a writer in Serbia in the AWIN school means to read theory and write experimental texts. Also, it means that you sometimes meet writers from other countries, share experiences with them and take part in literature festivals abroad. Sometimes you are invited to the festival and you do not have time to take part.

But you can always play with the text . . .

Your own hypertext verses out of order die in understanding . . . inside the voice without diaphragm from the throat . . . verses appear automatism is stopped by the desire . . . moving together . . . verses outside the voice inside the text dies hypertext understanding . . . without voice automatism from the throat out of order appears desire . . . stopped by the verses outside the text without diaphragm your own voice . . . moves stopped by disordered verses . . . desire moved by automatism hypertext without voice dies inside understanding from the moving diaphragm desire . . .

# Jelena Savić

*politics*

politics in every field is about who can get a position in the institutions of power and then take some money from the state budget and to get as much of their family supported by this institution also. this is done without any concept of responsibility for the work or any readiness to learn.

*power*

it is well known who has the patriarchal power . . . it is the elderly bohemians who have their throne, are on every board, get every directing or critic's position. they treat poetry as a brotherhood and help each other. if you want to establish yourself as a male poet, go and have a glass of anything, although preferably domestic alcohol, with your fellows. you want to be on their mind in case some opportunity for professional cooperation emerges. loyalty is an acknowledgeable virtue. and after you show your manhood by getting seriously drunk, nationalistic, not educated, and sexist, nothing will spoil your tender friendship.

*dichotomies*

as for dichotomies, everybody knows that poets are inspired by the higher creature.

that a poet is a sensitive and sensual man, one who is not coping very well with the reality of everyday life, but because he speaks of the essence, he is forgiven.

he is represented as having a pure heart of reality given to him by the divine.

also he uses his words to express his stormy emotions. he is a strange and beautiful camera that is filming different parts of our so-ordinary lives and connecting us with our deepest emotions. his sensuality captures the most wonderful parts of our nation and he represents the essence of our glorious people's spirit.

he is a special kind of person, sensual, finding his inspiration in food, drink, and women. he has absolutely no need for any kind of education, which might interfere with his ability to depict the character and history of his people.

*hierarchy*

male poets have an elaborate hierarchy determined by age. elderly bards of Serbian poetry, especially dead ones, sing songs from our history and they deserve all respect and piety and should be talked about respectfully because of their important role of representing the hard life, the sacrifice to the motherland and her people in our proud nation.

elderly gentlemen in institutions of culture are the next in line.

and then younger poets are packs of horny not cultivated dogs, products of an almost twenty-year-long deprivation of any civilization and proper education, working to raise their position in the hierarchy with the help of the biggest fucker.

*history*

poets and history have, on the surface, a very subtle relation-ship, full of tenderness and mutual worship and idolization.

and as in patriarchal society, marriage is a sacrilege, full of violence that no one should know about

still, it is not clear who would be a man and who a woman in this constellation, seems that both sides are torturing each other in an agony of death. a relationship full of scars, leather, and spikes, but without consent on either side. they are in a net and hurting each other because they cannot release themselves.

so there are all kinds of poetry nails that stick deeply into the flesh of history and vice versa. sucking the blood of one another like decasyllabic poetry, sociorealistic romanticistic nationalistic war-pushing poetry and history full of names of big poets that made this kind of poetry.

but in reality, every citizen, every Serbian, is a poet, is a gardener of the best flowers of our highly moralistic, proud, peaceful people.

*economy*

poets and economy.

poet as homo ecomomicus is hard to think about.

pictures of poets as well-known roosters and easy hands in spending money puts poets in a really hard position.

especially in a destroyed and poor country that is in the middle of a transition.

elderly poets, if they are seen as real representatives of Serbian culture, of course manage to get positions in institutions of culture and they carry this role with pride. being a poet is not profitable, but it can lead to acknowledgement.

to be a real poet and not to be a drunk is often too hard to resist, especially since younger poets tend not to have any money, but if they do the appropriate work, work that follows the rules of real Serbian poetry as presented by some already acknowledged Serbian poet or professor of literature or publisher, they will soon be given a chance to publish and get some money to be a real modern poet, a proud man and a Serbian, one published in Cyrillic.

but really, education, especially education in literacy and economy in modern times, have no link whatsoever to poetry, and poetry should not to be mentioned in such sacrilegious contexts.

*religion*

religion and Serbian poets, together with history, are old friends. from the Serbian army's attacks on Kosovo, we learn from our big Serbian poets that being a Serb is to be an orthodox Christian and to cut the heads off Muslim Turks.

also we all know that poets are mediums, guided by intrinsic conditions, states, and emotions, or that they are born with talent, or some kind of special capability with words, or they receive some special enlightenment from nature or god, especially after sociorealism.

symbols of religion are very effective in that context, so a poet cannot miss if he adds some of this spice to his poetry. it will give it the potent taste of a real Serbian porridge.


*culture*

the culture elite of poetry is very much defined by patriarchy. to be a member of the elite, you have to prove to a members of this elite that you are writing as a follower of their work. then you have doors opened for you in every institution of culture.

so, you can write about everyday life, or about little things, or about what it means to be modern. but you have to be careful when you choose a theme. you can critique the poverty of life but politics and activism are not supported, since poetry should be a peaceful place, like a vacation.

and not too much experimenting or complicated words for the same reason: we don't want to bother our reader or listener

it is recommended to use pastoral themes, narrative structures, confessional styles, to use strict rules of not mixing genres, transparent usage where language is treated as responsible and respectful and serious.

if you are at poetry night you should sit quietly and read poetry when it is your turn, in a stately way, from inside your being, not communicating with the public in any other way.

if you know your verses without having to look at them on the page . . . perfect.

*education*

education is not good for poets. they become estranged from their true self. their poems become fabricated and lose their representative power.

the only thing poets should learn about is history. the late history of literature. especially Serbian literature. real poets are not to be questioned but appreciated as a treasure of our educated and proud nation.

*poetess*

context.

feminism is treated as separatism.

it is connected with NGOs and as such it is nonpatriotic and traitorous.

it is also connected with different nationalities and religions and, because of that, it is also nonpatriotic, foreign, and dangerous.

also being in an avant-garde movement is treated as destructive, for you are ready to ruin the precious tradition.

looking for change, avant-garde movements are always questioning assumptions. they are very often interdisciplinary and connected with philosophy especially postmodern philosophy. and as we know, anything that is connected with new tendencies in any field is asking for it, asking to be treated as annoying, indecent, immodest, obscene . . . as showing off.

*characteristics*

to be a poetess in Serbia means that you are a woman with a diary, deeply embedded in gender, an emotional woman dealing with irrelevant concerns, not at all political, and also ready to be fucked all the time. you are a sexual object and you should be pretty, tender, and obedient.

also, poets should follow the rules and use classical forms with rhymes, although it is tolerated not to rhyme all the time. but poets must follow the themes, forms, symbols, metaphors, and genres that are traditional to Serbia, and use proper Serbian grammar, use narrative, present well-known truths about the world, and present these truths as something like objective reality, use writing that is pure, transparent, natural, unmediated, and free, use counterpoints and dichotomies, but ones that are neither too complex nor too understandable, use stories about something that has happened to you, that is deeply personal, and then read it slowly, as if it came from the deepest parts of your soul.

however your work doesn't exist and/or is not treated as publicly worthy if some man from the institution of culture doesn't come and give it a blessing.

you will get a blessing if you socialize and/or fuck some man from some institution of culture. and, of course, if you write poetry that is nationally acceptable.

if you present your work publicly in any other manner, you will be put in your place by benevolent but patriarchal comments made by worried elderly gentlemen poets, laughter behind your back, and/or harsh sexist comments made to your face by your peer male poets, or uneducated critics will try to stick their pencil dicks in your work, or worried elderly poets will ask what is this world coming to . . .

still, there are some things that others and feminists can write.

about _urban things_ but not in a narrative way.

about global things, about poli(tical things, about activism

private things but not in a confessional or easily understandable way, activist things using swear words AND br%utal descripti%ons of the consequences of violence against women and minorities living in Serbia today

introducing sca.............................................ndal by questioning of poetry

mixing genres

on serbian/latin/croatian/english/spanish

without big capital

letters or withALLBI GL A TTE   RS WI     T H O U T commas grammatical

sem   an tic   al ru lesma      de

b y o t h e r s INTRODUcing her one words and symbols signs meanings

~~using~~ alignment as she wants, schedule words on a paper as picture, playing with their look and meanings, using fonts and colors, shapes

merging poetry politic philosophy/ poetry and prose, drama, film mathematics . . . whatever she wants,

she can use film ppt picture Internet as constitutional part of poem

&r

reading her poe*try on the surf*ace, repeating words, in reverse/yelling screaming, whispering, playing not from emotions, putting to the words separate pattern of meaning

*keep these arrows yellow and text in color, to keep the colorful meaning i gave them*

using first person ~~without~~ hiding, building male figures in her works, speaking in male gender

speaking about construction of poetry, un suing her and using her on a different way at the same time

where she can speak with a public about poetry giving their meaning a space in building it together

where she doesn't have to fuck or be cute or listen to stereotypical jokes from somebody to get a space

where she ((((can find her own (c)(a(n)o))-n and bu+ild it up /further building ,,,,,,,,,,,,+**********herself by doing that

where she can perform and not declaim her poetry

where she can write her one critic of her own texts

where she can deci*************de when p"oem"s stops when different p!eriods of writing begin and where does it stop

where she mustn't be***************** god Serbian+ god *Orthodox Christian ?god wo!men? mot*her and only then poetess

where her sexuality? b********ody?work can be loo*ked through discourses that suit* her

these places are rear..and****** exist mainly as *I know in a heads of few* poetes in Belgrade

unfortunately      *****

        ****

         ***

        **

       *


DONT CUT OFF OR SQUISH WITH ABOVE THIS STARS IF SOME OF THEM ARE NOT FITING TO THE PAGE THEY ARE INTEGRAL PART OF THIS WORK AND COURSE FOR EVERY MINORITY PLACE MUST BE MADE IF IT IS A WHOLE NEW PAGE WITH JUST FEW STARS LET IT BE THIS IS THE SPACE I GAVE THEM THEY HAVE A RIGHT TO IT maja solar

# Not to Be a Poet in Novi Sad (to Be a Poetic Object for Modeling and an Always Grateful Good-For-Nothing/Rotter/Wastrel)

> Someone, *that's not me*, is coming and saying I'm interested in . . .
> —Jacques Derrida

The poetry scene in Novi Sad is dominated by male poets. It doesn't mean that women poets don't exist (women in a biological sense, which is certainly a reductive definition for women), but if they are not present in the public, that means they don't exist as female-poets. Those few female-poets who manage to be a part of the poetry scene in Novi Sad write classical lyric poetry or, on the other hand, urban poetry that uses common language. Female-poets who write activist and intellectual poetry almost don't exist. Therefore, Novi Sad is poetically an anti-intellectual and antifeminist sort of town. This is sad because Novi Sad was once the center of an extremely relevant neo-avant garde, full of many postmodern poets (during the 60s and 70s), who constructed interesting, innovative, poetical and theoretical practices and made (represented, established, and sustained) an alternative tradition.

I would characterize my own writing as philosophical, corporeal, activistic, neofeministic, and experimental. As a female-poet who has lived in Croatia and Bosnia and Herzegovina, I use a mixed Croatian/Bosnian/Serbian language and refuse to recognize any "pure" language. I believe that there is no such thing as a "pure" uncontaminated language. Nothing can be "pure," there's no pure discourse because everything is interlaced and intertextual. In writing, I combine ordinary language with scientific and philosophical language, and I also use different graphic and visual constructions, neologisms, onomatopoeia, made-up words, words without meaning, etc. All of this further complicates the understanding and acceptance of my writing. In poetry, I have more chances for language experimentation, while, in theory, the dominant paradigm leaves no space for that. This situation manifests in a strict distinction between theory and poetry, and allows theoretical writing to express itself only in canonical literary language. Although Novi Sad is a multicultural center, it seems it produces language that is homogeneous and transparent. All my theoretical texts that mixed Croatian, Bosnian, and Serbian languages were translated and corrected into the established Serbian literary language and spelling.

The problem with the relationship between theory and poetry is present at all sorts of different levels. Poetry in Novi Sad is either traditional lyric poetry, which is quite archaic, or modern urban poetry, which mainly uses puns and uncultivated speech. Whenever poetry uses theoretical discourses, it gets discarded, and intellectual male- and female-poets become abject beings (rejected beings, castaways). Furthermore, there have been objections that my writing is obtuse, hard to understand, too philosophical, too long, etc. The literary establishment privileges short forms and an absence of complicated conceptual thoughts. If I write things that are light and amusing, I touch my audience, but if I present serious writing in a serious way, I'm hard to understand, an experimental, abject, female-poet. There is still an allegiance to mimesis in the poetry of Novi Sad, even as, in some other discourses, it is under question.

Dominant discourse does not allow me to be a female philosopher and a poet at the same time, at least not institutionally. Philosophy professors at the university are not pleased with my experimental poetic occupations. Poetry is not compatible with moralistic and logical academic philosophy. According to them, performing as a poet ruins the reputation of the faculty, and it's not compatible with classical philosophy. Several times, I've been  blackmailed and verbally attacked, reminded not to forget "who feeds me and who gave me my job," clearly put in situations where I had to choose between working under their rules or losing my job. Moreover, though I'm very active on the literary scene in Novi Sad, my position is still inferior to the male-poets, writers, editors, professors, organizers, etc. In these hierarchies, I was often in situations where my discourse was in tension with and diverged from superior discourses. It is obvious that I do not have the actual power to make decisions and be creative. For all my success, it was repeatedly emphasized that I should not to forget "who brought me here," "who discovered me," and "who gave me my job."

Activist poetry in Novi Sad is often not acceptable. There is a general opinion that poetry is apart, is detached and isolated, from ideology and politics. After each of our activist performances, the audience reacted very intensely. Some reacted with enthusiasm, but the majority with animosity. In general, no one was indifferent, which indicates some kind of unique cultural shock for a milieu where archaic poetic models are dominant.

I have not published my poetry yet, nor my collection of short stories (it grows dusty and grey-haired in my computer), owing to direct threats and the fear that I would become unemployed. Therefore, I am not a female-poet, philosopher, performer, and even when I look like I am, it is not because I deserved it, but because someone made me such. Only in permissive limits. Dogmatic frames. Only as it is possible to be a female-poet in Novi Sad and fit into prevalent streams of Great Poets and Great Philosophers.

# Liana Sakelliou

responding to and translated from Greek by Tatiani G. Rapatzikou and Liana Sakelliou

*Feminism constituted a powerful and creative part of the American literary scene since the 1960s. Do you believe that it has also influenced poetic/writing creativity in Greece? If yes, in what way?*

Feminism does not seem to have influenced the established, mainstream of writers and critics in Greece; but it is affecting a new generation of writers, and also university students who are finishing their degrees. They are writing dissertations on women writers and use feminist critics in their work.

*How often do Greek literary magazines publish articles about contemporary American female poetry? Do you think that Greek academic publications keep you up-to-date with the contemporary American poetic/writing scene?*

Rarely. Greek translators focus mainly on the American Modernists and several Beats, only the ones they are aware of. It is only the Greek professors who concentrate on the work of American women poets.

*What's the rate of Greek translations of American female poets published in Greece? If you spot certain inadequacies, what are the reasons that cause them?*

Very few translations of contemporary American women poets circulate in the Greek market. Poetry books, in any case, do not have a large market outside universities and schools. In Greece, there would be an even smaller market for foreign poetry, not to mention the more specialized category of women's poetry, partially because there are many Greek poets and translations of traditional English-language poetry for readers to be interested in.

# George Zarkadakis

*How does it feel to be a male writer/poet in Greece today?*

Call me bipolar. I have been vacillating between hopelessness and mindless tenacity; and being bilingual does not help. Helplessness creeps in every time I realize the degree of corruption in Greece, a terminal social cancer affecting bodies and minds at every level. Mindless tenacity takes over when I get some historical perspective. I then feel that one should keep on writing regardless, and that being a "realist" (whatever that means) does not help the artistic output.

*Do you think that gender influences contemporary Greek poetic/writing creativity?*

I do not believe that we ever had a sexual revolution in Greece. We are still a very patriarchical society, and individual liberty is a very confused concept. As a writer, I am more interested in describing rather than interpreting, so my job is easier because it is less ideological. However, there are some polemical voices amongst women and gay writers who place gender at the epicenter of their milieu. And yet, my general feeling is that most contemporary works abound with trivial stereotypes.

*responding to and translated from Greek by Tatiani G. Rapatzikou and Liana Sakelliou*

## Phillippa Yaa de Villiers

## Writing Yourself into the World

I remember being told that a woman has to do twice as well as a man in order to be thought half as good. It makes sense! Especially in patriarchal South Africa. These conditions are like the weather, pervasive and not easy to change (it's taken us 150 years of hardcore industrial abuse to alter the weather). I think women are culturally invisible except for the brief time when they are sexually interesting to men. They have also been silenced for too long. Silences and invisibility are the main themes that attract me; they are what I am exploring in my life and my work. Overcoming cynicism, apathy, and despair is the small hurrah! I give myself each time I make a new poem, essay, story, play, or script.

I am interested in people who want to change conditions for women, and I am interested in creativity, so I also like the many ways that they propose to make the change. Artists hold up a mirror to themselves and the context gets reflected too. For example, under colonization and then under apartheid, black people were constantly told that they were inferior. Guides and thinkers arose, like Albert Luthuli, like Steve Biko, who offered a different mirror that included us. But the mirrors of African Nationalism and Black Consciousness are tools, not an end in themselves.

Feminism is also a tool. I like to think of feminism as a sieve, compass, scalpel, microscope, drum, torch, oven and ele-ment. It is a useful tool that we create and refine as our con-ditions vary and change. Feminism completes the picture that humanity has of itself. It has been shaped to incite protest about inequality, engage advocacy for women's participation, slice through myths and illusions about women, and celebrate the contributions that women have made to society.

The powers that be want us to be compliant and ignorant, so it's hard to get to a good mirror. If it weren't for protest politics, we would still be in the doldrums of racism and sexism.

Sometimes it looks like feminists count the advantages that men have and call up the injustice via pointing to the numbers. But comparing numbers leaves me depressed and uninspired. Just because twice the women now have access to publishers, doesn't mean that the system has changed. South Africa boasts that it has more female parliamentarians than any country in the world. Our Minister of Arts and Culture (a woman) appears to believe that lesbian photography is pornography. We also have terrifying rape and femicide statistics.

There are contradictions in our society that are not captured by a simple numbers analysis. Here's a story that might shed some light on the complexity that energizes, and simultaneously tears apart, our society.

I wrote a play called *Where the Children Live* that came second in the national scriptwriting competition. The play that came third, written by a man, was produced and toured the country. On the surface, this is pure sexism, where merit was rewarded with money and a prize, but no future. Penis—one, Vagina—nil. Honestly: when we returned, all flushed from the festival, we faced the cold fact that the play needed tons of work to stage it. Here's why. The story was based on my almost unbelievable true life story: I was adopted by a white family under apartheid. I grew up in denial of my race and adapted to the situation by losing my African language, contact with my people, the context of history. I was twenty when my father told me that I was adopted and that I was black; it was during the 1980s, a period in the struggle where the conflict and contradiction of racial segregation came to a violent head. In my life, the personal was intensely political.

What I learned from writing this play was that lying and duplicity, which were survival mechanisms in my home, were also a theme in many people's personal scripts. I discovered that it was not even a national dilemma, it was a universal one. By telling the truth I discovered a community that resonated with my words. This milestone got me a chance to practice what I dreamed. But the thing was impossibly complicated. I had to rewrite.

The writing of the play gave me work for three years. How to extract the salient bits? How to make a new, easier play? I wrote a one-woman show, *Original Skin*, under the guidance of a white, gay, director, Robert Colman. In a very visceral way our stories intersected, and we created a work of which I am rather proud. I have toured it and I am currently doing it in a schools program.

It has not received very good reviews. In the context of African Nationalism, it may say things that people don't want to hear. As in the case of Theresa Rebeck,[1] one damning review killed the show, except it was a review by a woman. Ironically, the best review I got was from a white man.

I am not arguing against what American sisters are saying about equal representation in the fields of writing and what Theresa Rebeck said about theatre in the US. I am simply saying that the numbers game takes us only part of the way towards our vision of a free field in which all players get an equal share of support. This work is very important, the lobbying and the activism—the squeaky hinge gets the oil, as Malcolm X said.

As an individual, I have to jump through my own hoops in order to achieve my goals. In some way, the marketplace cheapens us when our presence on the shelf depends on the things we cannot change, our gender and our skin color. We write what we like, and how we would like the world to be. We create culture as we write ourselves into the world script. I want white men to be moved by my words. I want everyone to have access to them.

I am constantly inspired by new writers that I meet on my travels. This month, I attended the Harare International Festival of the Arts where I was privileged to meet Blessing Musariri, Rumbi Katedza, and Irene Staunton, all women who are busy writing themselves out of the invisibility that patriarchy confers on us. Also, Rumbi and Irene have created platforms for other women to shine. Rumbi is a film-maker and a writer who works with actors, writers, and producers, making space for new stories. And Irene is a respected publisher as well as a writer in her own right.

Working across three continents, with the help of the internet, Isabel Ferrin-Aguirre, Kaiyu Xiao, and I have created an anthology of African poetry to be translated into Chinese which contains my work as well as Veronique Tadjo, Fatima Naoot, Shailja Patel, Makhosazana Xaba, Joyce Chigiya, Tjawangwa Dema, and Lebogang Mashile. The men represented are Wole Soyinka, Kofi Anyodoho, and Keorapetse Kgositsile, among others. Viva the invisible made visible!

Because of the liberation of our country in 1994, we had an opportunity to change the world. And we have, in many ways. Meanwhile, lesbians are routinely beaten and murdered, with few consequences because the system infers that their sexuality is "non-African."

It was brave of Theresa Rebeck to speak about the obstacles that she has to gracefully leap over as a theatre director. Here in South Africa, we are fighting to breathe. We are not even near the door of opportunity that American women are opening for themselves through their struggle. You in the first world are the kind neighbors we can call on, and maybe sleep over, when our abusive husband beats us up. But we can't move in with you; we have to fix up our own house.

I want to change the world I live in. I want to be a better writer and I want opportunities to continue that work. I am happy to be part of a global feminist conversation: I think you are pointing out important inequalities in your house. In our house, the dogs are sleeping on the furniture and peeing on the food: marking their territories. We are still in the basic house-training phase of living with patriarchs and their ways. We need to hear more voices talking about these things: love, power, food, money. It inspires us because it reminds us of possibilities.

We need more platforms to share our work. We need to interrogate the platforms that are available: the packaging of creative products demands that people specialize; it's easier to market a poet than a poet-playwright. The system crushes our creativity. Locked into a cycle of create, package, market, sell, we can already smell the outhouse. As we kiss the face of our latest newborn, we can already hear the earth thudding on to the coffin; all that we now despise was once new, fresh, delicious, and desirable. So it goes with all the stuff that we make: if it only means something to the market.

Any Google search of poetry reveals hundreds of links of poetry by women. But still the sisters are not satisfied. It feels like our worlds are so far apart, yet the principles remain the same, and the struggle naggingly familiar. They want to be taken more seriously for their contribution, for these works to be seen as part of the world canon of reflections on the human condition, written in a million languages by the universal human genius. They want to be paid what men are paid for doing the same work, paid money and attention and acclaim. Women want their work to be valued equally.

Aha . . . the V word. (No, no: the other one.) This conversation is not really about literature, or politics, or theatre. It's actually about values. For values to change, it requires a revolution. Without feminism, this is very unlikely—imagine the liberation struggle without Biko! Toothless and incoherent.

And if we use feminism as a torch to look behind the tragic icon of Biko, we discover Mamphele Ramphele, his wife and partner, the activist who still continues to write herself into the fight for social change. Who else is out there in the shadows? I write to make the invisible visible.

In the hierarchy of needs, I want social change more than I want politically correct language. As a black woman transracial adoptee writer/performer, I live complexity.

*I know that our souls are deeper than our skins,*
*that love conquers all seasons of despair,*
*and the reasons why we do things*
*is not always clear. At mother's knees*
*we learn our first stories*
*of who we are and who we are meant to become.*
*I was cradled by a dream*
*and I am the invisible black daughter*
*risen from the ashes of fantasies to take a human form.*

Just that. After that, we can talk, we can dream, we can become the possibilities that we create.

1. womenandhollywood.com/2010/03/16/text-of-theresa-rebeck-laura-pels-keynote-address

# Olivia Coetzee

I write the way that I want to write.

It is rare that I find a mainstream publisher that will want to publish my work in my own voice, without telling my stories using the English-white man's directions for poetry or writing.

The cliché "this is a man's world," well, the saying may be old, but it is the hard-core truth for me as a young writer/poet.

For me as an activist and feminist, it is one of the greater challenges not to be silenced by "their way."

I even find it in poetry workshops facilitated by women, for women; that there is no challenge of patriarchal structures in creative writing, as these "ways" are accepted by a majority of women as the way that things are, and things should be. That I as "woman" should get in line if I want a chance to be published, what a lot of bullshit.

I want to start poetry workshops that offer women the opportunity to just grasp creative writing for what it is, and for them to use it as a tool to express themselves. But even then, it is a challenge to define it and, through that process, I came to the conclusion that, yes, language itself may be structured patriarchally, but I still have my own voice as "woman" and, through doing things the way that I believe I should do them, I am challenging this right way of doing things.

"His-story" tells the story of Poetry, which was employed as a way of remembering oral history and story-telling from all over the world in tribes and different cultures all over the world.

Rhyme, verse, prose, and all other forms of poetry have been a part of us, since the beginning of time. Some of the earliest poetry is believed to have been recited or sung. This teaches me that poetry is a great medium for story telling, highlighting issues, and raising consciousness amongst ourselves as women, but these stories were told by men to men and most poetry sites that I visit give me the same feeling that yes, we are still very much living in a male-dominated world, and this is not just with poetry or creative writing but in all sectors, that the numbers of women working in sectors may have been equaled through laws and business regulations, but the jobs they get are usually junior positions. I have not experienced anything different in poetry circles.

I would like to reach a point where all "women," be they lesbian, straight, transgender, black, white, mixed color, Christian, Muslim, Jewish, etc., are represented in mainstream publications. And that we are represented by our own style of writing, our own formats, our own structures of poetry that are not intoxicated by the patriarchal system's way of writing. That being said, it is very difficult to challenge these structures as most mainstream publishers are run by men who want a certain style of writing and, unfortunately, I believe that by writing in these "styles," women's voices are silenced. They have to tell their story through male-created poetry structures, never having the opportunity to just "say things" in the way that they want, as women.

Writing from a "woman's perspective" or from my own voice, the voice that challenges the patriarchal way of things, is important for my voice/story/reasoning to be heard, to be able to write in my own way, filled with emotions, realness, and matriarchy.

Even if it means never finding a publisher for my work.

This tells me that I have a long way to go as a poet and writer, that women writers in general still have a long way to go when it comes down to challenging the way of things.

This will be difficult: women writers in general will not challenge the way things are. That may sound harsh, but if we look at work produced, we will see that published women in poetry have submitted to the white man's English way of writing poetry and this is a problem because women will never be able to "speak" through a man's way of writing; they automatically kill their work because they need to write in a certain way and publishers can easily say that work not written in this way is simply not good enough.

Even when it comes to self-publication, our voices as women are not strong enough to be heard by mainstream society. We ask people in general to challenge the status quo, which often leads to very difficult questions about this patriarchal society and who are the "privileged ones" in it.

Maybe the challenge is not being a part of this system, but actually challenging it, using my own voice as a woman, writing in my own style, publishing my own work, using the world wide web to get my voice heard, and not being caught in this game of how we as women can be more like them, how we can be accepted by mainstream society.

As feminists, we have fought for this for such a long time that we have forgotten about our own voices, which are being shut out by wanting to be equal to them, fighting for the right to be a part of their system, the same system that is shutting us up as women.

I don't see much sense in it. Not to disrespect the work done by all the great women of my time and before my time, but I just don't see how equality in their society can offer women the opportunity to be, the opportunity to speak, write, recite in the way we think best, the opportunity to be heard as the "beings" we are, the Women we are.

# Myesha Jenkins

## An Aging Feminist Becomes a Poet Too

responding to Philippa Yaa de Villiers

"Wow, I feel like I'm flying," I said to my sister poet, walking off a stage in 2005. There was only a glimmer of the woman who had left her activist, lefty lifestyle to become a development worker, 12,000 miles from home. When I left the San Francisco Bay Area to live in Johannesburg in 1993, the most creative thing I had ever done was lead chants at marches and demonstrations. Moving here, where I had to start afresh, gave me the space to discover another part of myself, a part that has revealed the very essence of who I am.

With time on my hands and not knowing many people, I indulged my "vague" interest in writing by going to poetry readings organized by the now-defunct Congress of South African Writers. In one of those sessions, the coordinator said, "We're just a bunch of writers, getting together to share our work with each other." I was stunned because I'd never thought of myself as a writer. Within a week, I had written my first poem.

Then I started speaking them at those very same COSAW readings. And then, actually seeking out other readings where I could listen to poetry and share my own work. I was published in newspapers, magazines, journals, and finally in my own book.

At a workshop one day, I met up with some other women, complaining about the lot of women poets in such a male-dominated genre. Our comments were the afterthoughts, our performances the add-ons to the programme. We continued to dialogue when we returned home and decided to do something that really featured women. Along with another woman, the four of us created a hugely successful performing collective, explicitly because we gave voice to the issues and visions of women. Amidst this male-dominated, largely hip-hop world, we stood out and stood up for women. We were on radio and we performed at the national arts festival, at luncheons for government ministers, in classrooms.

That woman's poetry group, Feela Sistah, became the launching pad for my spoken-word career. My first poetry collection, *Breaking the Surface,* was launched in the same period, cementing my relation to the written word in the minds of many many people.

Now known publicly as a feminist and as someone who pushes the issues of women, it's almost as if my age isn't an issue. I am sixty-one and usually in the company of people half my age. I neatly fit in with the poets because, even though so much older, I started writing late in life and many of my juniors are actually my elders in the word. Because I am a feminist, I do treat others honestly and equally, which has won me much respect amongst my young peers; I respect them, so they respect me.

I often laugh that someone like me can be on a stage, performing my own poems for 150 people, not one over 30, and be appreciated, receive a standing ovation. And after a gig, when a young boy shyly approaches, I am astounded that my words have impacted a twenty-something. Women have come to me crying after shows. I don't fit the mold: older, ex-pat, African American, slightly disabled woman, speaking with an accent, fattish and graying. I'm aware that in this same country, older women, who live alone, with one eye (and who might stay up late at night writing) are being killed as witches, burnt alive by young men the same age as those who applaud me when I perform.

On the other hand, these young men and women I deal with in halls and on stages also inspire me. I think I thrive on their energy, that sense of possibility and seizing opportunities, the confidence and drive to be successful that so characterizes youth. I've been tempered by age and living, but that youthful energy is vital to me as a writer, performer, and colleague.

These young poets, my peers, frequently try putting me into their boxes. I'm a woman, so I must be a mother. I must have a husband. I must cook Sunday lunch every weekend. Gently, I make it very clear that I'm no one's mother and that I've been single much longer than I was married. My arms don't ache to hold a baby. I prefer for them to think of me as the auntie they wish they'd had, and I watch people visibly relax and engage when they do. I am open and accepting, so people find a safety in my presence and in my words that they generally don't have in their lives.

So that's my story, amazing even to myself. From activist to poet and performer. I truly found flying. Breaking boundaries, promoting women and black people, being for real with everyone I meet, building community—these are the things that I speak about in my writing, the same ideals that people see in my daily life. These are the things I want to be remembered for . . . and my written words.

AM I A WRITER
Do I have the right to call myself a writer?
Because I like words
Because I wonder if there is a way
to say the essence of what I feel

Do I have the right to fly around the room
a moth, a balloon, a bumblebee
bouncing off the walls
wild out of my body and mind

Do I have the right
to be aroused by new sight

to grasp for fleeting truths
respond to the provocation of light
to share myself, open my spirit

Ribbons blow loose in the breeze
Clouds float gentle in the sky
My heart rages in colors
and the words come out

Do I have the right to call myself a writer?

## Makhosazana Xaba

## We Need Money and Time: Putting Women on the Biography Agenda

*responding to Philippa Yaa de Villiers*

I have come to the conclusion that unless writers have simultaneously dedicated money and time, biographies of women will remain at the bottom of the list of priorities. The genre—by its very definition—is time intensive; it's someone's whole life, after all. In the South African context, women continue to receive less public value than men, despite their constitutionally entrenched voting rights, their rising earning ability, their increasing numbers of seats in decision-making boardrooms, and their growing public visibility.

Telling the lives of women through biography is but one way of valuing them; their lives and their contribution to the tapestry that is our story as a country, as a continent, as a people, and as women of the world. I have always believed in this, but my personal journey with the genre is taking an unsettling and painful halt and I tell it here as a concrete case study to demonstrate how I have come to the conclusion that opens this piece. I then ask what I consider to be a fundamental question that, if answered, could possibly lead to other interesting actions, and I end the piece with my suggestions on what needs to be done.

In 2006, I submitted a research report entitled *Jabavu's Journey* to the Faculty of Humanities at the University of the Witwatersrand in partial fulfilment for the degree of Master of Arts in Writing. The first table in the literature review section of this report shows a list of biographies of Black South African women in four columns: name and profession of the biography subject; book title; author; and the year the book was published. The list was nine rows long.

The book titles were: *Winnie Mandela: Mother of the*

*Nation*; *Nelson and Winnie Mandela*; *Nokukhanya: Mother of Light*; *The Calling of Katie Makhanya: A Memoir of South Africa*; *Bessie Head: Thunder behind Her Ears*; *Zulu Woman: The Life Story of Christina Dlamini*; *Walter and Albertina Sisulu: In our Lifetime*; *Patricia De Lille;* and lastly, *Winnie Mandela: A Life.*

The first book on the list was published in 1985 and the last one in 2003. I gave this table the heading *A Preliminary List of Biographies of Black South African Women* because I was finding it hard to believe that what my in-depth research uncovered was such a miserably short list. I was convinced that, had I had more time (I had two years for this degree) to dig where no one had dug before, I would unearth other sources. Had I done a comparison to Black men's biographies, I no doubt would have seen a multi-fold gap; men being represented more in biographies. This much is obvious on general shelves in bookstores. As I write this piece four years later, I am thinking: it would be great if I had a bit more time to update this table. I don't. I am in a day job that pays me monthly and I use early mornings (my crystal clarity time slots), weekends, stolen moments during work travel, and alone meal times at restaurants for my creative writing.

When I decided to undertake this writing degree I resigned from work, took on short-term consulting jobs that did not require more than three days per week. I was in class once a week and had weekly assignments: reading and writing. I had consciously carved out time in my life to do this. The consultancy jobs I took were enough to put unbuttered bread on my table.

In May 2006, I started a year-long writing fellowship at the Wits Institute for Social and Economic Research (WISER) to write Noni Jabavu's biography. The stipend that came with it made it possible for me to put homemade bread on the table using affordable ingredients. The total amount for the research budget that came with the fellowship made it possible for me to undertake one ten days long research trip within South Africa. I did not take on short term consulting jobs as I wanted to focus on this once-in-a lifetime opportunity. I was living a writer's dream. I had all the time to dream, create, research and write. I had an equipped office and the university resources to back my research. And, I had a blood-red bank balance rolling from one month to the next, for a year.

I managed to raise enough funds from outside the university to travel and undertake research in 2007. I went to the UK, Jamaica, Uganda, Kenya, and Zimbabwe, countries where Noni had lived for at least five years. The shortest trip lasted a week and the longest four weeks. When I was back home, I took on consulting jobs so I could pay my bills. By the end of that year all my savings, which I had started digging into little by little in that first year of my MA studies, were wiped out completely. By the end of that year, I had lots of raw data, but I had to continue to write this biography through my travels, my mothering, and my putting bread on the table. I had no extra/spare/leisure time to write. In January of 2008, I started in my current job.

I have always known that creativity and intense and long writing projects like a biography need more time—but I never had to face it as I am facing it right now.

Interestingly, the most frequently asked questions (by friends, family, acquaintances, and complete strangers) whenever the subject of my biography writing, the fellowship and travel came up, were about money. Phrased varyingly: Where did you get the money from?; How are you paying your bond/mortgage and your car and the school fees?; Who is your patron?; Just how did you manage to take so much time off? Everyone knows that the middle-class salaries we earn do not match up with such expenses. Then, I heard the interesting "concluding" comments that often followed these conversations: You must care so much about her; She must be such an important person; That's a lot of sacrifice; Oh, I could never do what you did, I love my life far too much; You sure love your writing. Many told me in no uncertain terms they would sooner die than accept a fellowship that pays a "poverty" stipend.

I have been a political and women's rights activist since my youth. In my late twenties, I began to focus on women's health using a feminist agenda within the South African context. In all these years, I participated in fund-raising activities, receiving money from various donor agencies and organizations. Every single non-governmental organization I know survives through this perpetual struggle of having to raise funds to do work that everyone agrees is urgent, necessary, and honorable.

I have never had the opportunity or privilege to be in conversations about how women can amass enough money for themselves, in their own names to undertake this work, and thus determine their own agenda. Why? When I have heard money conversations linked to women within the feminist movement, they have all been focused on microlending schemes and survival for women. No doubt honorable. My interest is, however, different: Should feminism not advocate for women to have more money to line their pockets so that they can do with it what they want? And I am talking about lots of money that can support, in this case, the creation of women writers and artists' residencies, the establishment of women's fellowship and scholarship programs, so that women can put aside the money problem and have enough time to reflect, create, and dream through their projects.

# Zethu Matebeni

## An Uncanny Union: When African Lesbians[1] and Feminism Meet

A recent five-day meeting on what seemed to be a "forced marriage" between "isms"—lesbianism, feminism, and Africanism—held in Maputo, Mozambique left many of the participants asking more questions about feminism and lesbianism in Africa than there are possible answers. More than sixty participants from a number of African countries gathered in the Portuguese-speaking city for a donor-funded Institute on *Building Lesbian Feminist Thinkers and Leaders for the 21st Century*. The Institute was specific to lesbian and feminist participants, including trans men as well as heterosexual, and bisexual women.

Though debates on lesbianism and feminism or lesbianism and the continent exist and are widespread, they are always contentious. The former is also a contention experienced in other parts of the world.[2] The latter (in its generic form: Africa and homosexuality) is a well-known political battleground (or rather scapegoat) for many African statesmen, including those in Zimbabwe, Uganda, and Namibia to name a few.[3] Many of such have claimed that homosexuality is not synonymous with being African, that the former is a Western import even for those born in Africa. Another contested terrain is that of the position of feminism in Africa. These contentions are the focus of this contribution, which aims at questioning the workings of these categories in a space such as the Institute.

Having never attended one of these types of Institutes before, or having been "developed" into a lesbian feminist leader, I wondered and was highly curious, possibly skeptical, about how such "development" would take place. Our first morning at the Institute was to introduce us to a concept of African Feminism, as prescribed in the Charter of Feminist Principles for African Feminists (Charter) developed by the African Feminist Forum (AFF).[4] My skepticism was further ignited. Reading about the AFF reminded me of a newspaper article published during the AFF conference in Accra in 2006 by *The Heritage,* a Ghanaian newspaper. The newspaper had as its headlines and front-page article "After Blockade of Gay Conference Lesbians Meet in Accra. They Meet as NGO for Women's Empowerment."[5] The article's sensationalist tone clearly reveals the journalist's pre-occupation and fascination with lesbians from South Africa, who were three of more than eighty participants attending the AFF conference. Unfortunately, the article missed mentioning or even slightly suggesting the conference's main content: "feminist" or "feminism." The article's omission of the words "feminism" and "feminist" forced me to ask about the relevance and position of feminism in Africa. It also allowed me to wonder about the general silence on feminism in many parts of the continent, including South Africa.

To understand how to be an African Feminist is to master and adopt the Charter, which starts by naming and defining feminists, and recognizing the diversity of those who call themselves African Feminists:

We have multiple and varied identities as African Feminists. We are African women—we live here in Africa and even when we live elsewhere, our focus is on the lives of African women on the continent. Our feminist identity is not qualified with "Ifs," "Buts," or "However." We are Feminists. Full stop. This intention, both clear and somewhat contradictory, caused some discontent at the Maputo Institute. Participants felt that this conceptualization of a feminist was too rigid because it implies that adopting feminism (or rather an attachment to feminist ideology) is more valued than other categories. "Ifs," "Buts," or "However" were interpreted as: one is feminist only to the exclusion of all other categories and a feminist category had to stand-alone. One participant, after going through the principles of feminism as specified in the Charter, articulated, "I agree with some of the principles of feminism, but from what I've seen with regards to feminists, I do not want to call myself that." This comment raised tense discussions about class, gender, race, and sexual orientation in relation to African feminism, which remain unresolved. They also point to the origins of African feminism, which was distinctly heterosexual, pro-natal, and exclusionary in its practice and conception (Mikell, 1997:4). Not only is the language and terminology of feminism problematic for many women in Africa, the definition of feminism is by no means fixed, and many African women are at odds with feminism (Oyewùmí, 2003). Even though they may carry out a broad feminist agenda, many women eschew the label "feminist" for different reasons (Frenkel, 2008), including that: feminism, as a named category, lacks significance for many; it represents a foreign concept; and, for some, it enacts exclusions, many of which were highlighted in this Institute (Reddy, 2004).

The battle between "lesbian" and feminism does not end there. In some situations, where class and racial division are less emphasized, the fusion between the two is less complicated. At another part of the spectrum is the lesbians' challenge to feminism or vice versa. It is not obvious that every lesbian is a feminist or every feminist pro-lesbian. On the contrary, because both categories are so contested, they can be at total odds with each other. A general question I hear being asked, and even posed at the Maputo Institute, is whether a lesbian in Africa should be fighting for advancing women's rights or for their rights to be a lesbian, which is a silenced category or identity label. Even in South Africa, where constitutional advances protect the rights of lesbians on paper, at a social level this is a different case. Homophobia, hate crimes, sexual violence and torture, and murder of black lesbians in South Africa and other parts of the continent give us little faith in the demands of African feminism. The marriage of "lesbian" and feminism is a heavily contested position both within feminist and lesbian circles as well as in general public discourse. As experience in the West has shown, it is not enough to think that lesbianism meets feminist in lesbian-feminism (Butler, 1990). So, the challenge continues for us as we dip our feet both in lesbian and feminist worlds while standing solidly on African grounds. Are the struggles of lesbians in Africa separate from those of feminists? Can we make progress on these battles concurrently? Or is this a situation of who comes first: lesbian or feminist?

### Where to from here?

There are no conclusions to draw from this complexity. What is clear is that both feminism and lesbianism, as political and social categories need to be further interrogated and made more easily accessible and relevant to the lives of ordinary women in Africa. This process may take more than a five-day intervention. These categories need to be understood in dynamic social and political terms. It may be necessary first to dismantle the "essentialist positions" on what it means to be African, and an African Feminist. The diversities within African, feminist, and lesbian are as diverse as Africa's people.

The irony of this is that such Institutes, even though relying on essentialisms and "unifying" categories, remain the few spaces freely accessible to Africans, lesbians, and feminists. But they should be cautious of their own "false" achievements, which may go unnoticed, such as counting the number of feminists by the distribution of free T-shirts with "feminist" slogans. If such interventions continue without a thorough reading of the context, then they would even miss the telling sentiments of many participants of such Institutes:

"We're not feminists, but we'll take the free T-shirts!"

1. I am using "lesbian" here to refer to a woman who is erotically or deeply emotionally attracted to and involved with a member of her own sex. There are diversities within this category that this piece does not go into. These are dealt with in another piece exploring black lesbian identities and sexualities in Johannesburg.

2. In the United States, bell hooks' *Feminist Theory from Margin to Center* (Boston: South End Press, 1984) and Cheshire Calhoun, "The Gender Closet: Lesbian Disappearance Under the Sign 'Women,'" *Feminist Studies* 21:1 (1995): 7–34 explore these debates. In South Africa, many early activists saw feminism as "divisive" and "concerned with 'exotic' and distant issues such as sexual preference" (see Jacklyn Cock and Alison Bernstein's *Melting Pots and Rainbow Nations: Conversations about Difference in the United States and South Africa* [Urbana: University of Illinois Press (2002): 188-162]. Similarly, see discussions between Audre Lorde (US) and Astrid Roemer (Netherlands) in Gloria Wekker, "Matism and Black Lesbianism: Two Idealtypical Expressions of Female Homosexuality in Black Communities of the Diaspora" in *Journal of Lesbian Studies* 1:1 December (1996): 11–24. *Our Caribbean: A Gathering of Lesbian and Gay Writing from the Antilles*, edited by Thomas Glave [Durham: Duke University Press (2008), 368–381] highlights similar positions.

3. See Mark Epprecht's discussion of African presidents and their stands on homosexuality in Africa in "Black Skin, 'Cowboy' Masculinity: A Genealogy of Homophobia in the African Nationalist Movement in Zimbabwe to 1983" in *Culture, Health & Sexuality* 7:3 (2005), 253–266.

4. AFF Charter of Feminist Principles, wwwafricafeministforum.org.

5. Ana Karimatu, "After Blockade of Gay Conference Lesbians Meet in Accra," *The Heritage*, November 20, 2006. The NGO referred to is

the Forum for the Empowerment of Women (FEW), an organization in Johannesburg serving and promoting rights of black lesbians in South Africa. The journalist had interviewed one of the founding members of the organization. The rest of the article's tone points to feelings that some in the continent have towards South Africa's lax constitution and access to human rights for everyone.

Butler, Judith. *Gender Trouble: Feminism and the Subversion of Identity.* New York: Routledge, 1990.

Calhoun, Cheshire. "The Gender Closet: Lesbian Disappearance Under the Sign 'Women.'" *Feminist Studies* 21:1 (1995), 7–34.

Frenkel, Ronit. "Feminism and Contemporary Culture in South Africa," *African Studies* 67 (2008), 1–10.

Mikell, Gwendolyn. *African Feminism: The Politics of Survival in Sub-Saharan Africa.* Philadelphia, PA: University of Pennsylvania Press, 1997.

Oyewùmí Oyèrónké (ed). *African Women and Feminism: Reflecting on the Politics of Sisterhood.* New Jersey and Eritrea: Africa World Press Inc., 2003.

Reddy, Vasu. "Sexuality in Africa: Some Trends, Transgressions and Tirades," *Agenda* 62 (2004), 3–9.

# Maram al-Masri

*Did the international movement for women's liberation have any influence on women's social conditions in your country? What does this movement mean to you today? How can it be dealt with in the present time?*

Certainly, the international movement for women's liberation has influenced the social conditions of Arab women to a great extent. In my city, Lattakia, which is the main sea port of Syria, I will take my mother and the women who were living in the same era as an example. My mother was born in 1927, after WWI, which opened the door to the example of European women, and, along with the great need for workers, provided Arab women with increased freedom to network, work, and revolutionize traditional concepts.

My mother took off her head veil, which was the compulsory traditional dress of Muslim women in Lattakia; she went to the public movie theaters (for men and women); in addition, she was a school director and an active member of the Women's Union for elimination of illiteracy, teaching girls in villages and opening hand-made carpet workshops. At the time, I could not recognize that my mother was an ardent activist and I did not have an awareness of the importance of her actions. But today, I find that even when she cut her long hair very short in 1968 (which enraged and angered my father), this act was also a challenge. She taught me a kind of silent and effective revolt, and implanted in me the passion for freedom.

I believe that the women's liberation movement led by women, in particular by Muslim women, was more assertive, challenging and daring, in spite of the fact that this movement was slower than the movement in Europe. Even Arabic Christian women who lived in the Islamic-oriented community had to pay a high price. The movement was not only opposing worn

*responding to and translated from Arabic by Simone Fattal*

out traditions, but also leading a revolt against religion, which is more oppressive and suppressive. In my opinion, since freedom is a human need, and an impulse for creativity, it should be created by someone who is in need of this freedom.

This movement did not cover the whole of Syria, since it only captured some well-educated and cultivated bourgeois women who were in direct contact with western culture, such as the writer Ghada al-Samman (the counterpart of the French writer Françoise Sagan), who has influenced and still has an influence on the minds of young women, not only in Syria but also in the whole Arab world.

Women's liberation is still a controversial issue or cause. All rights obtained by Arab women are fragile and could collapse at any time, despite the exchange of ideas through the internet and the ability to travel. Travel is still difficult and impossible in some countries. In these countries, women suffer from the conflicts that arise in their minds between what they see on the screen and their hard reality. Some women revolt because they have no choice, some tolerate the conditions, others revert to dreaming, and still others hide themselves behind the veil, rejecting the freedom of rich communities that are transmitted by television as a morphine to the hopeless nations.

The rights obtained by women in our countries so far, in spite of the high-level jobs attained by some women, do not mean that they are liberated from the burden of traditions and religion. Some women are turning against the new woman, her freedom and her rights, claiming repentance in the name of religion and traditions, returning to the literal interpretation of the scriptures, and rejecting the European model.

Perhaps women's liberation is connected to men's liberation, which unfortunately is still imprisoned behind the bars of the political conditions that affect the economy, and the economy that affects ethics and everything else.

*What are the issues faced by Arab women, as a creative person and a writer in your country?*

I can't talk about this issue, since I have left my country and lived in France since 1982. I came to France fleeing a heavy and rigid tradition, which I revolted against and challenged from my early years, partly due to my free inborn nature, partly due to the open-minded family climate in which I was born and raised, and partly due to the influence of my reading. I was in love with a young man whose religion was different from mine. I danced, swam in the sea, traveled, wrote poetry, married, and after that divorced. I paid a high price, as I was denied access to my first baby who was stolen from me. In response to this denial, I went far in my revolt. I rejected the values of my community and married a French man, believing that I would be treated with due respect and recognized as a female writer, but unfortunately, when I declared myself to be a newborn writer, I was punished again. My French community did not accept a free Arab woman. They thought that freedom is a right granted to them exclusively.

For the sake of my mother, I will proceed and go on, in spite of all losses. This is a true struggle for justice and for creating a better community.

*How was your work received in your society? What are the problems you faced to achieve recognition?*

My writings were acclaimed by both critics and the public throughout the Arab world. All the newspapers wrote about them. They were acknowledged by important literary figures, translated into eight languages, and reprinted in many countries.

The role I want my writings to play as a whole are still the same as all literary works: I look forward to being understood and recognized, to improving human relations and conditions. I know from the readers' letters and from their reactions the extent of love they have for me.

One of my poems was selected for the curriculum at schools in Palestine, for children between twelve to eighteen years old. One teacher in some French school wrote in his report that after studying the poem, one girl student pulled herself together and disclosed a deep secret that she was suffering from.

I think both cases prove that poetry is a way to touch the unconscious and play an effective role in liberating human beings, improving their conditions and relations, and consequently improving life.

# Maha Hassan

*responding to and translated from Arabic by Simone Fattal*

*Did the international movement for women's liberation have any influence on women's social conditions in your country? What does this movement mean to you today? How can it be dealt with in the present time?*

I don't think the international women's movement had any influence in the Arab world, because of the predominance of religion, the weight of social traditions, and oppressive political institutions.

Women come into the world completely devoid of freedom. All citizens are under the scrutiny of other citizens, and this scrutiny makes one a prisoner of the opinion that others have of one. One has to conduct his/her life under this gaze. Society rules the individual. The individual in the Arab world does not know personal freedom. It is quite common for institutions to interfere with the person's behavior, and to deliver judgments on him/her, through religious or political associations. And the Fatwas we hear are the best indication of that trend. The Fatwas target world intellectuals or scientists, and women are the worst off because their condition is taboo, and no one speaks about it.

*What are the issues faced by Arab women, as a creative person and a writer in your country?*

Male imperialism is the biggest problem, because men always expect women to follow their instructions. Women's exchanges with men are always that of a follower. Religion has consecrated this in one ayat from the Koran, for example: "men have the upper hand on women." Which remains a subconscious reference in men's dealings with women.

The woman writer is treated first as a woman, whereas the male writer will always be regarded first as a writer, then as a man.

I, for instance, consider myself first as a novelist, and having to talk constantly about the topic of the liberation of women bothers me and takes me away from my main preoccupation, which is to write novels. Addressing the issue is not part of my creative work, but as I cannot bury my head in the sand and ignore what is going on. I am forced to deal with it. Let us take the killing of women for instance. I wrote two articles on this subject for my blog: www.maisondesjournalistes.org/dossier_femmes_maha_itv.php.

*How is your work received in your milieu and what is its impact on your society in general?*

Because of distribution problems, my novels do not reach the Arab reader easily.

My articles, on the other hand, have a great resonance. I receive feedback. Readers write to me. A Syrian woman wrote to say that she feels my articles express all of what she has to say and that she follows what I write. I feel that people in our society are ready for change, they are waiting for signs, but fear keeps them down. They are boiling under the surface, waiting for someone to listen to them, without any ulterior motives beyond wanting to give themselves the right to express themselves. A last word: I would like to thank Simone Fattal and the two American writers for their questions, and their help in the liberation of women and the dissipation of fear and abuse, whether it is about women's intellectual achievement, their personality, or the way to conduct their lives.

# Hala Mohammad

*Did the international movement for women's liberation have any influence on the social conditions of women in your country? And what does this movement mean to you today? And how can it be dealt with in the present time?*

I have never dealt with the liberation of women per se, in exclusion from its relation to the liberation of society as a whole. Since I was a young woman, I related to the Marxist view that life is a human endeavor aiming at social justice and the suppression of the causes that produce an oppressor and an oppressed, with the help of the intellect.

I looked for a place for myself in this world not as a woman, but as a human being. My feminine side is the side engaged in one's sentimental life. I am, besides this, a poet and a filmmaker whose project is free from ideology, set programs, and political power.

As a woman, I have to engage with the ideology that has deluded men into thinking they have an imaginary power over women through privileges given to them by this ideology. I do not want to try to get a man to recognize my rights. These rights must be only given and guaranteed by social laws. No one can give anything to an other human being. My effort consists in refusing anything that considers me or a man tools for building a society that is alien to our desires. In this place and time, I cannot allow myself to be defined as a woman, i.e. something contrary to a man. I favor therefore the word: *insana*.[1] *Insana* is the feminine for *insan* and not its contrary. In that sense, there is no liberation movement that is not for humankind as a whole. And so I am able to love my son, my friends, my lover as being my other half or halves and not my competitors or my enemies. It is a question of communication and opening my consciousness to the ideas that circulate in the world. We can work together to see beauty, and fight ugliness, to laugh, and to create new spaces for free human beings, create a large horizon and not a narrow one.

When I say that I am against oppression and dictatorship and injustice and for social justice and democracy and freedom of expression, it means that I am with all the diverse liberation movements in the world. I am the daughter of these movements, but they are not my mother. They will, with time, relate to me as well. Thus the relationship is free from imitation, but becomes subject to commitment. I commit to them freely.

I commit to freedom like I commit to music. We become like nature and its components: trees, flowers, wind, water, and beasts.

And thus we can achieve our part, which is not to play the part of animals, but to carry beauty and magic hopefully.

I am far from the direct political struggles and create for myself a program large and free, refusing as a matter of fact all laws that consider woman an inferior being. I don't support any of the fundamentalists ideologies.

I don't consider the laws that oppress women any worse than the laws that regulate the lives of the Palestinian people under the Israeli government, or the occupation of the Iraqi people by the Americans. They consider the other as an enemy, who should be either tamed or abolished. The only solution is through just laws that consider all humans as equals. And this solution will come from an awareness of the issues, and from the defense of this consciousness. This awareness will mean respect for the freedom of the other in their life, their beliefs, their choices, within a social organization led by civil laws that treat all people equally.

*How was your work received in your society? What are the problems you faced to achieve recognition?*

In our society, we do not have independent cultural associations, and therefore it was a long time before I found a niche, a place that looks like me and in which I find people like me. But we are in the margins. We are marginalized. The real strength is with political power and with money. We are simple individuals who dream together and, in that field, we are numerous.

My films have certainly met with respect and approbation. I would like the same for my poetry. If only a foreign publisher would defend this poetry abroad, this success abroad will come to nurture success inside the country and strengthen it.

1. Translator's Note: In Arabic there is a word for "human being": *insan*; it is different from man or woman and it has a feminine form too, *insana*.

# Fawziya Choueich al-Salem

*responding to and translated from Arabic by Simone Fattal*

*Did the international movement for women's liberation have any influence on women's social conditions in your country? What does this movement mean to you today? How can it be dealt with in the present time?*

Indeed, the International movement for the liberation of women had a big influence on the social conditions of women in Kuwait. It was immediately reflected in the political sphere; it propelled the issues and the solutions forward much quicker than the struggles that had taken place prior to it. We see it clearly in the participation of Kuwaiti women in international conferences, which brought about an exchange of ideas and underlined the necessity for women to be part of the political management of the country. But we must not forget the role of the Arab and national influences, and their importance at the beginning of this movement. The movement started here at the beginning of the twentieth century, with the beginning of social enlightenment and reforms that played a role in the establishment of women's associations. These associations were at the center of the social and political transformations that happened in Kuwait after independence. Through them, women were able to gain political rights and equality in the Constitution. But we have to say that, because of the tribal system and its hold on the social customs, women do not enjoy the political rights given to them by the Constitution. And this prevents them from entering the political arena fully. Women played a big role in the liberation of Kuwait. They reached out to the international movements, and that created pressure on the opposing parties, leading to women obtaining their rights for real: the right to run for political office and the right to vote.

*What does the movement mean to you in particular? And how do you see yourself in relation to it?*

International solidarity means a great deal to us. We are at the beginning of our effective presence in the political life of our country. Therefore, we need help to stand up against the forces that try to derail our march towards fully gaining our rights. And we also need to provide our movement with all the expertise, tools, and means necessary to our development and our march forward. These exchanges and these dialogues can truly bring people of different countries and cultures closer together.

*What are the problems that the Arab woman faces as a writer and a creative person in her country?*

Our greater problem is the existence of the tribal mentality and culture, in the general sense. For in this culture, man considers woman to be his shadow and that her station should be inferior to his. And this attitude has nothing to do with religion or with constitutional rights, but it is seen as a masculine inheritance.

We know that, from the beginning, the female presence was always linked to prohibitions and fear about exposing the forbidden parts of her body. These concerns had the consequence of completely hindering her freedom of movement and making it difficult for her to even walk down the street.

As for me as a writer, I refused to use the common language and so found my own voice. That did not appeal to the male writers. The agreement on a common language would have opened the door to the men's welcome and praise. But it was something I refused from the beginning and continue to this day.

*How does your society respond to your work? And what is its role?*

When I started in 1988, my work was met with intense surprise, especially on the part of the association of Kuwaiti writers.

The audacity and modernity of my writing was a big shock. And so they responded with a real war in the newspapers, and inside the association. The criticism grew when the Iraqi director, D. Aouni Kroumi, chose my texts to be performed in the National Theater of Baghdad and at the Theater festival of 1990. This hostility brought the members of the association together. They were united in their hostility towards me. At the same time, I became more and more accepted in the Arab world, especially in Morocco. Eventually, that led to my getting accepted. And now there is a book on my work published by the association.

As for my society, I think that my writing had a big influence on the new generation, and not only in Kuwait, but also in the Gulf and the rest of the Arab world. I know that through the letters I receive. There are now studies on my work, at the master's and doctoral levels at the universities, which study the modernity and openness that I found so early on.

# Rati Saxena

responding to Farideh Hassanzadeh-Mostafavi, collected by Pramila Venkateswaran

*Reading your poems, I feel poetry is your lost half. How did you find it?*

You are very much correct, my poetry is what I lost. But I can not say that I could get everything back in poetry. In fact, every minute I lose myself and every minute poetry tries to bring back me to myself. Poetry gave me a shelter, where I can sit for a moment and talk to myself. While talking to myself, I can talk to whole world.

How I found her is really a long story, because I was born in a family where no one even talked about poetry, I married into a family where poetry was never liked, I am living in a family where writing poetry is a form of madness. Yet poetry and I found each other.

I could not write for more than fifteen years . . . that was when I was passing through a black tunnel. But when I started writing, poems came to me like butterflies. I am grateful to poetry. . . . that's all.

*Please tell me more about this black tunnel. It seems your life has been an epic made by your own hands. Please let us know about details.*

This is a very difficult question.

Well, I was born in a beautiful city in Rajasthan called Udaipur. I was the fourth daughter in a middle-class, educated family. In Indian communities, the birth of a daughter is not appreciated by society. So, I was almost an unwanted child. When I was quite young, my uncle (mother's brother) took me with him to Bhopal. I can say, that was the best period in my life. I had a real carefree childhood. I stayed with them until I passed my fifth standard, but I do not remember anything regarding study because those days, I was too busy playing. My uncle taught me some math, that's all. When my father heard about my getting spoiled, he was furious. He brought me back to my own family. My own home was a prison for me; all my sisters were very sophisticated and well-mannered girls compared to me and there was no chance for worthless playing. (My poem "girls from good family" alludes to this story!) It was a tough time for me. I was put in an ordinary government school, but my sisters were studying in good schools, so they opted for science because they were good students. I opted for arts because I did not want to study in a boys' school (in those days there was no science in girls' school and studying in a boys' school meant living in a jail) and I was more interested in other activities like debate, elocution, acting, etc.

Even though I studied in a very ordinary school, I was always the star of the school. I won a number of prizes. At the same time, I was a very quiet and reserved girl at home. On school days, I was always busy with all types of extra activities and never bothered to study. Somehow, I got good marks. In 10 standard, I got good marks in math, so I wanted to opt for math for my higher studies, but my elder sister made fun of me, saying that an arts student could not handle math. I was upset and so decided to study a subject in which I had minimum marks and that was Sanskrit. I managed to learn this language; and as usual, I was a star in the class and a foolish girl at home. Then I opted for BA honors in Sanskrit. In college I again became popular as a debator and an actor, and also did other activities. I won a number of prizes in these competitions. Then I finished my MA in Sanskrit. As soon as I completed my master's, I applied for a doctorate, but soon I got married. I could complete my doctorate after marriage, but I had to deal with a number of problems. I had to go through a number of family adjustment problems with my in-laws. I had to behave as a middle-class village daughter-in-law, so I had to massage the feet of my mother-in-law, do the cooking, do stitching and embroidery work, etc. I had to live without any books.

Even though I had studied in ordinary school, I was very fond of reading. Words always hypnotize me. I do not remember when I started, but I always found myself reading. I was so fond of reading that there was a joke in my home that went: Don't ask Rati to sweep, because if she finds any torn paper while sweeping, she will stop her work to read it. So my passion for reading was not going to let me be a good daughter-in-law for very long. After thirteen years of marriage, I started my studies again. This time, I passed teachers' training exams and started working in a school, then a college. I left the job after seventeen years. From early childhood, I was always writing and then destroying what I'd written because I did not have the courage to support the writer in me. But at the age of 40, I started writing openly and started getting published. Unfortunately, I write in Hindi and I live in south India. So I never had any direct communication with my readers. But in ten years, I have published almost fifteen books and five to six hundred pieces in journals. And I still have a lot of work that is unpublished.

*So you deny Isadora Duncan's statement: "I wonder if a woman can really be an artist, since art is a hard taskmaster who demands everything, whereas a woman who loves, gives up everything of life." I am curious also to know if, in your life, "the imperious call of art" has ever put "a tragic end to love"?*

I think my background is different than Isadora Duncan, because, for me, art is not limited to writing only. In my childhood, I saw my maternal aunty smearing cow dung on the floor of the courtyard with her fingers. The courtyard used to get polished and the lines she made with her fingers made it more human. That was when I first thought about art. I also saw my aunty drawing on the walls with a rice paste of cow dung (it was a part of a festival of women). Those lines are stuck in my mind. I have seen the women in my family singing while working at the grinding stone, while cooking, and while celebrating. Art was an important part of woman's work in my childhood. But, of course, these women were never called artists. They were only women or mami or nani or didi or chahi.

It is true that I could not become a full-time artist for a long time because I had the responsibility for my family and expectations from my in-laws. But even in those days, I was living a life full of art, doing embroidery work on my daughter's dresses, etc.

*To understand your ideas about the difference between women's literature and men's literature, I need to recall the restrictions for women. And also remember that, even in societies where equality is not the slogan among men and women, women can feel uneasy when they sit behind a desk to write. They feel unusual, as if they have betrayed others. Their consciousness can suffer from the guilt that they might have robbed others' rights.*

No doubt writing is more easy and natural for men than for women. It is more difficult for a woman to completely devote herself to writing. Most of my writing has died before birth, because ideas came to me while cooking or doing other things for family. And I could not write for fifteen years, that time was completely devoted to my family. And when I started writing, I felt guilty for writing. I could not prioritize my writing until now. Still, even now, writing is my part-time job and my home comes first. Sometimes I feel like I am working in a circus, doing so many things at the same time. But sometimes I feel that this pressure gives me energy to write.

I often feel guilty for not reading or writing. And that makes me write better. I could never sit behind a writing table and think. I always think while doing something like cooking or driving. I could never follow a timetable for writing; when I want to write, I ignore everything. So, I feel a woman has to train her mind for writing. I am popular for my serious prose writing and serious articles too. They need a lot of time and energy. I could never write them in one sitting. But breaks give me time to think and that is why I can write more strong and serious prose. Sometimes, when I have plenty of free time, I can't write a single word. I feel that god has given more energy to woman than man and that is why she can do so many things at a time.

In Malayalam literature, a great poetess called Balamani Amma (the mother of Kamala Das) had the opportunity to get the time to write like a man, time without any family burden because her husband supported her. Her writings are good, but sometimes I feel she missed so much in life. Another poet, Ayyappa Paniker, looks after his family as if he is the lady of the family (because of certain family problems), but he did not regret this. He said "the kitchen is the place where you get all the rasas" (salt, sugar, hot, etc; Indian poetics talks about nava rasa, the nine rasa/emotions) "so working in the kitchen helps me to write better. Because of cooking I learn to use rasa in better ways." I feel that he is correct. When a woman cooks, all the majors are within her, so she does not need to be overly careful. At the same time, she has the ability to experience life deeply. And that is why, unlike a man, she does not need a timetable for writing.

It is not always true that women's literature is different from men's. But there is no doubt that most of the time a woman writes about her own world. But I believe that women should do serious writing. I am sure that serious writings by women can be very powerful.

So, I am not unhappy for having less time. Because I feel lucky to get a lot of experiences in my life.

*Is it so difficult in India for a poet to make a decent living?*

Decent living? My God! It is difficult to live with poetry in India. If a poet is completely depending on poetry for his livelihood, he will not get a single meal in a month.

Most poets have other jobs. There are very few who completely depend on their writings, and even they find this difficult. I left my job for writing and started a web site. Every single paisa for the site was spent by me from my pension. Luckily my husband has a job, so I did not need to worry about food or shelter, otherwise I would be on the street. Even for my site, I could never make a single penny. The strange thing is that people often ask me, where do you work? I can not say that I am poet or writer. If I say I am a poet and a writer, then their next question will be: but where do you work? And if I stay at home, then they will say: oh, you are a housewife then.

How can I explain to them that I work more than any working woman? I work for ten to fifteen hours a day It is not that there are fewer poets in India; a number of people are writing poetry. But writing poetry is not a respected job these days. In my social life, nobody knows that I write serious things. They do not know about any of my writings. It is difficult to get published in India. You have to pay to do so. But there are clever people (who are often very bad poets) who manage to grab big awards and get lots of money (because of their political connections).

I think this is the situation everywhere in world, isn't it?

*If you were me what would you ask from Rati Saxina?*

I do not think that I am as knowledgeable as you are. You have asked very important questions. And you are a clever interviewer. But there are so many things that people from outside India or the Indian continent can not understand. For instance, being a poet is not respectable work here for a woman—most of the poems written by women are seen as autobiographical. Even though we had great woman poets like Meera, Habba Khatoon, Lal Dad, Akka Mahadevi, and many more. All these woman poets suffered badly in their lives. I don't think that things have changed here. Society still does not give women poets proper respect.

## Pramila Venkateswaran

Kutti Revathi's second book of poems *Mulaigal* (*Breasts*), published in 2002, created a storm of protest among male writers in Tamil Nadu. What Kutti Revathi endured was a witch hunt—obscene phone calls, letters, threats, and a call to burn her poems in the city's center, Chennai's Mount Road. The reaction of the literary establishment, particularly the male writers and lyricists, was conventional: How dare she write unashamedly about the body!

I find this reaction odd when there has been a long literary tradition of women poets in India depicting the female body in poetry. One only has to read the poems of Avvaiyar, Akka Mahadevi, Sule Sankavva, Mirabai, Muddupallani, to name a few, to understand the depiction of the erotic by women poets. Of course, both in the devotional and in other classical poetry written by men, women's bodies have always had a sacred place. But the erotic has never been purely a male domain, even though the list of male poets writing erotic poetry perhaps is longer, partly because in the history of selection, preservation, and, finally, dissemination and translation of extant editions of poetry in all the Dravidian literary traditions, many women poets were excluded.

It is important to note that what in the West we separate into sacred and profane does not apply to Indian poetry, where nothing about the body is profane. Revathi's title poem, "Breasts," is evocative of the sensuousness inherent in us, and the poem urges us to become conscious of the breasts' sensations—the fullness and the fulfillment that is not dependent on a partner; the owner of the gaze is herself:

> Breasts are bubbles, rising
> In wet marshlands

I watched in awe — and guarded —
Their gradual swell and blooming
At the edges of my youth's season

Saying nothing to anyone else,
They sing along
With me alone, always:
Of Love,
Rapture,
Heartbreak

To the nurseries of my turning seasons,
They never once forgot or failed
To bring arousal

During penance, they swell, as if straining
To break free; and in the fierce tug of lust,
They soar, recalling the ecstasy of music
From the crush of embrace, they distill
The essence of love; and in the shock
Of childbirth, milk from coursing blood

Like two teardrops from an unfulfilled love
That cannot ever be wiped away,
They well up, as if in grief, and spill over.


As Kutti Revathi explains, her sole concern was to explore
breasts as an "inhabited" living reality, rather than an "exhibited" commodity (india.poetryinternationalweb.org).

This aim of women wanting to be the describers rather
than the described is found in much of the poetry written by
women in the Indian literary tradition, particularly in the south.
Take for instance the following translation of one of the poems

of Muddupalani, an eighteenth-century poet, from her volume, *Radhika Santwanam*:

> Move on her lips
> the tip of your tongue;
> do not scare her by biting hard.
> Place on her cheeks
> a gentle kiss;
> do not scratch her
> with your sharp nails.
> Hold her nipple
> with your fingertips;
> do not scare her
> by squeezing it tight.
> Make love
> gradually.
> Do not scare her
> by being aggressive.
> I am a fool
> to tell you all these.
> When you meet her
> and wage your war of love
> would you care to recall
> my "do's and don'ts," Honey? (Tharu and Lalitha)

This poem, along with the rest of the volume, is replete with the knowledge of the pleasure of the female body, presented in the format of a sex instruction manual to the male lover, here, Krishna. In Muddupalani's poems, the woman takes the initiative in love-making, she is not the passive recipient of love or the object of the male poet's description of her sexuality. Unlike the typical rendition of the Radha-Krishna story, Muddupalani takes the liberty of imprinting her experiences of her daily life and sexual pleasure onto the Radha-Krishna story, thus impishly suggesting that her story is perhaps the more interesting one.

The twelfth-century poet, Akka Mahadevi, wrote erotic *bhakti* (devotional) poems in Kannada. Here is one poem that addresses the man attracted to her body. She affirms in this poem that she is the mistress of her body, and will decide how she wants to be seen: she declares she has chosen god (Chennamallikarjuna or Vishnu) as her lover:

> Brother, you have come
> drawn by the beauty
> of these billowing breasts,
> this brimming youth.
> I'm no woman, brother, no whore.
>
> Every time you've looked at me
> who have you taken me for?
> All men other than Chennamallikarjuna
> Are faces to be shunned, see, brother. (Tharu and Lalitha)

One only has to look at recently published volumes of Indian literature, such as *Same Sex Love*, edited by Susie Tharu, *Indian Love Poems*, edited by Meena Alexander, *Women Writing in India*, edited by Susie Tharu, and many volumes of poems in Indian languages that have yet to be translated into English and other languages, to understand the powerful contribution of women poets in the tradition, who locate the pleasure and pain of the body within the text of human experiences.

Fortunately, Kutti Revathi's story does not end with the angry reception of "Breasts" and calls for its censorship. Filmmakers Anjali Monteiro and K.P. Jayashankar from Mumbai decided to make a film, *SheWrite*, about four censored South Indian feminist poets, Kutti Revathi, Salma, Malini Maitri, and

Sukirtharini (indiadocu.blogspot.com). The controversy and the film has spurred Kutti Revathi to write her next book, *Udalun Kadavu,* "The Door to the Body," due this month (*The Hindu,* 2/7/08).

Feminist poets can take courage from poets like Kutti Revathi and from the rich literary tradition.

Perhaps we can learn from this story that the best way to dispel stupid ideas about the "F" word is to disseminate feminist poetry via the internet—blogs, youtube, listservs, and websites, —and to network with mainstream magazine editors to publish more feminist poets from around the world in their magazines.

I take courage from the stories of women poets in the Indian tradition who explored the beauty and the strangeness of life, particularly women's lives, in a language that expressed their truth, without giving in to the stylized expressions set within the male tradition. To do that required guts and self-assurance, which inspires feminist poetry today.

# Padcha Tuntha-Obas

First of all, the world of poetry in Thailand is small. Talk of publishing poems, poetry books, poets, or readings are normally limited to select small groups, the "in" people, who are generally regarded as noble and beautiful by everyday society, but not really mattering much. Still, poetry usually shines during times of political crisis—when poems begin to be seen as "speaking to the people's heart," when a few words can produce a large impact. And then our nationwide popular political weekly magazines—comparable to *The New Yorker* and the like—begin to publish a few poems in each edition. Still, walking into a bookstore, one will find few poetry books.

With the little authority that I have on this issue, it seems possible to say that the division between men and women writers in Thailand arises at a mysterious point where there is no form of recognizable "anxiety," especially among younger writers. (As for poets in particular, it is sad to say that perhaps poetry here is not "big" enough to have many people—both men and women—anxious about it.)

It would be very surprising to see a woman writer nowadays worried that being a woman would lower her chance of becoming published or successful. This is not to say we have perfect equilibrium between men and women writers—a look at some statistics does show men writers have been more celebrated in history and received more formal awards and such. But this does not appear to have prevented writing by women. Flipping through a new anthology of emerging writers compiled by Matichon, a large and respected newspaper and publishing house, I was very happy to see even more woman writers.

To try to explain: A male colleague of mine, who is also a writer, made an observation that writing is relatively new for Thailand. For both of us, in our late twenties, we see the current writing scene as having emerged most strongly at a time when  women already enjoy comparable social and intellectual status with men. I agree with him. Young women writers today might not even realize there is such thing as anxiety or struggle between men and women writers, here or elsewhere.

To me this is a great start. More can definitely be done. It would be wonderful if poetry beyond the traditional forms were promoted and embraced here. Young writers, who already seem unaffected by gender anxiety, should liberally be exposed to the idea that poetry is not only verses that rhyme that are mostly used at political rallies. Poetry could lose some rigidity. It could start to be recognized as "cool" as well as beautiful and noble. Poetry should be included in Fine Arts departments as well as in Literature and Literary Criticism. We could use more writers able to teach writing and nourish young writers.

# Moon Chung-hee

## The Flow of Korean Women's Poetry

*translated from Korean by Clare You*

With five thousand years of Korean history, Korean poetry has a long past.

Modern Korean poetry—contemporary, free-form poetry—had its start about a hundred years ago in the early 1900s. During the past one hundred years, Korean poetry has undergone various transformations in theme, language, and form; especially noticeable changes and developments are found in women's poetry.

As a nation with a deep-rooted Confucian tradition, Korean society was centered around the male and did not allow for the education of women. During the last century, however, educational opportunity has reached Korean women. Accordingly, women's poems, gradually shedding their reliance on the often romantic and emotional sphere of the existing poetry world, started to establish and solidify their identity, and define their uniqueness.

As women were drawn into the consumer and production market in full force, they took on an important role in mainstream society. This development went hand in hand with the historical progress made after being emancipated from Japanese colonial rule, enduring the Korean War, surviving the military dictatorships, and finally achieving the democratic society that exists today. Women's social standing has advanced with the speed that brought about the Korean economic miracle in the midst of the North and South division of the country. As women poets were breaking out of the traditional woman's consciousness of the early 1920s, they led the period by expressing for the first time their womanly self-awareness through poems. This intellectual breed of women, the so-called "new woman," maintained their rarity. Nonetheless, Korean women's poems largely belonged to the world of lyrical sensibility and emotional response until after the Korean War. Since then, recurring social unrest has also influenced changes in all areas of literature.

In the 1970s, as the country became an industrial society, Korean women's poetry began to unfold in a way uniquely its own, moving with the entire society toward freedom. Women poets, with a talent and maturity that challenged the male-centric world and the linguistic taboo placed on women, emerged with the struggle against the military dictatorship and its evident restrictions. This emergence of a new group of women poets—Moon Chung-hee, Kang Eun-gyo, and others—brought *women's* language, not men's, into poetry.

While these changes in women's poetry were taking place slowly alongside the economic development of the nation, the upheaval against materialism during the eighties also became manifested in poetry and went further to expose human alienation and the sterility that the society imposed upon its citizens. This new generation of poets, which delineated itself from the previous generation of the seventies and the eighties, includes Choi Seung-ja, Kim Hyesoon, Kim Seung-hee, and Kim Jung-ran. Their poems cast sardonic smiles on the earlier poems of congested self-awareness and self-consciousness during the military dictatorial regime. This new generation of poems spread like wildfire as they sang and glorified the common people's imaginations as the poet's own voice (like Ko Jung-hee).

In the 1990s, the rendering of browbeaten women's lives in women's poems once again had an effect on Korean poetry. Poets like Hwang In-Sook remained relevant with verses of simplicity and keen sensibility; other daring young poets expounded their unconscious desires in colorful and responsive language. New young poets like Ra Hee-duk drew attention with poems that, with delicate diction, grasp moments of feeling and provide penetrating insights into life. Choi Youngmi's modern and critical imagination and Choi Jeong-rye's strong metaphor also drew much attention. A new generation of Korean women poets, including Huh Su-kyung and Kim Sun-u, are expanding their horizons of activity with a variety of strong themes and language skills.

The first poem written by a Korean woman appeared around the second century BC in an ancient tale. The song is a tragic and beautiful story about a woman singing to her husband, who had drowned in the river. The song known as "Baek-Su-Gwang-Bu's Wife" appears on the first page of middle-school textbooks. Recently, for the first time, a woman appeared on a Korean paper bill. She is Shin Sa-im-dang, who lived about five hundred years ago in the Yi Dynasty and was a well-known poet who wrote many heartbreaking poems of longing for her mother.

During the Yi Dynasty, *kisaeng*, a distinctive class of women poets, left ninety beautiful poems. Kisaeng, who sang and danced as they entertained men, could join the scholars and upper-class men, yet had the unique status of the socially sub-jugated. They were women poets par excellence. Their limited poems are considered far superior as literary works to the over four thousand poems left by the scholarly male literati.

Contemporary Korean women's poems have gone beyond issues of identity and feminism, and having established their voices in the literary world, they are reveling in their talent. This talent is no longer relegated to a page of decoration in the male-dominated history of Korean literature; it will soon sing of human happiness, anger, love, and joy in a solid and definitive language, like that of our great Mother Earth.

## Choi Youngmi

# A Thirty-Year-Old's Hope and Despair

*translated from Korean by Clare You*

At thirty, I felt my life was at the edge of a cliff. There was no time to fall into the sentiment of already being a thirty-year-old. I was fighting a survival battle. I took a leave of absence from graduate school and had just started to learn the trade at a small publishing house, after going to great lengths to land the job. I'd been working barely three months when I called the company after a few days off, and was told that I was no longer needed. The company had a new president and my job was eliminated.

1991 was the worst year of my life. Before the reality of the lost job sank in, my boyfriend of a few months dropped me. A couple of months after I lost the job, he called me to say, "It's best if we no longer see each other." There was no explanation or excuse, just a short, matter-of-fact statement. I responded with equal brevity, "okay," and put down the receiver. That was that. I felt wretched. I'd just been dropped from society's workforce, and by the man I trusted most and to whom I felt closest.

When it rains, it pours. My family was in a mess, too. As the oldest of three daughters, almost thirty, unmarried, unemployed, I was a tumor and the black "duck" of the declining family. When I woke up in the morning, the hours I had to face each day would rush in like dust piling up in the corner of the room. I felt suffocated. My infrequent phone conversations with friends in similar situations were my only link to the outside world. No, there was no one to see even if I wanted to. No one was looking for me; no one was calling for me or asking my name.

For me, it could've been day when it was dark, or night when it was day, in my windowless room; it was dark at midday.

I was caged in the smoke-filled room, killing day after day, when my mother abruptly opened the door. She kicked casually at her daughter's feet under the comforter covering the lazybones who lay swaddled under it, and said, "Your life is a failure, Youngmi-ya. At thirty, you have no man, no child, no money, no fame. What have you done till now? You are a failure, only a shell."

F-a-i-l-u-r-e. Shell. As the words shot out of her mouth, I popped up as if I've had an electric shock. It felt like a nail had punctured me.

From that day on, I was sick with the "thirty-year syndrome." My heart lightened like a feather; the next second, it fell hard, burdened with a heavy load of my worldly problems. Around this time, I went to a disco, which I had previously only heard about and danced alone in a frenzy.

I wanted to craft a critical tally of my life—what I had dreamed about, what I had lived for, what I had gained or lost, what I still had... I wanted to weigh my worth—my life's worth—on the world's scale.

For that, I had to get away from this suffocating house. I could no longer take Mother's scorn for not bringing home money, or my younger siblings' disdain and condescension for living off them. I went to a friend after agonizing over the thought of asking for help. "Could you lend me money?" "How much?" A million won.[1] How difficult it was to say it. One million, like a piece of gold in hand, I left the house without direction.

At thirty years old, I lived in a kosi-won, a dormitory for the civil service examinations.

I was not there to study for the exams; I had no place to go. A kosi-won was, as it is now, the cheapest and safest place for a thirty-year-old woman. For 20,000 won a day, it provided a room with three meals. It was small, but big enough to house one body; it even had a window that let fresh air in. It was a paradise, for me. After paying five months' rent in advance, not much was left. All I had were a few jangling bus tokens and hundred-won coins.

The fall had left and the winter arrived. One cold day, I caught a brutal cold. I had no money for the cold medicine, ssang-hwa-tang.[2] What bitter emotion I felt as I dragged my fevered body, went to a bookstore, sold Marcel Proust's *In Search of Lost Time* and held a thousand-won bill. But not all was lost time during this period of twenty to thirty. It was a precipitous time.

December 30, 1991: The night that hungry snow was piling up, useless and silly, I wrote in my diary: "My life may be a failure, still there is 'I' in me, and am alive, writing poems." The poem I first wrote went like this:

> Is the road for a professional revolutionary
> the road for a jobless man?
> I don't even have such a common thing as a career,
> a business card with a worthy title.
> Without a cheap lover I can cuddle with in the cold,
> I'm going around, around on a distant road.

From the fall to the winter of that year, utterly alone, I ruminated over my acid youth and spit out my first poems. The poems, like lumps of blood or the shrieks of wounded animals, were put together and published. With the publication of *Thirty: The Party is Over*, my unemployed career came to an end, and I became a poet. Contrary to the title of the anthology, however, for me the party had just begun. It was not a party that someone had prepared for me. It was a party I'd prepared for myself. I chose the ingredients and cooked with my own hands. "Thirty" was such a time for me.

Looking back, I may have never been young; on the other hand, I may have always been young. Because I never enjoyed a normal youth, am I unable to get old normally? As I am about to turn forty, I still feel from time to time as though I'm in my thirties. I dress like a thirty-year-old, shake like a thirty-year-old, think and act like a thirty-year-old.

I had nothing to hang on to while crossing over the river of "thirty-year-olds." I had to navigate it solely on the power of delusion and the sighs of attachment. Tonight, I desperately long for that time, the time I stood against the arrogant force of the oncoming current with a resolute, combative spirit.

1. One million *won* in Korean currency was about $1,000 at the time.
2. *Ssang-hwa-tang*: Korean herbal medicine good for a cold or to boost the immune system.

# Emelihter Kihleng

Dr. Evelyn Flores and I are collaborating on an anthology of writing by indigenous writers from the geographic region known as Micronesia, which encompasses many islands that are diverse linguistically and culturally. We are following in the footsteps of other Pacific Island anthologies, such as *Lali: A Pacific Anthology*, edited by Albert Wendt (1980), *Nuanua: Pacific Writing in English since 1980*, edited by Albert Wendt (1996), and *Whetu Moana: Contemporary Polynesian Poems in English* edited by Albert Wendt, Reina Whaitiri, and Robert Sullivan (2003), that strive to promote writing by indigenous Pacific Islanders. There has been more writing coming out of Polynesia and Melanesia than Micronesia, and Evelyn and I felt that creating an anthology of writing from our region would be an important step for getting our voices heard in the Pacific Islands and beyond.

As in all "firsts," it is a challenging undertaking, but also quite exciting. Micronesian cultures, like all Pacific Island societies and most indigenous cultures, are oral. In much of Micronesia, knowledge continues to be passed down orally and is not written. Creative Writing is therefore still a fairly new phenomenon in Micronesia. Evelyn and I both live on Guam, and we put out a call for submissions in local and regional newspapers, online on various Micronesia and Pacific-related websites and listservs, and through word of mouth. As expected, most of the submissions received were from Chamoru writers from Guam, some of whom live on-island and others who live in the United States. Guam has a unique colonial history that often separates it from the other islands in Micronesia. The island is an unincorporated US Territory and has been greatly affected by American colonialism since 1898 when it became a US military colony. The other islands in Micronesia, with the exception of Nauru and Kiribati (former British colonies), are now under compacts of free association with the United States. The anthology is obviously quite focused on indigineity and other issues surrounding it, such as identity, language, and colonialism.

Representation is an important issue that we have to deal with. Because this is a Micronesian anthology, we need to represent the region as a whole, and this is quite challenging given that we only received a few submissions, if any, from other islands, and we may not even accept what was submitted. It is quite impossible really. As editors, we are striving to include the best writing that Micronesia has to offer, and in doing so, we realize that we may not be able to include writing from all Micronesian islands, but only writing that best represents our region of the Pacific.

Our project is not a women's anthology project. The anthology will include writing by indigenous men and women from Micronesia. We have received more submissions from women. I suppose one could assume from this that there are more women writers in Micronesia at this time. Also, it is worth noting that both of the editors are women, and we are both poets. Evelyn is a Chamoru woman from Guam and I am a biracial Pohnpeian woman born on Guam and raised on Guam, Pohnpei, and in Honolulu, Hawai'i. Hawaiian poet and scholar, Brandy Nalani McDougall, is our outside reviewer for the project. Essentially, although this is not a women-only project, it is women-run. I think this is especially appropriate given that most islands in Micronesia are matrilineal, and women tend to have a lot of power. Micronesian women are oftentimes the leaders in important movements in the region. In this case, it is two Micronesian women spearheading the first anthology specifically for and written by indigenous Micronesians.

# Rocío Cerón

responding to Lila Zemborain

Experimental poetry in Mexico is still marginal. Just a few poets over the last twenty or thirty years have appeared. Ulises Carrion, one of the most representative figures (he wrote the manifesto "The New Art of Making Books"), left Mexico to live in Holland (until his death). One of the reasons he left was that he thought the Mexican literature scene was very solemn. Also, the idea that one can be an experimental poet and be a woman is, in a macho society, seen as very strange. Since 2003, we have had a collective, MotínPoeta, which means "poet mutiny," that was founded by Carla Faesler and myself. Our idea is to make interdisciplinary projects that take poetry as a departure point. We have produced two CDs: "Urbe Probeta" with poets and electronic music (poems-landscapes of Mexico City) and "Personae" with poets from different places in the Mexican republic and electroacoustic composers. Our third production is "Empire," a book of poems by Rocío Cerón, music by Bishop, video by Nomada, and graffiti and stencil by Tower. It was launched in late June 2010.

From the beginning, we have had complaints; some poets (many born in the Forties or Fifties) think that our work is trivializing the idea of poetry. We keep going. And we've even gotten some supporters now. My personal work is with visual and object poetry. I think this type of work across different "continents" or formats doesn't trivialize poetry, but to the contrary, permits access to other words, poetry, and language. Now other young poets have been working with poetry, but in diverse forms. Women in Mexico have been the ones to really make breakthroughs in the poetry scene. I am thinking here of the visual poetry of Myriam Moscona or the art books of Minerva Reynosa or the poetry projects of Abril Castro and the video-poems of Carla Faesler. We represent the new idea to create and express poetry not only on the page, but also in music, in the relation between objects, in the streets.

We need more spaces, more magazines that will really support our works (in Mexico leading literature magazines, like *Letras Libres* are just looking at work by male writers). I use the term "guerrilla action" for what we do: small press books, poetry readings in contemporary museums, street poetry actions, CDs, parties with poetry bombardment, and radio poetry bombardments. We also use youtube and myspace. Another thing I do is teach workshops that focus on poetry in unconventional formats so I can show young people that poetry and language can live in the places and spaces they want.

# Gidi Loza

## I Am a Woman-Writer

I'm interested in several things. I'm a woman and I write. I use language as a medium for discovery. Language in my body has always felt different. Right now, language works in me as an instrument for discovering. Me = my body. My body is primordial to me. Through it, I experience the world. I experience the world I have created and the world created before me that is in me.

For some time in my life, my condition of woman-female didn't matter. I was taught (which is in part unconscious and part conscious) to forget about me, to think more of the exterior, of the outer reality-world than *my* inner world. For me, right now, it works differently. I've learned (in the process of learning about myself as a complete self) that to begin with something one has to begin with oneself. I needed to begin with me. Me: body, history, past, symbols, thoughts, thinking, voices... My world is connected to everything I am (I as a multiple being). In this way I can know and experience myself as a whole.

My body is my first connection of me with me. And knowing myself (an important thing for me in my writing because I discover myself through it) leads me to the connections I'm part of, the connections that are always happening, the connections that happen through a language that appears within the body, an autonomous language that is not rational. The body has its own language (or several ones). Discovering my body helped me discover the world inside me, it helped me reach it, see it, experience it. My body is a source of wisdom I need to listen to.

Society tells me my body (a female body) is not important (therefore I'm not important). Society tells me the last thing I should care about is myself. Society tells me I must forget myself and reach the otherness which is in itself a fantasy.

I have learned, through my body, that the things I've learned are totally the contrary of the living of a *totally great experience* (I take these words from Kathy Acker). Education in the country where I live (Mexico) is not education, is degradation. In Mexico I can translate education as: television-sleeping-not thinking-sex-money-belittling-stupid-reality. Mass education is these things. This is an incomplete way of living, not autonomous (and at the same time collective). Depending (as education teaches us to do) is to forget we are here. We try as hard as we can to separate ourselves, to see what is not primordial, to give a shit about our ancient culture.

I am, as a woman-writer, who lives in a created-divided-land (Tijuana-US), learning that boundaries and limits only limit-centralize: they are prisons. Thinking, feeling, experiencing, and knowing myself through my body has opened the limits of *me* in *me*. Has opened the limits in the limits. And one of the things this reveals to me is that *me* is a wider, multiple being in a wider and multiple reality that is wiser and richer (in the sense of perceiving, feeling, thinking, receiving, giving . . . ).

I need, in order to live a fulfilled life, to realize what and how I've been taught, to see the pattern I have been set into. To realize there is something else besides "this," and I'm not against "this," but "this," in the deep bottom of "this," is just cement, objects, gossip, roads, maps (all that is already shown-known, all that we can see without effort).

As a woman who writes, I feel that the world is an infinite, connected weaving that is taking place right now.

# Jussara Salazar

responding to Lila Zemborain

*What should US poets know about the living and working conditions of Brazilian women poets?*

In recent years, here in Brazil, poets and media have been questioning, in a general way, the presence of women in the literary world, mainly in poetry. Out of this discussion, the expression "feminine literature" was created, as if women wrote from a distinct reality and we could not think about writing except as a woman, despite the many social and cultural differences of a big and contradictory country as ours. The great Brazilian writers of the tradition are men, and because of that, poetry written by women is assumed to be confessional and thus subordinate. Our generation here and now is the generation where this is changing. There is a new approach that regards the feminine condition in a natural and respectful way that acknowledges all its aspects and differences, and that will enable us, maybe, in the near future, to say that Brazilian literature is also produced by women writers. Today we are limited to a few isolated examples of women writers. I remember, for example, Clarice Lispector and Lygia Fagundes Telles.

# Silvia Guerra

*What should US poets know about the living and working conditions of Uruguay women poets?*

I think we know nothing or very little.

None of us know them.

I believe that the conditions of life and work of Uruguayan women poets are also varied and depend on the age of the poet.

For example, women in the so-called Generation 45—Vilariño, Vitale, Berenguer—I get the idea that they have not felt the wound of gender.

Those of the next generation—Marosa di Giorgio, Circe Maia, Nancy Bacelo—were more combative, and although they have not often raised the issue of gender, it appears in their work.

The poets who follow these age groups belong to the dynamite age, that is, the time when the country is completely out of it politically and economically; they are almost all single women who have more than one job and who have dependent children, so the label "poet" is quite difficult to accommodate. Now, people who are younger, are in another age. They are trying to work on some things related to writing, trying to recover when things occur, and trying to get paid when the job allows.

# Ana Arzoumanian

responding to Lila Zemborain

Poetry in Argentina is very isolated work. The universities don't take it as a subject of study. There is not a "canonic reading" of poetry. This reality makes poetry a land of freedom, on the one hand; and on the other, a land of eternal marginality. The publishers don't encourage the publishing of poetry and there are no literary agents for poets. Men support each other, and when I say support, I am talking about places ruled by men: newspapers, magazines, etc.

# Romina Freschi

*responding to Lila Zemborain*

*What should US poets know about the living and working conditions of Latin American experimental women poets?*

I don't know what US poets should know. Or what other poets from any country, including my own, should know. I think women in my country, and me as a woman, feel discriminated against so many times during the day that we don't even notice. Being a poet is difficult. There's such utilitarianism that poetry is seen as pointless. There is also so much poverty that many people reject it as an activity of the oligarchy, and it is, most of the time. Being a woman poet is something so thin, it seems almost an illusion. There are a lot of women writing poetry in my country, but none of them are taken seriously. Women get to be published by a "serious" editor (that is someone who would pay for the edition, sign a contract, has contacts with the local press and will pay honoraries or rights) at the end of their lives, almost as a favor (if they're not dead already). Doing something different from a narrative, figurative, simplistic form in poetry is many times an object of mockery. Being an experimental women poet is being invisible, when not crazy or just silly. We get excluded from papers, contracts, anthologies, even dialogues. The intellectual field is really aggressive to women, and women themselves are very aggressive and competitive with each other, even for the tiniest and most chauvinist rewards. There are groups of women who work together, but they seem not to exist for papers, magazines, academic studies, or the very few commercial editors.

# Liliana Heer

*responding to Lila Zemborain*

*What should US poets know about the living and working conditions of Argentinean women poets?*

I will answer these questions but with one condition: I hate generalization, so I will express my viewpoint, absolutely subjective, driven by the enthusiasm of this proposal.

I think there is much to be known, from both shores, about the poetic writing phenomenon, so much that it is almost impossible to cover it all. One of the most important things that I observe in Argentinean women poets is their work with language. They use sound and meaning to search for the trove of disruption, to be awake to the halo of the real.

Many times, art goes against life conditions and one writes in any state, but one writes better when one has time on one's side.

# Lila Zemborain

*What should US poets know about the living and working conditions of Argentinean women poets?*

I have lived in New York since 1985. I started writing poetry again in 1987, after a gap of almost ten years. When I lived in Argentina in the seventies, during the military dictatorship, I was not connected with the poetry community, and I wrote poetry almost for myself. In 1993, I published my first book of poetry in Argentina, and began to establish longstanding relationships with Argentinean poets. At that point, I was not interested in the US poetry community at all; my interlocutor was Argentinean: men and women poets. Later, in the nineties, this group got expanded to writers who wrote in Spanish, either in Latin America or in Spain. Finally, in the year 2000, I started to connect with poets in New York and I found a very welcoming community, especially, in the Poetry Project, and Belladonna, who published my first book in translation in 2007. As you can see by my experience, I consider myself an outsider in both communities, since I really began to develop myself as a poet here in New York, but writing in Spanish. The main difference that I see between women poet communities in New York, and in Buenos Aires, is that poets here have the possibility of working in academia while developing their own poetic work, which gives them an economic release, even in these times of crisis. In Buenos Aires, where the economic crisis is constant, poets do all different kind of jobs, many times not related to their creative work. But this doesn't mean that there is less activity: there is an incredible abundance of readings, small and big presses, and websites run by women, that are not especially selective in male/female terms. Nevertheless, it seems that, in Argentina, the need for women's poetry anthologies is still there, as shown by the anthology *Poetas argentinas (1940-1960)*, edited in 2006 by

Irene Gruss. Experimental poetry, though, is less understood, so experimental women poets have less visibility. This might have to do with the lack of understanding that political writing can also be (of course) experimental.

*What can be done? Is there anything to be done together?*

Promoting dialogue between Spanish-speaking women poets and US poets through translation would obviously be very productive. There is a lack of knowledge in the US about the work of Latin American women poets, even of those residing here. To bridge this gap, in 2000, I started a very small summer reading series, called Rebel Road (after the street where our house was in Shelter Island), where I invited three poets: one American, one Latin American, and one in-between, Latino poet. The reading was held in English, and with the help of a sponsor I published a chapbook of every reading. Through this, I met and befriended a lot of American poets, and a community was being created. With this experience in hand, in 2003 I started curating the KJCC Poetry Series at NYU, which is held in Spanish. I always include a couple of bilingual events, even a Catalan/Spanish/English one. But if the invited poet is not well known to Americans, the English speaking audience is not very big. I think that Cecilia Vicuña's *The Oxford Book of Latin American Poetry*, published this year, will be ground breaking in this sense, opening American audiences to new voices. But in terms of integration, the only way to achieve it is by organizing cross-cultural events and projects.

Translations of the work of American experimental women poets into Spanish would also be very influential, in breaking a certain formal homogeneity in women's writing. There are many Spanish-speaking women poets and translators, who live in this country, who could be able to do this work. But this should be done with a project in hand: an anthology, a website, a reading series, etc.

The freedom that I found in American experimental poetry has widened the possibilities of my own poetic investigations. And living in this country has also allowed me to connect through my writing with poets from all over the Spanish-speaking world (as shown by the poets that have answered your questions). As a Clinical Assistant Professor at the new NYU MFA in Creative Writing in Spanish, I promote cross-reading of American and Latin American experimental poetry. And the students really take advantage of it.

American academia's economic possibilities (contrasting with the lack of money in Latin American countries) could also be used as a medium to establish the much needed dialogue between Spanish-speaking women writers and American women writers.

# Can We Do Together?

*Ana Arzoumanian, Romina Freschi, Liliana Heer, Silvia Guerra, Jussara Salazar, Rocío Cerón, and Ainize Txopitea are esponding to Lila Zemborain. Fawziya Choueich al-Salem, Maha Hassan, and Hala Mohammad, are responding to and translated from Arabic by Simone Fattal. Mahhosazana Xaba is responding to Phillippa Yaa de Villiers. Demosthenes Agrafiotis, Katerina Anghelaki-Rook, and Liana Sakelliou are responding to and translated from Greek by Tatiani G. Rapatzikou and Liana Sakelliou. Sanja Pilić and Barbara Pleić are responding to and translated from Croatian by Ana Božičević. Jana Kolarič, Breda Smolnikar, Nataša Sukić, Iva Jevtić, Barbara Korun, Meta Kušar, and Vida Mokrin-Pauer are responding to Stanislava Chrobáková Repar and translated from Slovene by Iva Jevtić. Stanislava Chrobáková Repar was translated from Slovak into Slovene by Stanislava Chrobáková Repar and then from Slovene into English by Iva Jevtić. Etela Farkašová, Jana Bodnárová, Eva Maliti, and Dana Podracká are responding to Stanislava Chrobáková Repar and translated from Slovene into English by Iva Jevtić. Mária Ferenčuhová, Uršuľa Kovalyk, Jana Pácalová, Ivica Ruttkayová, Anna Grusková, Derek Rebro, and Zuzana Mojžišová are responding to Stanislava Chrobáková Repar and translated from Slovak into Slovene by Alenka Šalej and then from Slovene into English by Iva Jevtić. Jakuba Katalpa, Lenka Daňhelová, Daniela Fischerová, Pavla Frýdlová, Tereza Riedlbauchová, and Božena Správcová are responding to Stanislava Chrobáková Repar and translated from Czech into Slovene by Bojana Maltarić and then from Slovene into English by Iva Jevtić.*

## Ainize Txopitea

Blogging has become a way to tap into public opinion, so I will suggest to build a blog where the views of US and Hispanic women poets are connected. Create a forum, an online community centre of analysis, discussion, education, publications, arts, reviews, etc. A directory where feminist poets of all continents can be viewed.

## Ana Arzoumanian

I do think that making a "community" is a political answer to the oddness of literature written by women (as it is called in so many places). Plurality, the way of making a tradition that could give us a place in the world of letters. I mean not only reading each other, but also allowing us to be read by men, not as gendered literature but as literature. People don't say: literature written by men, do they? Being translated is one of the issues. Making room for readings out of the academy. Having a voice that could rule.

## Romina Freschi

What really works for me is trying to stay in touch with the people I intensely value and to maintain a conversation. But that can be difficult and sometimes it feels like starting over all the time. The internet is a very useful tool because most of the people I try to stay in touch with do not live in Buenos Aires. I think, therefore, that experimental poetry is not a local phenomenon but a global one; it has no boundaries. Even though I often feel frustrated, I cannot think of a better way to have contact and conversation. I think experimental or alternative—or whatever we should call ourselves—poets should experience the commitment and responsibility of sustaining dialogues between each other and face together the material and social barriers we have to deal with every day alone and often in anguish.

## Liliana Heer

The first thing that comes to my mind is proposing an interchange of readings and translations. That is to say, to create a poetry factory with our own texts. Through this, we would penetrate the convergences and differences that link us beyond any classification.

## Silvia Guerra

To start, try to read. US women should read Uruguayan women and the Uruguayan the US.

## Jussara Salazar

Nations and regions produce arts centers that determine what is excellent, determine what or who should be published, and thus build hierarchies. I believe that decentralizing this would widen support for the subaltern, for literature written by women. The exchange of ideas and information is interesting because they always throw the center, and the center's concentration of "power," off-balance, injecting oxygen into it as they open a discussion to the different views in the world, where they meet and where they become distant.

## Rocío Cerón

I think that a relationship and a dialogue between experimental women poets from the Americas are very important. To share experiences is to enrich. Also, seeing the works of other poets opens the possibility of feeling that you are not alone doing something "strange." I hope in the near future that the American and Mexican universities will open their doors to symposiums or gatherings where experimental poets can present their works.

## Fawziya Choueich al-Salem

I expect the American woman to open herself to our culture, the way we are open to all cultures from around the world. We would like her to help make it known to the American people and to show them that racism against Arabs and Muslims is wrong. Terrorism is not a necessary aspect of religion and it has goals that have nothing to do with religion; its roots are totally political, even though it may hide under a religious veil.

We believe that the American woman, free from numerous ideologies, and open to humanism, is the best and most appropriate person to fulfill this role, i.e. bringing together different points of view, establishing dialogues and cultural exchanges, which could bring us closer together, and abolish the idea of the clash of civilizations, the Muslim other, etc. Humanism is above all these considerations.

## Maha Hassan

As for what the American woman can do: she should read our work, and take our opinions back to her society. The Arab woman is very present nowadays in international forums, which is good and compensates for her absence at home. All the independence movements in the Arab World, in their struggle against imperialism or colonialism, did not help the liberation of women. Those movements wanted to please their followers and did not address the taboos of gender. Unfortunately, the movements in favor of women came from the West.

## Hala Mohammad

I think that translating the work of Arab women is the great difficulty before us. The obstacle between our knowing each other. We should be translating much more than we are now. This is the only independent way to get cultures closer together, to make our cultural understanding vaster, and to encourage dialogue. I would like the humanistic American woman, the one who is a citizen of this world, to commit in all freedom to her own independent cultural project and to add to her freedom and dreams. In that way, we can both be a part of the ideal homeland: creativity. Again, translation would make this possible, would bring our creativities together, and make our voices freely heard, would allow us to do more than follow the political powers that always give recognition to those already in favor. And, hopefully, we will achieve change.

## Olivia Coetzee

It is important to be able to do workshops highlighting issues of patriarchy and how it is silencing our voices as women.

Help women to understand their own voices by creating forums, using the internet to its full potential.

Newsletters to the parts of the country where internet is a luxury, highlighting our issues and at the same time, creating more consciousness in women's circles; it is a sad day when we have so many powerful women in this country, but so few who are challenging the system and the inequality it holds for women poets.

Challenge the system on public platforms, challenging mainstream publishers.

Create platforms for dialogue with women writers published in the mainstream and women who are not published.

Challenge this patriarchal system's way of writing by writing in our own voices, highlighting women's issues that are not considered important enough by mainstream publishers.

## Makhosazana Xaba

My challenge and suggestion to all individual feminists of the world is this: We need to start taking the idea of amassing enough capital for ourselves seriously. We must stop relying on others and complaining about "donor agendas." Never-ending pitching expeditions are not sustainable. Women and feminists need to make their own money if they are serious about being composers of their music, publishers of their books, architects and designers of their own galleries, directors of their own movies and plays, and holders of their own destinies. We need money and time to write. Stories of the world will not be complete without biographies of women. We need lots of money and lots of time to write biographies. Self-sacrifice cannot be the answer; it should be erased from the agenda of feminism.

*Demosthenes Agrafiotis, Katerina Anghelaki-Rook, and Liana Sakelliou are responding to the question "What is the message that you would you like to send to your American female co-poets?"*

## Demosthenes Agrafiotis

Audacity and bon courage.

## Katerina Anghelaki-Rook

The message that I would send to the American women poets—and to all the women poets in the world—would be: keep it up! Because while it seems that our times have turned their back on poetry, the times to come will be, it seems, very difficult—psychologically, atmospherically, economically—and then I am sure human beings will turn again to poetry. And maybe to women's poetry even more so because women, by nature, know how to give birth to a new world, of poetry as well.

## Liana Sakelliou

To American women poets I would say that if they express the depths of their experience, and perhaps this might mean female experience, then it would have relevance to all readers, or in some cases to all women, including those in countries around the world. Furthermore, if their writing should forge new visions of experience, then it would be important beyond the time of the writer.

## Sanja Pilić

from "How to Save Yourself…"

To begin with, procure the most expensive lingerie and start a magazine where you can publish your own work. Become an editor, because to be just a writer is for losers. Find a handsome companion (gay's ok), and quit being romantic. Join many clubs and political parties. Find, at long last, a tribe you can belong to! Hem your skirts and practice walking in high heels. Nod your head a little more and be nicer to the boring gentlemen you were indifferent to before. You don't have to say to their faces exactly what you think of them. Start having fun. Take dance lessons. Invent a new literary movement. It would be nice to nab a position in the Ministry of Culture. Or find a young lover. He's better for the ego than newspaper eulogies or your collected works on the shelf. Life is trivial, I'm sorry! Sartre, if he was any less ugly, would never have become a philosopher.

So, start participating in sports and talk to your financial adviser about investing the money you inherited from your grandma in Sutivan. Change your hairstyle. Change your writing style. If in the past you were a drama queen, if you moralized and ruminated, have some fun for a change! If you really have to spend time at a computer because you're too tired to be a waitress and too old to become a pianist, at least enjoy writing. Life's short. Be economical. Rational. Pragmatic. Cheery. Have fun. Your male colleagues might still not respect you, your female colleagues might not take you seriously, but you'll enjoy yourself.

Come up with your own style! The style makes the man, as someone said. Praise yourself, since others do it too. Stop being so well-mannered; if someone smacks you, smack back. Don't let writing rule your life, let your life guide the writing. Make friends with guidos and players because they know how to make it and survive, and turn your innate sensitivity into a strength. Keep playing and take no one too seriously, not even yourself. When you're in a bad mood, go get a massage.

If your book sales don't increase, at least you won't be sorry you're not the new Sylvia Plath. And even she had to stick her head into an oven to get noticed. You take your head out of the oven, since you don't have to suffer to write. And if you're unsuccessful in the literary world, you won't be sorry because you will have had some fun. If you do succeed, in spite of everyone and everything, buy some stock and nestle into a good investment fund.

And don't forget to take your aunt from the nursing home on a cruise to Greece and Turkey. You are still that gentle, empathetic, ancient soul who once, so long ago, decided to become, oh, a regular, boring woman writer!

## Barbara Pleić

I wonder if our situation would be easier if we had a more solid "family tree," an uninterrupted tradition of women's literature to lean on. It exists, of course, but when will it become a deserving part of the canon, and no longer an alternative underground current, a hidden history reached only by those whose interest surpasses standard Croatian literature courses? Subversion is great, but I wonder to what extent this approach to the creative work of Croatian women writers can be considered subversive, and how much of it is a matter of simple neglect and the ossification of the inert structures of official curricula. Considering the number of exciting women authors emerging in our midst, it's time for a change: to our great joy, it appears that future anthologies will have to make plenty of space for the likes of Kristina Kegljen, Marija Andrijašević, Dorta Jagić, and all others who follow them. It's undeniable that we are luckier than the "vanguard" of women who preceded us; the sudden growth of the alternative media (particularly the internet) allows women authors far better possibilities for collaboration and the public presentation of their work. As one of the many shining examples, I'd like to mention the web portal cunterview.net, which, in the words of its founders, provides a "virtual space created to address the lack of systematic research, documentation, and presentation of women's creative expression in Croatia and beyond," and which "pays attention to creative women because of their absence from the media." The portal includes a database of artists in different genres, from the visual and dramatic arts, to music, new media, and literature. The "do it yourself" approach is well-known to women throughout history, and virtual communities of this sort are ideal for strengthening both the mutual exchange and the awareness of one's own status; this is certainly one of the methods of solidifying the backbone necessary to the future continuation of the line.

*The remaining writers are responding to the question "Where do you think the hidden reserves or the potential to im-*

*prove the situation are located? Do you believe a joint action is called for, either at home or internationally? Do you have any specific suggestions?"*

## Jana Kolarič

To tell you the truth, I have no idea how to overcome this state of affairs. As long as everything remains on the level of principle and verbal endorsement, all is fine. It is different when one enters the world of material concreteness. When you become active with the intent of changing the situation, you are accused of only looking after your own interests. I tried, for instance, to change some of the ways in which stipends are awarded by the Slovene Writers' Association, of which I am a member. Statistics do not lie: even though the membership of the Association is divided equally in terms of gender, only a fifth of the stipends, sometimes even less, are given to women. When you demand a reason, an explanation, you are told that women have less to show: fewer articles, reviews, prizes, quotations . . . This is how the committees protect themselves from charges of prejudice and bias. And why do women have less to show? Well, we return here to the original cause: it is said that it is the inferiority of women's writing itself that is to blame.

## Breda Smolnikar

The only solution is individual work. Sooner or later, the results will show. That is, if you are a true artist. And there are few of those, so very few of those. It has always been that way. But it makes me sad to see a young name disappear or drown, just because it was not nurtured at the right time, if only by a letter or a kind word. When I was young I had the luxury of being noticed, recognized. Then, later, I had to find strength inside me to persevere. And the strength to fall.

## Nataša Sukić

I believe that some sort of joint action or projects that would aim at the promotion of women's literature are necessary. The promotion of women's literature is important, since it opens up social spaces and breaks stereotypes. At the same time, it encourages women to finally send off "all those letters that have remained hidden in their drawers for so long."

## Iva Jevtić

A lot has been done. As far as literature is concerned, I see future potential in the shaping of a new generation of critics and theoreticians who would be capable of placing unrecognized work, contemporary work, and the works of the Slovene canon into new theoretical frameworks. However, we should be aware that our possibilities remain severely limited as long as there is no wider consensus on the role and value of both feminism and women in Slovenia. Considering the many excesses and imbecilities that we have witnessed over the past few years, the future does not seem bright at the moment.

## Barbara Korun

The general state of culture is worsening each day, in all aspects: there is neither glory nor money to be found here. In our postwar society, culture does not matter, politicians pretend it does not exist (except as scenery for symbolic state events, such as our cultural holiday, Prešern Day) and very few political parties even mention it. As an artist you cannot live off your work (the situation is best for some theater people and museum curators); the fact that Simon Gregorčič could buy a house and a small vineyard with his fees or that Lojze Kovačič and his family could live for three months with the money he got for a short story is now a distant dream. . . . Oh, but I am sorry, all I do is complain. The solution is to persist, on your own and with others. The solution is to help, encourage each other. Every literary word is important, priceless. We witness and that is what matters: the story of mankind and womankind should continue to be written.

## Meta Kušar

If I understand correctly, this is a question about a call for political action, but such action cannot work unless we are truly aware that we all, each and every one of us, only see around us that which is already inside us. I imagine such a movement should confirm women in their uniqueness and in this way encourage other women, bystanders and potential co-workers, to join. I would be very sad to engage in something that would negate the deep femininity of men around me.

## Vida Mokrin-Pauer

I do not know what advice to give to us, the community of women poets. I am terribly tired of calls to action, of being called upon to find a way to help myself and other women . . . Through quantum mechanics and Transcendental Meditation, I discover within me and everything an infinite field of possibilities. I am directed at its humorous and animist-cosmic-playful wave-lengths . . . And in-between, I rest! As a feminist, I urge you to have a look at these two films, at least!: *Tom & Viv*: a biographic movie about T.S. Eliot and his wife Viv; and *What the Bleep?!* (subtitle: *Down the Rabbit Hole*), a film on quantum theory. There are two versions of the movie, the one with the subtitles is better. Apart from my books and translations of my poems in various journals—it would be downright stupid and self-denying to propagate the books and thoughts of other writers, but not my own—I also advise women to read the great books of my friend Andrej Detela and the book by Urban Kordeš, *From Truth to Trust*. Hahahaha, but truly, this is one of the most feminist, scientifically philosophical books that I have ever read. And it does not even mention feminism. And there are many more books and movies . . .

## Stanislava Chrobáková Repar

I am becoming increasingly skeptical and strive to set goals only on a personal level, since they seem more reachable that way. I notice, even with those closest to me, this incredible complexity of everything, even change. I am still fighting the idea that weariness (death?) resolves everything, and yet my path inward is growing shorter and shorter. How well I understand a younger colleague of mine who once said: *"I am so fanatically feminist I even find the idea of feminism insulting!"* And yet, is there any other avenue of addressing gender injustice? I seriously doubt it.

I believe an important condition of improvement is the recognition of our feminist colleagues from the West, who have travelled a road much longer and have more experience. They should not forget their colleagues from the East, i.e. the countries of the former Eastern Bloc. And we should not be used to satisfy the ambition and goals of others, as we usually are (even within the space of, for instance, research projects funded by the EU). Another, and equally important, condition is for feminists from Central, Eastern, and Southeast Europe not to forget themselves, both on a political and a personal level. Without the necessary, wider social consensus, gender equality and justice remain a utopia of the few, cultural and intellectual if not political and economic elites.

A propos (to be more specific): I publicly propose JJ and JC from *Aspekt*, for the second time already, to be awarded the Dominik Tatarka Prize—for their feminist work and achievements. I believe Mila Haugová to be the next favorite—for her poetry. I do not think Dominik would mind. He respected women—in his own (dis)loyal way, of course. I cannot say this is reflected in the award bearing his name.

## Etela Farkašová

I often think about how to create more opportunities for the publication and distribution of women's literary works. The organization of joint projects could be one of the ways, so I support the organization of joint, internationally coordinated projects that would contribute to the distribution of literature by women authors, as well as enable the development of international contacts among authors from different countries. In September, I attended a conference of Central European women writers and poets in Budapest, and there was common agreement between the twenty participants about the need for such association. I believe that the organization of similar international seminars is useful; only in this way can there be an exchange among writers that can lead to the discussion of potential strategies for the future. I believe that the creation of joint research projects would be useful, aimed at, for instance, the comparative analysis of the representation of male and female characters in one or the other literature, the relations between the sexes not only in the private but also in the public sphere, intergenerational relations of men as well as of women, and so on. Such research projects could also entail the analysis of sexual stereotypes in texts by men and women or the analysis of the subversive possibilities of texts based on the presentation of stereotypes. The findings of these projects should be presented within universities of different countries and in this way instill a developed sense of gender issues in our future intellectuals. It is only then that the special organizations or women's associations would prove unnecessary and the understanding of women's literature or women writers (in itself not a result of female but male critique) would lose the grounds necessary for its existence. Women authors would gladly discuss literature only in terms of its being "good" or "bad," as our male colleagues never fail to do. This is just one of the reasons why it is necessary to create conditions of true equality (but I do not mean equality in terms of uniformity) of genders in the literary field. I hope this survey will also play a small part in this endeavor.

## Anna Grusková

The question implies that there is a universally bad situation in need of improvement, and this may be true. I am sure there is need for joint action. First, it would be best to meet and get to know each other, and out of this, ideas and cooperation would arise. Or maybe there should be an international literary competition for women that awards a local woman (Slovak, Slovene, Czech, German, etc.). The results of such a competition could also be presented in the European parliament.

## Derek Rebro

The more I am familiar with our academic world the less I am inclined to engage with it. I see a way forward mostly on an individual level in the sense of continuing my work as a literary critic and in the dissemination of a different view on the work of women authors. This also concerns our feminist activism: its agents, both male and female, are gradually losing the will to progress both mentally and as individuals (sometimes this is also due to a mind-numbing amount of paperwork that allows them to survive, but at the same time drains their energy). Of course, the younger generation of feminists could help here but I sometimes get the feeling that it is precisely these feminist youth who our "mother feminists" are ashamed of. The activism and enthusiasm of the young is not enough unless fed on the widening of our intellectual horizons, a sense of distance, and humor. Carefree laughter, not cynicism. I sometimes get the sense that the younger feminists have taken over from their predecessors their strictness, intractability, and sharpness, if not paranoia, and this, in my opinion, is not the way to bring feminism to the people—and not only to those already in the know. There is a lack of a creative dialogue between groups with different viewpoints (it is not enough to declare: feminism means feminisms!—it would help to live this diversity) as well as a lack of an honest self-reflection that feminist circles in the West have been practicing for a long time. I see the future in more people taking seriously the demands of feminism, but at the same time not forgetting to dance.

## Jana Bodnárová

Women writers definitely express, sometimes even define the lives of other women, no matter what country they live in. This is why it would be adequate—at least from my view as a woman author—to publish international anthologies of women's writing. There is a blank here, at least in Slovakia. This is equally true of theoretical reflections on the state of feminism. It would be useful to have more publications of an international nature (the journal *Aspekt* cannot cover everything). Outside the capital of Bratislava there is a definite lack of talks by theoreticians from abroad despite interested, enthusiastic women living all over this country.

## Mária Ferenčuhová

I believe there remains a lot to be done on many levels in the area of gender issues. I certainly believe that any community of writing women could benefit from group action (the publication of thematic issues, public readings, etc.) especially with adequate media support: this is the only way to stop the discussion of gender issues from being explained away as a form of minority cultural phenomenon.

## Uršuľa Kovalyk

The situation is going to improve once we, women writers, show more solidarity with each other and are no longer afraid of being labelled as feminists. Also, it will get better as soon as there are more women's presses and more sympathetic women in high places and committees that distribute funds. Maybe someday there is going to be a sort of international organization with, for instance, open competitions for women authors on various gender or feminist issues. Or maybe we'll have a female version of the Pulitzer or Nobel Prize. I think all this would help.

## Eva Maliti

Writing is a very personal, intimate thing. I am not a fan of big group actions, even though they are sometimes necessary . . . When writing, a person is alone, with paper, or these days more likely a computer, and in this way one develops and forms thoughts that need to be communicated. However, it is obvious that with the help of feminism many things have changed and moved forward; women all over the world are gradually coming into their own. Personally, I am more a witness of these processes around me, but I welcome all positive endeavors. I believe it is important that women continue to work from the standpoint of humanism, which I believe is an essential part of being a woman.

## Zuzana Mojžišová

The struggle to help women has the character of Sisyphus's work or Don Quixote's fight against windmills. For people of my kind, who feel an inborn (and maybe adequate—but here I go boasting) responsibility towards others, and who try to be socially engaged, even if not in the field of feminism but in other arenas (with me this is ethnic xenophobia and violence against children), it is good to have around us people irritated enough by the situation of women to fight it. To raise the awareness of a society takes a long time. But I am sure that each step on this path, unless completely stupid, is a step in the right direction. I feel deep respect towards women authors who are advocates of women's rights. In books and texts by women that I am reading, I am discovering more or less clear vindications of the daughters of Eve. Could it be that all of us women authors are feminists, since it cannot be any other way? Or alternately, because literature talks about the world around us?

## Jana Pácalová
I do not see any possibilities for the improvement of the given situation and, as a skeptic, I do not have a more concrete idea of what such a solution could entail, either individually or in cooperation with others.

## Dana Podracká
I see potential for improvement only in the raising the awareness about women and the quality of women's writing. This should be based on a spiritual foundation and not declarations or theoretical proclamations that disregard male emotions and thought. Women have to write about who they are and always write analysis that goes deeper and deeper. When I read male autobiographies, memoirs, or traditions, these are always traditions passed on by men to other men; women act as companions in parts of their lives and then gradually disappear, change into icons or Pandoras.

## Ivica Ruttkayová
To me feminisms are a way of life or, to be more precise, a way of questioning myself, life, culture, and, inevitably, feminisms. I try to get at the root of this mode of critical thought. It is an inner need of mine. In case there are more of us who feel this

need, and I believe this questionnaire to be proof of this, the number of challenges ahead should prove enough of an incentive for each and every one of us. And then, hopefully, some issues might be taken for granted; hopefully, we will not have this constant feeling that we are beginning from scratch . . . an incentive to create space and connections, since this is how literature works: as an organism.

## Jakuba Katalpa
Since I do not have an intimate knowledge of the feminist movement in the Czech Republic, it is difficult for me to say where there is scope for improvement.

## Lenka Daňhelová
My standpoint in this matter, both my ignorance of these issues and my personal contentedness, is based on my relationship with a wonderful man who takes utmost care not to limit me in any way. And I try to do the same with him. We can work on any issue that we come across in our relationship. Maybe it is easier for us because we do not have a large family. But I do not think this would significantly affect matters.

## Daniela Fischerová
I love meeting my colleagues; I would like to see more of my Slovak colleagues. Rather than group actions and institutional manipulation, I believe in interpersonal relations. Experience tells me that small groups work better than mass action. What if we organized a meeting of Slovak and Czech women writers, twenty people or so, where we talked informally about the ups and downs of our profession?

## Pavla Frýdlová

Czech women are mostly unfamiliar with the concept of female solidarity, so there remains a wide field of possibilities for joint action, either at home or in connection with women from abroad: the exchange of experiences, study stays, seminars, colloquia, getting to know each other, creative residencies, translations, reviews, readings . . .

## Tereza Riedlbauchová

In the Czech Republic a writers' association should be established, maybe more than one, a group that would have the necessary funds to support the writing and publication of fiction, the publication of literary journals, and the organization of literary festivals and readings. It should no longer be expected that an author will read their work for free. We authors should be able to make a living from our readings, like so many of our colleagues in the West.

## Božena Správcová

What do you mean by to improve the situation? The situation is not at all bad, at least here in Europe it is not. I would not even consider improving some aspects of it. I like it when a man opens the door for me or greets me first. I am always wary of news about "sexual harassment" coming from America or women's quotas. I wish for the world to finally come to grips with the fact that men are men and women are women and that no sex should hanker for the advantages of the other one. The only thing truly worth improving is labor laws. At the moment I have no plans for political action in the name of women's rights.

# Undoing Numbers

PAUL FOSTER JOHNSON
JULIAN T. BROLASKI
E. TRACY GRINNELL

## Undoing Numbers

Within the constellation of factors upon which we base our editorial decisions, we have made a perennial effort to balance male and female contributors to *Aufgabe*. The process always seems to be accompanied by a certain unease about the right way to get to at least a 50/50 split. We're perfectionists! So, naturally we followed with interest the recent exchange between Jennifer Ashton (in her essays "Our Bodies, Our Poems"[1] and "The Numbers Trouble with 'Numbers Trouble'"[2]) and Juliana Spahr and Stephanie Young (in their essay "Numbers Trouble"[3]), which was followed by considerable commentary on poetry-related blogs. We decided to use the conversation as a starting point for this editors' note and what follows are responses from each of the poetry editors for *Aufgabe*. Each of us felt it important to distinguish between (biological) sex and gender in these responses. Johnson and Grinnell use "male" and "female" rather than "men" and "women," since demographically speaking, the ratios discussed reveal the sex rather than the gender of the writers and rely upon names, which are changeable, without accounting for queerness in any form. Brolaski uses neither in xir response, which explores questions of authorial legibility and the breaking down of gender binaries.

*Paul Foster Johnson*

Spahr and Young's "Numbers Trouble" was written in response to Jennifer Ashton's "Our Bodies, Our Poems." Ashton argues that the concept of "women's innovative poetry" in current practice is essentializing and outmoded. In her initial essay, Ashton supports this argument by claiming that in the mid-1980s, female poets had achieved parity in publications and editorial and faculty positions. Spahr and Young focus their response on this assertion, analyzing the ratio of male and female poets who have published in (mostly US) anthologies and presses and who have received awards. They find that despite limited improvements, female poets were not only underrepresented in 1985, they currently remain underrepresented in the areas studied. The study goes on to solicit and report responses from poets regarding the desired role of the "poetry community"—presumably constituted by people and also by poetry institutions—in "engaging with the living and working conditions of women in a national/international arena."[4]

These essays provoked a wide range of online responses, many of them organized by Elizabeth Treadwell on the blog Delirious Hem.[5] For the most part, the responses agree with and extend Spahr and Young's conclusion:

> [T]he experimental/postmodern/avant-garde/innovative poetry scene needs a more radical feminism: a feminism that begins with an editorial commitment to equitable representation to think about how feminism is related to something other than itself, and to make writing that thinks about these things visible.[6]

Spahr and Young's poetry scene is anti-essentialist in its implication that "feminist interventions" operate in the same field as other movements and ideas, as opposed to, say, woman-centered projects associated with 1970s cultural feminism. This anti-essentialist conception is tacitly affirmed in the blog responses. The methodology of Spahr and Young's essay is another aspect about which the blogs are generally silent. Among the exceptions, Joyelle McSweeney considers the patriarchal "anthological thinking" surrounding the quantitative disparity alongside a non-hierarchal editorial approach through Deleuze's concept of the assemblage;[7] Dale Smith laments the businesslike task of "a poetics based on spreadsheets."[8] Yet tempting as it is to articulate a more democratic editorial vision, it is difficult to overcome Spahr and Young's success in realistically mapping the environment indicated by the general term "community."

Rather than staking out a pure position from which innovative writing can be delivered, Spahr and Young provide an accurate sketch of the existing conditions in which experimental writing is produced. These conditions include a necessary engagement with presses, journals, reading series, and blogs. For many, writing is also a livelihood, often in the form of academic teaching jobs. While many poetry institutions have strong progressive commitments, dominant attitudes about professionalism are always present in their organization and choices.

From here it is not a long leap to the (rightly) cynical conclusion that power in poetic communities is correlated with outcomes as measured in publications or awards. As it turns out, the structure of poetic communities has very little to do with formal allegiance or stylistic preference. In this particular conversation, this is indicated by the avoidance of analyzing any nuance or innovation in technique of the writing that turns up in experimental publications. The numbers have the final say on a publication's success or failure in the arena of representation.

This is not to say that writers are exempt from the burden. Poetic communities have adjusted to past feminist interventions and now accommodate a recognizable "but not exclusive" set of concerns identified with feminism. In the sociology of poetry there is a system of signs understood by writer, editor, and, ultimately, a niche audience. For example, an editor may be inclined to publish writing that exhibits certain hallmarks of a feminist project: poems that explore the erotic connotations of jouissance, poems that are well versed in the language of psychoanalysis and sexual difference, poems in which the body registers as a site of linguistic soundings. There may be much to admire in these kinds of poems, but their value to an editor derives at least in part from the specialized knowledge they contain, and the prestige that knowledge confers upon the publication among those who discern it.

Because of the increasing specialization of poetry as an academic discipline, it is not surprising that it does not connect with "the living and working conditions of women in the national/international arena." Only through the complete abstraction of "poetry" is it possible to make this broad connection. If this engagement is a central concern of the poetic community, it would be necessary for this community to examine its own social basis in relation to these living and working conditions. This would be a fundamental step toward finding some sort of common cause.

As an editor, I am drawn toward work that reflects, negates, or distorts the context of its own creation. With specific reference to the topic at hand, kari edwards's insistence upon "no gender" is a transparent and bold statement of poetics, but one that is ironized by the fact that edwards is a self-described gender activist. In this issue, Evelyn Reilly's rant about the customs of poetry readings and Brandon Brown's use of satire in relation to class and academia come to mind as other examples of writing that attends to the conditions in which it exists.

In the same way that Theodor Adorno argues that the only way we may form a concept of freedom is through our lived unfreedom,[9] the ideal of equality in the poetry world is given meaning only by the experience of inequality. It is important for writers and editors to consider the professional and institutional demands of the poetry community, and how these demands relate to what they are writing and selecting. This preliminary step would be necessary before applying this specific problematic to general struggles.

*Julian T. Brolaski*

> Gender is only one factor on which to base pairs ... In addition...gender is not a simple masculine-feminine binary as the use of many terms both toward and within the queer community demonstrates.
> —Anne Curzan, *Gender Shifts in the History of English*[10]

We all appear in "bursts of proximity" (Dwibedy, "jetsam"), or as Rumi observes, "Language is a tailor's shop where nothing fits." Is it possible to speak outside the confines of gender? Race and class are not always visible in names, so what is in them? Gender is often in them. We think of gender as "visible" and legible in language. That's how Spahr and Young conduct their study in "Numbers Trouble"—it is for the most part a study of names capable of being gendered—or names which are known to read as one or the other. It is a vital step towards addressing gender equanimity in poetry. But in order to dismiss the idea of gender as a criterion for legibility we must as Judith Butler puts it "undo gender" in favor of personhood:

> The very criterion by which we judge a person to be a gendered being, a criterion that posits coherent gender as a presupposition of humanness, is not only one which, justly or unjustly, governs the recognizability of the human, but one that informs the ways we do or do not recognize

ourselves at the level of feeling, desire, and the body, and the moments before the mirror, in the moments before the window, in the times that one turns to psychologists, to psychiatrists, to medical and legal professionals to negotiate what may well feel like the unrecognizability of one's gender, and hence, the unrecognizability of one's personhood. (58)[11]

As editors who confront head-on the problematics of "counting" gender—we (the *Aufgabe* team and others) must also consider those who cannot accurately be counted: Dana, Alex, Jess, Sean, Kit, Chris—whose abbreviations obfuscate gender—K.C., J.R.—who refuse to be counted—kari, Julian—ambiguously gendered names that one is eager to give a stamp to—to make them eligible for personhood, but as kaufman writes:

> this bridge splinters then gives way
> ("censory impulse")

Not that we could negate sexism by insisting on a gender neutrality—we must continue to be feminist editors and readers—to be personists[12] by considering ways we might end or at least undermine the myth of binary gender. kari edwards's insistence on "no gender"—echoed by Kate Bornstein and other trans/gender activists—is a functional paradox: the evacuation of gender as a means of becoming multiply or fluidly gendered:

> And stay for our way our way our way of safe
> safe is safer with superbugs bugged
> safe is safer than other is neither
> and other is neither much good or safe
> (Coleman, "We are going to talk about science with pictures")

The way to be multiple is to recognize gender variance in our books and in our lives: female, male and other. I use "gender" here because we are talking about political and poetical bodies—the body as it intersects with its artistic iteration—and how these are read by editors and readers. And then we have the cheat sheet biographical notes in which unknown gender is often revealed. Language determines gender and language is well known to be both structural and indeterminate. Gender, after all, is a term we get from linguists. What if we were all referred to by our patronym (admittedly still gendered)? What about those writers who can pass on the page, but not on the street? Or as Sailers writes:

> There is no way of seeing their daily lives
> among the voices. Or a queer exotic.
> It's as if their accents have been corrected,
> but who knows.
> ("Dogtown")

How quick we are to police gender! The poems themselves can be neither male nor female, so to what extent can we project a gendered persona on the text? And further we are in wartime—a time which has no respect for bodies or the persons that inhabit them:

> War in all its different guises
> How can the body take all the confrontation?
> hostility? the build-up of arms?
> (Rivera, "Poem With a Line Drawn Across the Body")

Should we be thankful or irritated that the draft is gendered? When war makes us devolve into disposable beings we turn to nonsense for sense—one tries to speak the president's name but it comes out gobbledygook:

> lam teevee pee bushchickenpok
> tak turkeybird gug dyinfeast . . .
> gug screwa sall gug slavendie
> (Rancourt, "image war")

We must concern ourselves with not only with gender equality but with the issue of authorial legibility—how one is read—to interrogate how the disembodied (poetically bodied) voice is gendered by readers and editors. So that "no gender" or "no race" or "no class" are not among the disappeared:

> these poems which can also describe the singularity of either an individual life, or socio-historical life and/or that instant and duration of their imbrication, their multiplicity, their affectivity . . . of the Disappeared
> (Light, from *Against Middle Passages*)

but occupy a necessary place on the spectrum, dismantling binaries by engaging the hybrid and the in-between. As Blau DuPlessis writes:

> And felt compelled
> to rip up the page and turn from these pronouns:
> I? you? we? Who cares about them!
> Who cares how they are linked!
> Push them over a cliff!
> ("Draft 88, X-Posting")[13]

. . . so that we might expand the distribution of pronouns. To say: out of many, many. Or instead of he/she to give name to the/

and, to trans otherly gendered, obfuscated, unknown or illegible persons: xe, xir, xemself.

*E. Tracy Grinnell*

> You should be interested enough in the world, with all its manifold strangeness and contradictions, oddities and possibilities, that your editorial/curatorial vision would organically support . . . an ecology of poly-verses.
> —David Buuck, Delirious Hem, Re: "Numbers Trouble"

I don't like anthologies. Two of the most important anthologies to me as a young, queer-female poet in the Bay Area were *Moving Borders: Three Decades of Innovative Writing by Women*[14] and *Out of Everywhere: Linguistically Innovative Poetry by Women in North America & the UK*[15] (the text taught by Leslie Scalapino in my undergraduate writing class at Mills College). These anthologies were undoubtedly important interventions for the reasons Spahr and Young cite in "Numbers Trouble." And they made accessible a feminist poetic avant-garde that I was searching for and demonstrated that it existed in the present tense across national boundaries. But anthologies are inherently, undeniably, always problematic. Even when necessary, they cannot be inclusive. And yet the compulsion to anthologize is pervasive. Whether for social, aesthetic, temporal, or corrective reasons, the compulsion always results in something that is dated (i.e. out-dated if not incomplete and exclusive) as soon as it is released into the world, hamstrung by its existence as a *singularity*. Anthologies are not capable of creating the "constant, necessary pressure" identified by Spahr and Young . . . but journals and magazines are.

Yes, we do numbers with *Aufgabe* because it is impossible not to register the lower number of submissions received from female poets and because it is impossible to separate one's own convictions, aesthetics, and poetic interests from issues of race, class, gender, orientation, and politics in general. We do numbers, however roughly, because each act of editing is an assertion of these positions in some form. The results are mostly imperfect but these things must line up: one cannot claim a progressive and inclusive—and feminist, if truly progressive and inclusive—politics and then proceed to publish serial volumes that fail to represent artists working from a range of circumstances, orientations, or positions. Our politics are essential and we reveal them in every editorial act.

Each issue of *Aufgabe* has presented its own dilemmas and I have discussed the question of gender balance and editorial process with several guest editors. What has been the case, and what we will continue to assert into being, is that the editors we work with, the contributors, and the readers of this journal are invested in a more dynamic poetry community that does intervene to impact social conditions, at the very least on the level of representation and accessibility in arts and letters. Journals and magazines make no claims—at least this one doesn't—to be comprehensive, but we can consistently attempt to create pathways, make connections, and put communities—poets, visual artists, translators, editors, readers—into conversation.

In issue #5, 4 female poets and 15 male poets appeared in the Moroccan section, and it was a struggle to get work by any female poets to begin with. In issue #6, featuring Brazilian poets, 7 females and 12 males appeared. In the Italian feature of this issue, there is work by 6 females and 10 males, including visual artists (see Jennifer Scappettone's foreword for her comments on "the male-dominated surface of Italian letters"). These are social issues. And again, these numbers say nothing about individual poets' gender or other orientations, circumstances or positions. However, what I can't ignore in these numbers is that the significance of publishing, say, 4 female poets—nevermind translating into English and publishing these writers in the US as representative of *a* living poetic reality in their country—likely registers very differently in Morocco, Brazil, or Italy than it does here in the US. And in any case, it is only a starting point. We must insist on the attempt at balance, even if, frustratingly, it only reveals the work that remains to be done seeking out otherly gendered poets in Morocco and other Arab countries, Italy, the Americas and so forth. The application of our poetic concerns has to consider context since this journal throws together artists and communities operating under very different conditions. This is part of what keeps *Aufgabe*—a publication for innovative writing—vital: the combination of contexts within which innovative writing is happening, and therefore the definition of "innovative" itself, changes with each issue. We cannot adequately intervene on an international scale unless we are at the same time recognizing different social/political/historical spheres and trajectories of innovation, resistance, and activism. And we cannot begin to address questions of access, unless we as editors are actively seeking out work from a variety of cultural contexts with attention to these disparate realities.

Constant, necessary pressure. Whenever we engage in editing of any sort—selecting, reading, recommending, discussing, blogging, curating—we must exert this pressure. It is simply not enough to express frustration with the lower number of submissions by female poets and then shrug or throw one's hands up. I don't know what combination of factors results in a lower number of submissions in the US, or why male poets tend to resubmit more frequently and persistently. What I do know is that editing is enactment, as much as writing is. It is proactive and must attend to the thriving and mutable sphere of polyverses.

—*Brooklyn, New York 2008*

1. Ashton, Jennifer. "Our Bodies, Our Poems." *American Literary History* 19:1 (2007): 211-231.

2. Ashton, Jennifer. "The Numbers Trouble with 'Numbers Trouble.'" *Chicago Review* 53:2/3 (2007): 112-120.

3. Spahr, Juliana and Stephanie Young. "Numbers Trouble." *Chicago Review* 53:2/3 (2007): 88-111.

4. Spahr and Young, p. 91.

5. Treadwell, Elizabeth, et al. "Dim Sum." Delirious Hem, delirioushem. blogspot.com/search/label/dim%20sum 7 February 2008. A comprehensive roundup of blog responses can be found at digital emunction, www. digitalemunction.com/2007/11/04/poetry-and-gender-following-numbers-trouble/

6. Spahr and Young, p. 100.

7. McSweeney, Joyelle. "Against Anthological Thinking" in "Dim Sum." delirioushem.blogspot.com/2008/02/dim-sum-joyelle-mcsweeney.html

8. Smith, Dale. "Re: The Name & the Paradox of Its Contents," Possum Ego. 1 November 2007. possumego.blogspot.com/2007/11/re-name-paradox-of-its-contents.html

9. Adorno, Theodor. *Negative Dialectics.* Trans. E. B. Ashton. New York: Continuum, 1973.

10. Curzan, Anne. *Gender Shifts in the History of English.* Cambridge: Cambridge University Press, 2003.

11. Butler, Judith. *Undoing Gender.* Routledge: New York and London, 2004.

12. Not like Frank O'Hara's personism—whose mock-manifesto names only Ginsberg, Whitman, Crane, Williams, LeRoi Jones and Alain Robbe-Grillet as cohorts.

13. *Jacket* 35. jacketmagazine.com/35/index.shtml

14. Sloan, Mary Margaret, ed. New Jersey: Talisman House, 1998.

15. O'Sullivan, Maggie, ed. London: Reality Street Editions, 1996.

Reprinted, with some minor edits. Originally published in *Aufgabe* 7 (2008).

# This is What a (Pro-) Feminist (Man-Poet) Looks Like

CHRISTIAN PEET

*How do you see yourself as a participant in feminism? How and when did you first recognize the importance of feminist issues? Have you ever felt conflicted about your relationship to feminism?*

I don't think about it enough, actually, so I am grateful for this opportunity. My recognition of "the importance of feminist issues" has developed slowly, over a long time, owing less to books than to the women who have shaped my consciousness. By extension, my consciousness of feminist issues owes something even to the men who have affected those women's lives. I think my consciousness began around the time my father started beating my mother. At the time I had no language for it, however; I was a child.

Later, as a teenager, two years in rehab opened my eyes a bit wider. Many of my women friends were prostitutes. I won't call them "sex workers" because it wasn't "all that," and because none of them wanted to continue working as prostitutes. Most of them were mothers as well. I enjoyed being with them because their Mom vibes were a great comfort, but surely my heart and consciousness also benefitted from their strength, and their wisdom, and their beautiful fucking senses of humor.

I didn't really began to study Feminism with a capital "F" until *after* college—if you can imagine such a statement coming from a Bennington College undergrad. My mentor at Bennington was Anne Winters, one of my favorite women poets, but I don't think the topic of feminism came up a great deal in our discussions: mostly she taught me all I know about prosody, capitalism, and the Bible. Not to say women haven't had tough rows to hoe, traditionally, in all three of those areas, but it wasnít the focus of *my* interest while I was in college. I tended more toward issues of class, coming from the working one as I do, and as Anne does, with a certain irony in our finding both refuge and outlet in education and poetry.

If you'd asked me, in college, I might have said: I tend to resonate with the work of men poets. I have no "problem" with most of the women poets I've read. I'm just not really "into" them. [NOTE: The number I'd read couldn't have gone far beyond 10.] I like Sylvia Plath just fine (*such chiseled lines! such exacting diction!*), and Elizabeth Bishop (*such navigation of form!*), and some others, but I can't see the fuss about . . . well, I don't know . . . Adrienne Rich, for example. She seems awfully direct. Didactic, even. Her metaphors kinda beat me over the head. . . . Etc.

At the time I was also fairly obsessed with all of Richard Hugo's work (much to the befuddlement, if not dismay, of Anne Winters). And I still like Hugo's work—mostly because it has a lot of trees and rivers and can be enjoyed by working class readers who have not spent $100,000 on degrees. That said, however, few would argue that his work does not evidence something of a "conflicted relationship to feminism."

I might have also said that my okayness with feminism was clearly evidenced by my obvious "love of the ladies" on campus. Who knows what I would have said, though, honestly—I was drunk a lot. Certainly I would have pointed out the feminism of my "Avenger Dildo" commercial, which I wrote and directed for my video production class: two scantily-clad young women kiss and fondle each other before trying out the Avenger Dildo, a stout strap-on they delight in severing with a kitchen knife. Buckets of fake blood ensue, and they can't help but smear it all over each other, laughing. *CALL NOW! 1-800-AVENGER.*

I was trying. I still am. It's difficult to see through Others' eyes. It takes a long time.

And also: there actually wasn't that much blood. I would have liked "buckets," but instead had only a plastic baggie filled with some red liquid, inside the cardboard boner.

My girlfriend at the time, now my *ex*—go figure—whom I'll call "Ex," for lack of a better name with which to address her while not muddying her internet presence as a professional in her field—has worked her entire adult life as an advocate for women, in one way or another. So, luckily, I was able to learn a bit by osmosis as she worked for women's crisis centers and eventually began working directly with perpetrators of domestic violence. Most "DV perps" are men, you will not be shocked to hear, but Ex was one of the few women "to have the balls" to address violence against women *by* women. A lot of her colleagues wouldn't admit that such a thing existed—go figure.

While Ex was studying for her Masters in Psychology, I also read her books, one or two of her surveys-of-feminism textbooks included, as well as Simone de Beauvoir and Betty Friedan, et al. I was most interested in Queer Studies, however, Leslie Feinberg in particular: *Stone Butch Blues* and *Transgender Warriors*. Reading the latter, I was fascinated by the history of *two spirits*, (Google keywords: *two spirit* and *berdache*—the latter being an offensive term, though widely used in academic studies). And I think this is key to my brand of pro-feminism—it's part of a larger desire to embrace and foster mixing and mingling and hybridity and coexistence of all kinds. (No doubt my interest in *transgenre* lit has roots in this transgender lit.)

In 2003 my current partner blew my doors off. What she had to teach me, what she continues to teach me, is mostly beyond words (like it or not, writers), in the realm of physical and, dare I say it, "spiritual" expression, but I can say this: her understanding of identity as regards race, culture, class, sex, and gender (and all else) is the wellspring of whatever I may try to call my own. Nothing prior, certainly no book, prepared me for falling bum-over-teakettle in love with an ethnically indeterminate bisexual immigrant woman writer and teacher born working class and now possessing experience and diplomas enough to lecture on all the above—meaning that she is, in short, still "Other."

Nothing prepared me to meet her friends, for that matter. Or for my hetero white guy self to live among them as a minority. Yea, verily I say unto you: this Christian was reborn in Prospect Heights, Brooklyn, NY. Feminist indeed. And a whole lot else.

*How do you support feminism in your role as teacher, mentor, editor, publisher, blogger, poet, etc.?*

I read and teach and am inspired by the lives and works of women: post-feminists, womanists, lesbians, biwomen, transwomen, housewives, whores, and witches; first wave, second wave, third wave feminism; the multiple orgasms of clit lit; L7 riot grrl Donita Sparks tossing her bloody tampon at an English crowd; madness, fornication with the devil, streams of consciousness, the ancient tidal river that swallowed Woolf; the late 1960s, Toni Morrison a single mother raising two boys and teaching full time while writing her first novel, *The Bluest Eye*; the early 70s, abortion and Margaret Atwood's firstborn novel, *Surfacing*; genital mutilation, murder, afterbirth; we look inside Annie Sprinkle with a speculum and a flashlight, and if a student says, "Um, gross," or "Fucking pussy," then I ask, "Why?"

We take a moment or two of silence after reading aloud a rape scene.

And when my women students want to discuss women's

issues in women's literature or in literature in general, I tend not to keep lecturing at them, but rather shut up and listen.

I also publish the work of women writers. A little more than half of the books in the Tarpaulin Sky Press catalog—including the press's next six titles—are books by women. I haven't done the math, but I'm guessing the magazine's ratio is somewhere in the same ballpark as the press.

In recent years, the magazine has been edited by four women writers whom I am deeply honored to know: Rebecca Brown, Elena Georgiou, Bhanu Kapil, and Selah Saterstrom. Two other women writers, Eireene Nealand and Julianna Spallholz, have been editing and otherwise supporting the press since 2002, assisted in a variety of ways by Caroline Ashby, Lizzie Harris, and Sarah Brown.

Soon I'll be stepping down as editor at *Tarpaulin Sky*, and though I don't know who she is, I have no doubt that my replacement will be a woman. Since I'm not actually paying anyone at the moment, I think that's even legal.

*What branch of feminism, model of feminist poetics, feminist icon, or etc. Informs your poetry? Or, from which of these does your poetry diverge?*

My fear, in discussing any *ism*, is that the discussion will become a discussion of an *ism*. My relationship to feminism is my relationship to women: present, living, and ever-changing. Rather than quote classic feminist texts, or pretend to be a theory-driven academic, which I'm just not, I'd like to quote a little bit of the great stuff I read however many moons ago, here at Delirious Hem, in the forum that birthed this one: "This is What a Feminist [Poet] Looks Like."

K. Lorraine Graham speaks for me when, in discussing the importance of French Feminism, she says:

I'm less concerned with how to get women into institutions and positions of power than how to change the way institutions and power are constructed. Those two goals are connected, of course. Sometimes having women with economic and cultural power can change power structures, but often women with power may identify with those structures just as much as the people who created them: Margaret Thatcher.

Graham could be describing elements of my writing process as well:

I never begin a project knowing how it will end—that's also part of what I consider a Feminist poetics: even though everything I write is going to be inevitably caught up in cultural norms and expectations, I want my poems to push against such expectations, even as they acknowledge that they are caught up in them. So, I don't start with conclusions. Or, if I do have conclusions, I start by questioning them.

Kim Rosenfield's feminism is also remarkably similar to my own, in that it embraces elements from a variety of movements—except that hers is tall and has a moustache, whereas mine is only 5'6" but has a bigass beard. Among other things, says Rosenfield:

Feminism is about reducing the impact of what comes out of the tailpipe of society, putting new systems in place to help it withstand the shocks that come so we can plot a path of elation rather than of guilt, anger, and horror. . . . My feminism can harness the "power of human energy," and address the world's gloomiest challenges without shoving them into denial or depression. . . . My feminism already lives a scaled-down life. It is quite tall, with a ponytail and moustache. It's already bartered, shared, and canned together. Tradesmen, workshops, cultural institutions, and farmland surround my feminism. I make my feminism as self-sufficient as possible. For a generation, feminists have told us to change our lifestyles to avoid catastrophic consequences. My feminism tells us those consequences are now. My feminism can be a bridge to carry us over the terrible time ahead and into a world we long for.

Presently my feminist icons tend to be living, are not always icons for other folks, and often include my friends. The following are but a few, off the top of my head (yet, strangely, alphabetized!): Dodie Bellamy, Aase Berg, Lisa Birman, Ana Božičević, Catherine Breillat, Jenny Boully, Rebecca Brown, Jan Clausen, Margaret Cho, Traci O Connor, Angela Davis, Ani DiFranco, Katherine Dunn, Danielle Dutton, kari edwards, Eve Ensler, Sandy Florian, Elena Georgiou, Renee Gladman, Kim Hyesoon, Brenda Iijima, Shelly Jackson, Elfriede Jelinek, Miranda July, Bhanu Kapil, Amy King, Joan Larkin, Joanna Lumley, Joyelle McSweeney, Harryette Mullen, Dolly Parton, Joanna Ruocco, Selah Saterstrom, Kim Gek Lin Short, Juliana Spahr, Annie Sprinkle, Heidi Lynn Staples, Shelly Taylor, Rosmarie Waldrop, Wendy S. Walters, Amanda Jo Williams.

Over the last few years, the work that I've studied the most, and that has had the most profound impact on me, has been work by women. The list is too long, so I'll stick to the living, focus on the most recent reads, exclude Rebecca Brown (whose latest book I just blogged), exclude TSky Press authors, exclude also my girlfriend, and from the remaining pick only a few: Aase Berg, Bhanu Kapil, and Selah Saterstrom.

I'm presently rereading Swedish poet Aase Berg's selected

poems, *Remainland* (translated by Johannes Göransson, Action Books, 2005), and for months now I've been walking around with her first book, *With Deer* [Hos rådjur] (Black Ocean, 2008, also translated by Göransson). Berg's is a feminism of the dark and surreal variety. Think Artaud, Breton, Ernst, as performed by Nico, post-Velvet Underground, making public her spectacular decay. Berg's feminism also springs from images of "the natural world"—but in the case of *With Deer*, think: watching The Nature Channel on a bad tab of acid. Or even The Weather Channel: today and tonight, nightmares; tomorrow, nightmares with occasional clouds. Think *When Animals Attack*, think demonic, human-flesh-eating guinea pigs. Think bedtime fables to keep you from ever having children.

Berg's feminism is an ecopoetics, and her ecopoetics not only collapses distinctions between the "human world" and the Other, but also makes room for—how should we say it?—the *less savory* elements of the natural world. The first line of my notes for an unwritten review of *With Deer*: "Look up 'putrefaction.'"

In Berg's feminist ecopoetics, there is no separation between disease in bodies and disease in cities, social structures, civilizations. No separation of blood and oil. Everywhere fucking and misery. Everywhere miscarriage and cancer. Everywhere, "The Gristle Day":

Black blood is coming. Out of that hole. Thick blood is coming. It looks like oil. And the squirrel screams in the tree.

Black blood is coming. Not very much blood, but undeniably out of that hole in the middle of the white. The hole has walls, swollen and flaccid, and doesn't dare bear down and push out. That's why the blood screams.

The hole doesn't dare open and push itself out of the

hole. Black blood is coming. Out of that hole. Mechanisms have stopped, the flesh hangs pale on the hook and has ceased resisting. The squirrel screams all alone as the tumor plug drops into the hole. The blood screams in the tree; the blood screams black in the white.

We are born in the sewers, out of the horrifying dough beyond good and evil. It smells like ghosts, it smells of slop flesh, it smells of placenta and uranium. Black blood is coming. Marsh gas and diarrheas bubble. Out of the hole that screams and screams as gristle encloses the embryo like an eggshell and a jail, and the little squirrel in my little hand has broken all the small bones of its whole skeleton. It lies still and its eye is the hole; the hole spread open and tired. Blood is probably still coming out of the black intestine on the bottom of the flesh.

Black blood is coming. Out of that black old hole. Marsh blood and sludge blood and creamy gunk blood. It looks like oil. And when the squirrel screams one last time in the tree, a moan slowly rises out of the hole.

Berg's feminism collapses distinctions as it explores symbiotic relationships, explores the dynamics of dualities rather than the stasis of antipodes. Excerpted from "In the Horrifying Land of Clay":

There was an evil horse that galloped along the evil river in the horrifying land of clay. There was an evil horse that galloped with me on its back. Beneath the hair-strap his muscles moved and chafed against the muscles of my taut inner thighs which clamped down around his body. . . . There was an evil horse that galloped through the horrifying land, an evil and dark horse with manhood and musculature, and I was thrilled to have him as my enemy.

In Daniel Sjölin's excellent introduction to *Remainland*, discussing *With Deer*, he could just as well be describing the work of Bhanu Kapil: "a bold style, in which water and earth—sorrow-death and the body—mix to form blood, clay, and tar. She detourns the theme of 'the girl in the woods' [a dangerous formula . . .]." As if speaking directly about Kapil's most recent book, *Humanimal: A Project for Future Children* (Kelsey Street Press, 2009), Sjölin describes "a hybrid between woman, language, and animal: a decomposition process at the same time as a creation process."

Kapil's *Humanimal* is a densely packed, highly-layered, and, I dare say, literally *magical*, slim volume of transgenre text that is, among other things, part palimpsest, part eulogy, part Shelley Jackson's *Patchwork Girl*, part nonfiction (cross-) culture study, and part hope. It maps the story of "Kamala and Amala, two girls found living with wolves in Bengal, India, in 1920," alongside Kapil's travels to the region—with her research itself, at that time, being recorded by French filmmakers attempting a documentary of human-wolf contacts. Kapil's source text is

> the diary of and Indian missionary, Reverend Joseph Singh, was first published in 1945 as a companion text to *Wolf-Children and Feral Man*, a book of essays by the Denver anthropologist Robert Zingg. In the jungle, on a Mission to convert the tribal population, Singh had heard stories of "two white ghosts" roaming with a mother wolf and her pack of cubs. He decided to track them. Upon discovering the "terrible creatures" to be human, he killed the wolves and brought the children back to his church-run orphanage, the Home, in Midnapure. For the next decade, he documented his attempt to teach the girls language, upright movement, and a moral life. Despite his efforts, Amala

died within a year of capture, of nephritis. Kamala lived to be about sixteen, when she died of TB.

Beyond the initial intrigue of the lives of these two girls as "subject matter," what inspires me is the text's hybridity, Kapil's approach to narrative, which smells a lot like poetry. Like poetry giving birth to biology. As in "nature," there are no straight lines in *Humanimal*, and a linear once-through of the text's seventy-odd pages will reveal only so much; it doesn't require multiple readings to be appreciated, but it certainly rewards them, and Kapil's narrative invites study from multiple angles. Were I to compare Kapil's form(s) to visual art, I might choose Cubism, except that I would call Kapil's style something like *Dodeca-hedronism*, or perhaps even *Great Stellated Dodecahedronism*, or perhaps, not to be so limiting, I would call it simply *Polyhe-dronism*. A hairy, mammalian polyhedronism.

On an angry day, I might see *Humanimal* as a polyhedronist approach to vivisection, an examination of men examining little girls; a polyhedronist approach to traditional dress, to cooking one's meat and using utensils in the name of God, to training frightening little wolfcunts to piss where the sign says so. But to see it *only* in these ways would be counter to the very idea of polyhedronism.

Not to mention that polyhedronism itself is an inadequate term. For all its angles, it is still, well, too angular. In the world of *Humanimal* all angles bend and curve.

Her two arms extend stiffly from her body to train them, to extend. Unbound, her elbows and wrists would flex then supinate like two peeled claws. Wrapped, she is a swerve, a crooked yet regulated mark. This is corrective therapy; the fascia hardening over a lifetime then split in order to reset it, educate the nerves.

In the world of *Humanimal* all edges ebb and flow, are "complex horizons," towards which "Kamala slips over the garden wall with her sister and runs, on all fours." They are the absurdity of the very idea of edges, something like the edge of night versus the edge of day; they are membranes through which we (trans)migrate, through which we are born. In the world of *Humanimal*

> Two panicked children strain against the gelatin envelope of the township, producing, through distension, a frightening shape. The animals see an opaque, milky membrane bulging with life and retreat, as you would, to the inner world. I am speaking for you in January. It is raining. Amniotic, compelled to emerge, the girls are nevertheless reabsorbed.

Indeed the surreal feminist ecopoetics of *Humanimal*'s curvaceous and permeable prose engenders all manner of worlds, and all manner of creatures great and small, and all in flux, inextricable from what some humans would like to call their world. In the world of *Humanimal*, "the moonlight illuminates the termite mound where the wolves have hollowed out an underground cave with their beaks. Sub-red, animal wolves and human wolves curl up with their mother, in sequence, to nurse." Elsewhere, "An animal flowers in the elements. It grows wings. A cat with wings alights on the doorstep, as if to say, I'm off. I don't need your food anymore." In the world of *Humanimal*, "the cook fed us meats of many kinds. I joined my belly to the belly of the next girl. It was pink and we opened our beaks for meat. It was wet and we licked the dictionary off each other's faces."

I dreamed that night I was crawling on the floor with a circus acrobat from the 1940s. He was Chinese and his eyes were ringed with black lead. As if in a trance, I left my seat in the audience and danced with him. It was a dance based upon the movements of a black panther and a white eagle. We crossed them. This was mating deep inside the market. We danced until we were markets.

It is this mating, this co-creating, this inspiring hybridity that allows me to read *Humanimal* and not come away simply destroyed, thinking Kamala and Amala simply destroyed. Or, in Kapil's words: "From these stories, I constructed an image of the dying girl as larval; perennially white, damp and fluttering in the darkness of the room."

I read *Humanimal* and want to write. I want to transform things, perform alchemy. I want to give back something in return. I want to *create*.

A word of warning to the reader: I mentioned already that *Humanimal* is a magical text. I do not mean "magical" in the sense of Disney's Ice Capades, or a great first date—though maybe I do mean love. What I mean is: this book has magical properties. It is a magnet and a torch. It is also medicine. And a portal. What I mean is: on the Amtrak to New York City a month ago, reading this book for the first time, I noticed in the seat adjacent to me an Asian woman. She looked around on occasion, down the aisle, out the window—the things we do on trains other than read or sleep. What was different, in her case, is that she had a long ribbon of cash-register paper unspooling from her desk tray, piling at her feet. On the paper there appeared to be scribbles. Closer inspection indicated that she was unreeling the paper ever so slowly beneath her pen, which bounced and jumped and zagged at the mercy of the train.

I've heard that one can be literally blind to things for which one has no language. I don't know if that's true, but I'm certain that I would not have figured out so quickly what this woman was doing, may not even have cared, if I hadn't just read the following:

> In the aeroplane from London to Kolkata and in the jeep to Midnapure, I put my nib on the page and let motion wreck the line. My notes were a page of arrhythmias, a record of travel.

Make of it what you will, but that's my kind of transgenre work: out of the realm of literature and dropped at my freakin feet. Huzzah! Which is also one of the many reasons I read Selah Saterstrom's work: both she and it possess an otherworldly ability to punch holes through this one. But I digress—that's for a Halloween piece I'm writing: "Feminists and Other Unholy Witches: Why Are We Still Scared?"

Selah Saterstrom's first book, *The Pink Institution* (Coffee House Press, 2004), examines generations of women in a particular Southern family, and their varied internalizations of, and rebellions against, the culture to which they belong. In the section "Maidenhood Objects," the whole of the chapter titled "Dining Room" reads as follows:

> Willie called his daughters into the dining room. He picked up a dining room table chair and threw it into a closed window. The window shattered. He said, "That's a lesson about virginity. Do you understand?" to which they replied, "Yes, sir."

The bulk of *The Pink Institution* is occupied by the lives of the women who precede the narrator—her mom, aunts, grandmothers—as well as the men who helped to shape their lives. The narrator does not become a character in the book until three quarters into the novel. Born and raised in a rich history of violation, addiction, and suicide, the narrator is fragmented, and thus, so is the narrative, moving from ablated captions on historical photos to genealogy as plot; from brief snapshots/scenes rendered in spare prose to highly wrought and deeply layered prose poetry; from a childhood sexuality and spirituality inextricable from a desire to write (masturbating via rubbing against a desk, a girlfriend kissing game involving paper, eating a pencil eraser which has stood in for God, the Host), to a hunger inextricable from vomiting and anal bleeding:

> Food becomes sublime. It geometrically squares into its complex statistics. This happens in proportion to my growing hunger. The more hungry I become, the more what food looks like and what one does with it becomes alien. Until all food is pure object and eating is apocalyptic Eucharistic. At this point I know I am hungry, but I cannot remember what one does to alleviate hunger so I put my fingers in my mouth. . . .
>
> Food is what you put in your mouth. You put it in your mouth. The rubber slide hidden in glossy food. Red velvet cakes stacked in a corner of a decaying house. Pork, too. Which is fatbread saturated with rancid.
>
> The first time was during the summer I was twelve. I put my fingers in my mouth and bit them until they bled. I was sitting on my mother's bed in the back of her new husband's trailer. I had never felt such relief. It was a cool passing through July's hanging heat.

My experience is this: post-trauma, new pain can be relief, can numb old pain; hypersensitivity transforms into catatonia and back again; that which doesn't fragment, morphs; that which cannot morph, fragments. When her grandfather commits suicide on the front lawn with a shotgun in his mouth, the narrator of *The Pink Institution* sees, in the aftermath, afterbirth.

> After he shot himself, my grandfather's face was a spangle bouquet that made grass die. What is difficult about looking at something like that is not that the mind resists fragmentation in general, but that it is confounded by textures which refuse the tensions one desires through edges. Even when they took his corpse away, his head was still there, some soaking into the ground, some in liver-colored strips and bits unable to be absorbed. It looked like the oversaturated pile of womb waste on the floor between my sister's legs after she gave birth. They could have been the same. They were not but light would not have known the difference.

The rendering of trauma, in literature, is a subject that interests me for personal reasons. The experience of trauma is individual; it takes many forms. It is difficult to render in language without making the reader want to turn away. Even Toni Morrison's expert handling of it, for example, in *The Bluest Eye*, routinely shuts down some of my students. At least at first. Not because they've experienced similar trauma, I should add, but because they would rather not experience even its telling. There are countless other reasons I am interested in trauma. Here are millions: Afghanistan, Bosnia, Burma, Congo, Darfur, Haiti, Iran, Rwanda, USA . . . ; women are abused, raped, mutilated, and murdered everywhere and every day and have been since the beginning of human history.

But I'm going to come back to that. My partner called while I was writing this. We talked about it and agreed that, sometimes, on "good days," we both like to believe that feminism in the US can safely take a backseat to issues of race and class and sexual orientation—but only in the US.

The US, after all, has Annie Sprinkle. In a perfect world, *The Book of Feminism*'s last page might say: "And then God created Annie Sprinkle and all was well."

Of course it doesn't work that way: even if the last page were written (with or without Annie Sprinkle), there would still be plenty of folks who'd yet to read it. As I said before, the discussion of feminism is always at risk of becoming a discussion of a static *ism*, rather than a dynamic discussion of dynamic women and their dynamic lives, and while feminism in the US may have come far enough to focus on issues such as not-quite-equal pay rather than systemic, horrific, state-sanctioned atrocities committed against women (for example), it is not difficult to see that almost every issue women have faced in this country, women still face, whether in the job world or in the literary world, etc.

As Juliana Spahr's and Stephanie Young's "Numbers Trouble" pointed out, and as discussed in "Dim Sum," here at *Delirious Hem*, the literary world remains far from equitable—even the ostensibly forward-thinking, small-press world. Personal example: I know an otherwise hip small press that's published books by fifteen men and two women. The publisher told me that he has nothing against women writers. He just rarely encounters women's writing that he *likes*. Obviously! Silly me! Not long ago I also had to call him up about a review he'd published online, to ask if he might not at least remove the word "mousy" from his already needless description of meeting the author in person.

One of the questions/prompts for this interview was *Do you have any concrete suggestions for altering the gender disparities in the poetry world?* That one's easy: support publishers who support women writers. Ignore presses that ignore women writers. Or give them hell. Whichever best suits your personality. I choose to ignore "things I don't agree with," unless those things are actively causing problems for myself or others. I'd like to believe that a press that fails to publish women writers will become only half the entity it might have been and will likely die alone and unloved, with its dick in its hand. And I don't mean only presses run by heterosexual men. See Richard Tayson's excellent article, "Joan Larkin and the Poetics of Lesbian Inclusion," in *Pleiades 29.2*:

> In a 2005 letter to the editor of the *The Gay and Lesbian Review*, Larkin confronted the magazine about its "Poetry Issue": "Maybe it's time you renamed the magazine *The Gay Male Review* or perhaps *The Gay & Token Lesbian Review*. I suppose I shouldn't be surprised—I've long been chagrined at how underrepresented women are in your pages—but I was stunned and insulted by the lack of any real discussion of poetry by gay women in something calling itself 'The Poetry Issue.' One piece on one lesbian poet out of seven articles. . . is even less inclusive than the abysmal record of *The New York Times Book Review*."

Nor is it just editors, says Tayson, but also gay men writers whose work ignores women—lesbian or otherwise. "Forty years after Stonewall," says Tayson, "a change of world is still in order. . . If gay men are not including many women in our poems, who and what else are we excluding?"

That said, the reason I tend to just plain ignore writers and editors who ignore women—well, that goes back several paragraphs to where I left *trauma.* One has to make decisions, I have heard it said, and more often than not, I'm inclined to apply a sort of triage system to my concerns. Given my limited time to write (or to be on this planet—either way), I want to make sure I devote at least a little of my presently unwounded, unsuffering self to people whose situations are not so lucky.

Hence, I can't finish writing *this* until I've said *this*: my thoughts on crappy publishers come and go, but daily I am destroyed inside, reading about ongoing atrocities against women and girls in _____.

In the five days that it's taken me to complete this article, it's estimated that 250 women and girls have been raped in South Kivu, in eastern Congo. In South Kivu, a doctor, in conversation with Eve Ensler, said the most common wound to a woman is a "traumatic fistula . . . caused by insertion of a gun, bottle or stick into the vagina or shooting a gun between the woman's legs," causing a "rupture between the vagina, bladder and/or rectum," and rendering "an uncontrollable leakage of fluids, secretions, urine or feces." The intent is not to kill the woman, but to shame her. This is a "strategy of war."

When I say "I am destroyed inside" it is only a metaphor. In this way, it is a luxury. As it is our luxury to visit websites such as Eve Ensler's vday.org, for example, to better understand and to help end violence against women and girls. As it is our luxury to debate what the US and UN should or should not do for the women in eastern Congo, or in _____.

It is also a luxury for me to read Saterstrom's work. She has done the difficult work. At times I read her second book, *The Meat and Spirit Plan* (Coffee House Press, 2007), as a sort of prelude to *The Pink Institution*—but it's more like chicken-or-the-egg. Part book-length, ekphrastic prose poem framing Rembrandt's *The Slaughtered Ox*, part sustained meditation on pain, *The Meat and Spirit Plan* features a narrator protagonist who has much in common with the narrator of *The Pink Institution*. A young white female from a heavymetal Dixieland, whose experiences with rape, drugs, and reform school precede her enrollment in state college, the narrator's interest in God earns her a chance to study for a Master's Degree in Theology in Scotland, where, when she isn't suffering postmodern dissections of Diderot and the like, she passes her semester sitting in a crumbling museum, getting drunk with a Holocaust survivor and watching the butcher in the town square.

A little more than halfway through *The Meat and Spirit Plan*, is a chapter titled "And Suddenly I Thought: This Is What It Means to Make a Movie in Sweden."

The Postmodern Seminar for the Study of Interpretive Uses decides to include film as text. . . . After one film I get in a fight with a master's candidate from Washington, DC who is doing his last year of research at the Seminar by invitation. At a departmental gathering to welcome new students he once reprimanded a Theoretical Studies girl for using "Heidegger" and "grace" in the same sentence. Never use the word "grace" he said. It shows your hand. By which he meant ass. He said it like her use of "grace" revealed her trailer park origins when she should try and marry better. Oh, said the Theoretical Studies girl, scribbling a note to herself on a napkin.

The film we got in a fight about ended with a woman being killed by a soldier. She was pretty much dead, but he did her in for good by jamming a gun in her vagina and then pulling the trigger. The film didn't show this but implied it. The question the fight hinged on was this: Did the woman, in the last split second of her life, experience the meaning of her suffering? Washington said yes. The possibility of experiencing such meaning, despite solitude and cruelty, was the rule.

I thought this was a romantic view of what the last split second of life might be like. And I thought it was unfair. It was stealing the woman's death from her, which meant in the end everything was taken. Taken and put in the ghettos of our intellectualizations. Soured thoughts counting more than smears of blood. Why couldn't we sit in the pain of not knowing? Maybe she didn't get the big meaning of her suffering. Maybe she just suffered, then died.

When the fight is finally drawn to a close by the head of the Seminar, Washington has won because he is smart and uses language like an exacto blade. He never raised his voice and has remained calm. My face is red and my voice shaky. As people leave the room they look at me as if they feel sorry for me and look at Washington like he is a great guy who understands theology.

Later, I look out the terrible room's bay window. In my head I say to the people who watch movies that it is a stretch to think that the witness knows what it is like to die. I say: may the story of Washington, DC be a lesson to you.

May it be a lesson to all of us.

Originally published online at Delirious Lapel under the forum "This is What a (Pro)Feminist [Man Poet] Looks Like" (edited by Danielle Pafunda and Mark Wallace), deliriouslapel.blogspot.com/2009/10/chris-tian-peet-responds.html.

# The Name & the Paradox of Its Contents

DALE SMITH

I am a footnote. I was in a campus bookstore yesterday and glanced through the new issue of the *Chicago Review*. In it I quickly read Juliana Spahr and Stephanie Young's essay on gender and publication, "Numbers Trouble." I was curious about it but short on time and did what I often do—I flipped through the pages rapidly trying to get a sense of the key coordinates. And then, lo and behold, I saw my name footnoted deep in the bowels of the thing. It referenced posts to the Buffalo Poetics list from 1997 in which I responded to critiques of gender and publishing.

I would like to respond to this "footnote" by way of a brief personal reflection. Recently on her blog, *The Well Nourished Moon*, Young writes that she and Spahr are interested in expanding the conversation they begin in their *Chicago Review* essay beyond the limited perspectives of US feminism. She writes:

> One of the things our paper does is end up being a catalogue of what's missing; a catalogue of some of the limits of a mostly white, mainstream US feminism in experimental poetry scenes. We see a myopic lack of attention to women's issues outside of the US and a lack of collective action. We need more feminisms.
>
> We end this paper asking people to write to us with suggestions about how to overcome this. Our intention is

to try and compile a bunch of these suggestions for publication in order to start a conversation.

Would you be interested in being a part of this conversation?

Since, in part, their article references me, and in order to respond, in my way, to this call for an extended conversation, I present here a self-evaluation as a form of response, since I am implicated in this problem to a minor degree.

## II

Ten years ago I began posting notes to the Buffalo Poetics List. Much of what I said then was influenced by many factors. Primarily, a novice as far as poetry was concerned, I perceived the list as being hostile to poets I found compelling. In the winter months of that year, many on the list made derisive comments about Edward Dorn, who had been recently diagnosed with pancreatic cancer. Some referred to him as a "bigot." Others publicly expressed their desire to provide Dorn with a "[p]unch in the mouth." And still others compared him with Hitler, and "waited expectantly for some coke-induced froth from his evil lips—did he ever post" a response to this online community of poets. In anger at the blithe list commentary regarding his work—commentary to which he could not respond due to his illness and indifference to online technology—I sympathetically appropriated his energy to begin entering conversations on the list from a position of anger. This, though acknowledged ten years too late, is not the best point from which to enter a conversation.

In one particular thread, written in September 1997, it was pointed out to me by Dodie Bellamy that one issue of my small magazine, *Mike & Dale's Younger Poets*, only published poems by four women out of the 24 writers our journal contained. I won't rehash what took place: the curious can troll the Buffalo archives if they wish. At stake in this particular thread, though, is the question of representation and equity on literary markets. Should editors publish an equal number of female voices as men?

## III

I remember reading Judith Butler in a class taught by Lyn Hejinian called "The Language of Paradise," at the New College of California in San Francisco. This was in the 1990s. I recall that Butler's theory of performativity influenced my thinking about gender tremendously. It appealed to my understanding of dynamic action—dramatism in Kenneth Burke's terms—as a way to engage the construction of identity in a way that focused on the act rather than on the metaphysical assumptions of ontology. Looking back over *Gender Trouble* today, the key word in the subtitle that still stands out for me is *subversion*. Butler's focus too on "the subversive and parodic redeployments of power rather than on the impossible fantasy of its full-scale transcendence" also appealed to me as a way to engage social bodies. Moreover, of great importance is the work she did to complicate any easy notions of gender as ontology, for, she argues, it is not biologically determined. Sex comes into being after the law. Representation of gender is performative, wrapped up in the complex weave of subjective identification with the disciplines of power that institute our cultural coordinates. And then from here our chances of representation come down to that "parodic redeployment of power." We can't assume the category: we must read the dynamic intrusion of subjectivity into other contexts.

Looking back at my posts of September 1997, I see a young man ill equipped to participate in the environment of the Buffalo Poetics List. I trust that person (my old self), and his instinctive gestures and claims: but I cringe at his "parodic redeployments" (though I embrace his lack of theoretical sophistication). Still, if his vocabulary had been better constructed, perhaps his entrance on the List would have been eased. And, thinking of Derrida's *On Hospitality*, it is true that we do not get to choose who enters our domains. This creates opportunities for discussion and reflection through confrontation with the other—in whatever context you want to define other. Theorized through this notion of hospitality, Derrida suggests that "tolerance" draws boundaries that prevent engagements with the other. Such "tolerance" is unproductive in terms of communication. By testing one's identity in a context in which the other arrives to challenge us, we can develop strong arguments that further conversation without retreating into the safe categories of being we claim to protect us from the dynamic arguments of others.

## IV

In 1997 I wore the mask and armature of the underdog. At the time, I was entangled in my emotional devotion to the systems of other writers while trying to find my position within these new social coordinates. Unfortunately, I worked out much of this social confusion publicly on the List. I think there was benefit in doing so, even if it alienated certain people—and continues to sustain a divide between others and me in our community. Mainly, I was torn between taking a position and resisting one, and to this day, I would prefer a poetics that remains open and dynamic to one that is closed under the category of a particular heading. Still, to communicate effectively, the lure of the category tempts me, though I often regret such things and turn back on myself in contradiction.

At stake though was this problem of representation. Recently it has become necessary for some to count the prize winnings offered by the various institutions "supporting" "poetry" in America. Also, as in the recent *Chicago Review*, a kind of body count goes on, comparing the number of women to men published in magazines over the last fifty years or so. Spahr and Young perform a kind of cultural critique, following Steve Evans' own brilliant analysis of prize data in *The Poker*, in order to respond to the inequities in North American publishing. But here's the problem:

Such critiques look at poetry as if it were just another business. A poetics based on spreadsheets rather than affinity and affection—or reflection and speculation—gives the game over to other disciplines. Read as another social discipline, the inner life of poetry—its formal and rhetorical components—are passed over in order to disclose its productive value on capitalist markets. The urge to count, however, is strong in us Americans, duped as we are by polls, elections, and faith in empirical orders of social measures. But this has never been my project: to count.

My wonderful co-editor through 10 issues of *Skanky Possum*, Hoa Nguyen, has argued with me about this. Her position is on the side of equity. Provide equal space for women writers in small journals. On the surface, of course, I agree: it is weird to see a magazine or a press publishing works that are written predominantly by men. Why would anyone even take a stance that favored some kind of skewed gender representation? Of course, in the economically and temporally "squeezed" moment of small press production, positions mutate, and much is forgotten or obliterated in the long hours of typographic layout, correspondence, and production. Much of my oversight as an editor was and is a tremendous reliance on velocity to help me accomplish some critical task. In the wake of that speed, crucial issues get pushed aside. And when questioned, the defenses mount, because the unconscious results conflict with the conscious goals of production.

Women find places today more than ever to publish their work. Many editors are committed to including women in their journals. It would be foolish to purposely exclude them on any grounds. The problem, however, becomes one of editorial intent: editors must make commitments to women writers or face some stern questions. And so we come to the counting game again: numbers. These numbers are based on ontological assumptions of gender. A genealogical approach to issues of gender, by contrast, looks at the dynamic actions—the performative capacity—of gender disclosure. The second wave feminist concerns for equity are important—but this is not my project. I remain instead committed to Butler's argument on the subversion of identity as a basis for provoking a "redeployment of power."

## V

At stake too is this: bodily pleasure. I support almost every combined notion of sexuality that can be imagined. Gender should be explored and pushed out in every possible way to liberate those desires that are so often repressed and condemned by the Law. Poetry is one key way to achieve this. As an epideictic genre, its main function is to produce reflection and speculation within the minds of its audience. All are welcome to participate, but some "subversive and parodic redeployments of power" work better than others in terms of producing reflection and speculation in the minds of an audience. This is where editorial decisions can be made. How will these words affect an audience? How might a journal be shaped to persuade an audience to speculate on other formulations of power?

Power? Poetry really pushes beyond power too. Foucault's arguments about power regimes are so compelling that reconciling them with notions of desire, affinity, and affection often challenge our perceptions of subjectivity within certain social relations. But by accepting the essentialist ontology of gender as somehow being determined prior to the intrusion of the law, and by asserting a platform of equity that does not value the impact of dynamic acts in relation to an audience, editors fail to accomplish political acts with their publications. Poetry becomes another product of disciplinary regimes rather than a genre of speculative feedback and reflection on those disciplinary forces. It is used to condone crippling ontological categories rather than to subvert power with its affective claims on desire. On the surface, my project is not radically different from the equity-centered feminists: but under it there lies another set of assumptions about power, affection, reflection, and persuasion in terms of an audience.

## VI

In my confused and over-complex manner of reducing these issues of desire and power to terms I could understand ten years ago, I fucked up. I'm still not confident that I grasp the issues here as well as others do. But I have always devoted my work in its many arrays to an open and vigorous critique of power and desire, and I've put my words out there to push thought into action. The success or failure of this can only be determined from our diverse perspectives and investments in the debates so widely straddled here. To my own "defense," let me add to this *apologia* a question offered a decade ago to me by Maria Damon, and then let me respond. Better late than never.

"Dale," she said, "I wonder if it'd be fair to say that your aesthetic sense may itself be the product of conditioning in an unjust society?"

This question, you might say, has pushed me the last decade when reflecting upon my role in the making of art and in publishing. Since that initial public "outburst" I have gone on to write about the work of many "women." And I have published others and worked with women to achieve the redeployment of power argued by Butler. Moreover, my work over the last decade, with some few exceptions, has focused upon the construction of masculine identity. By confronting masculine identity within the context of the hearth—marriage, childcare, and other domestic concerns traditionally related to women—I have worked to examine how performativity of gender is not just a queer concern. Butler's work pushed feminism toward an inquiry into the nature of subjectivity and it complicated gender as ontology. As a basis for queer theory it is great, but it also opens space to investigate gender across the board. I see no reason why such theoretical uses of gender study should not apply to straights as well as gays, women as well as men. The main thing is that such gender-specific constructions and desire-driven identifications are not categorically glossed but explored in a dynamic context of ongoing changes that are open to self-critique and interpretation.

If the world is "to change," gender relations must be explored and reinterpreted by those also who usually are lumped in with the oppressor class: white males. My work explores how white male relations to the hearth can be performed in new ways. My words may be perceived as confrontational in certain contexts, but I have pushed these concerns into the open for debate and reflection, with often uncomfortable consequences for me. It is through my own reflection upon events from a decade ago that I have worked to more radically appreciate and explore what's at stake not just for women, but for us all who are challenged to respond to our environments through complex identifications and judgments that ultimately contribute to our survival. This has been my project and it will remain so, for I find it more valuable than taking count and keeping score, which seems to be a goal of equity-based feminists—and that's not insignificant work. It's just not the whole picture, either.

Looking back after a decade upon the traces of one's self left in electronic media is kind of freaky. I realize too how unprepared then I was for electronic environments, for I had only begun to acquaint myself with the web in the summer of 1996. By writing this I wanted to point out that the context always shifts, expands, and morphs in ways few of us can anticipate. Our words, motivated within specific frames of reference, reach others and persuade them somehow to listen to us, or spur them into action, or reaction, to accomplish something, even if it's a reorientation to the issues at stake, or the generation of a reflective moment that can inspire other ethical acts. The point is we are dealing with complex dynamic surfaces. These are constructs of the imagination and the real. This is where my poetics begins, though I don't think this is a terribly subtle position. It is merely a beginning ten years in the making.

Originally published at possumego.blogspot.com/2007/11/re-name-paradox-of-its-contents.html, November 01, 2007.

# On "Numbers Trouble"

A. E. STALLINGS

I know very little about the status of women in innovative poetry (though I'd agree with Stevens that "all poetry is experimental poetry" I recognize that some poetry is more conscious of and focused on innovation than others), aside from, say, the vaguely condescending introduction to Marianne Moore by T.S. Eliot, or the crushing neglect and sad facts of Lorine Niedecker's life (Zukofsky does not come out smelling like roses). Regarding the more general bean-counting chart and graph, I can say that it is fascinating and suggestive, but that these numbers are absolutely meaningless as statistics without the related numbers of what percentage of submissions are from women.

Or indeed without knowing what the selection process in each venue entails. The *NYRB* is exonerated if it in fact received no submissions from women (unlikely); but more egregious if these numbers were largely the result of solicitation rather than over-the-transom submissions (true for many higher-end journals). And because it publishes fewer poems, the statistics are going to be easy to skew. The numbers given for the *Chicago Review* are tantalizing to extrapolate from, and my hunch is that they are probably roughly representative. If only 35% of the submissions were from women, but 37% of the acceptances are women, women are outperforming the men. But the bigger question is, we know women are studying poetry in large numbers, we know they are writing, we know they are seeking

MFAs: Why aren't we submitting? Or why aren't we submitting to the big leagues?

In other words, this looks to me not so much an issue of sexism at magazines—whose goal after all should be to publish the best poems they receive, regardless—as an issue of self-censorship and/or complacency by women, on the one hand, and on the other, the older problem of women and ambition, women and career, women and a room of their own, women and *time* of their own; that is, marriage and child-raising. This is something women writers are still contending with, and maybe always will be. One can say that having a child enriches the possibilities of one's writing, but I can name any number of childless writers whose work seems endlessly rich. I worry that it is no coincidence that almost all of my favorite writers (men and women) were childless and/or gay.

I think there is a much greater anxiety about the cost of child-rearing to creative output among women—the childbearing years and years of peak creativity have a lot of overlap—and I think it has to do with the fact that women still tend to be the primary care-givers, and the poetry world frankly isn't cut out to deal with that. I talk to male poets with small children in roughly my same age-group and publication-level (one or two books), and suddenly realize we are not so much living in parallel universes as different worlds. The wife is the one at home all day with the endearing but energy-sucking little one, while the male poet, admittedly underslept (he helps out as much as he can), still has an office to go to and hours sacrosanct for his work. This may also be because he is often the main breadwinner, and his career is something at stake for both of them. I know that I am being unfair; I expect a chorus of male poets to tell me so, and I myself know several stellar exceptions; but I would say on anecdotal evidence that this is still largely the case. After all, someone needs to be the primary caregiver, but this still seems to be de facto the woman. In dark moments I have my doubts about how compatible motherhood (read, primary care-giver) really is with being an artist—the one is all compromise, the other, for greatness, admits of none. I don't think we should kid ourselves about that. This pulls at women more than men, on the whole. As a friend puts it, "No one else can have my child, or write my poems." Do men agonize about this?

What would women poet-mothers need to better realize their potential? Grant money should be given as readily for babysitting or child care as it is for sabbatical travel or research projects—it should be as respectable to ask the Guggenheim for babysitting money as it is to ask for money for leave from a high-powered poetry teaching job. It would help if there were residencies and retreats that recognized that women might have to come with their children. Perhaps some of these things exist already, but not enough, and not with high enough profiles. And no, women shouldn't expect this to just get handed to us; we need to work on this for ourselves.

In an e-mail, Ange [Mlinko] mentions that perhaps men congregate in some way to the "extremes" of poetry—either end of the bell curve. It's an intriguing notion; although, actually, I'm not even sure we *have* a bell curve in the US anymore, since current US poetry seems all about the extremes with very little attention to the middle, the Main Stream, as Don Paterson discusses it in *New British Poetry*.

What is also strange about the US poetry scene to me is the association of political bents with poetic ones—thus innovative poetry would be on the left end of the bell curve and formal poetry on the right. This impression, however misplaced (is Ezra Pound left? Is W. H. Auden right?), has affected expectations of gender equality in both poetry camps. New formal poetry in the US has been accused of conservatism in politics and aesthetics (see Ira Sadoff's "Neo-Formalism: A Dangerous Nostalgia,"

*The American Poetry Review*, January/February 1990). Paradoxically, this may result in more "gender equality" in the numbers game, since there has both been a concerted and conscious effort by women to fight for their place at the table, and even an effort by the "establishment" (if you can have an establishment in a movement that is already marginal), sensitive to charges that it is all about dead white men, or white men who will one day be dead, to be and to *appear* to be inclusive.

I had not realized that the anthology of women writing in form, *A Formal Feeling Comes*, edited by Annie Finch, *predates* the seminal *Rebel Angels, 25 Poets of the New Formalism*, edited by Jarman and Mason. Finch's anthology, by bringing formal women poets to the fore, arguably makes possible the fact that *Rebel Angels* represents 11 women poets out of a total of 25, a pretty respectable ratio, though credit should also be given the editors of *Rebel Angels* for making a conscious effort to include women. (In the interest of full disclosure, I am not included in either anthology.)

I asked Annie about the rationale behind *A Formal Feeling Comes*, and the effects. This is her response (she has given me permission to quote):

Re your question, yes, there was definitely such an imbalance. When *A Formal Feeling Comes* came out in 1993, there were hardly any women represented in the formal poetry world. At the Hendrix Formal Poetry Conference, the precursor to the first West Chester conference (I think it was in 1990) the faculty was, as I recall, 10 men and 2 women, and the main faculty photo left out the 2 women because the faculty was modelling the host's collection of vintage ties. The first couple of years of the West Chester conference, most panels were routinely all male. Molly Peacock and I complained, and the standard answer was "but there AREN"T any other women formalist poets. If there were, we'd include them!" I was frantically editing *A Formal Feeling Comes* and I kept saying, "wait till my anthology comes out and you'll see that yes, there are women formalist poets."

When it did come out, things began to improve. The reaction to *AFFC* was intense from two sides: from women poets in the "outside world," genuine surprise that formal poetry could be fun (reviewers would write things like, "I used to think I hated stuffy formal poetry, but I had a glass of wine and started to read these diverse, down to earth women and I loved it!"), and from the male formal poetry world, a very quick (perhaps slightly embarrassed?) absorption of these women formalists they hadn't thought existed. The first edition of *Expansive Poetry* included no women; the revised edition includes a number of women by reprinting their pieces from *A Formal Feeling Comes*. Otherwise there would still be no women in it. I doubt that *Rebel Angels* would have anything like a 50/50 ratio if it hadn't been for the work done by *A Formal Feeling Comes*.

An e-mail to Dave Mason also confirmed that *Rebel Angels'* inclusiveness was conscious:

> We made a deliberate effort to represent women and minorities (including several gay poets) in the book. We wanted to combat the charge that formal poets were politically conservative.

But women still seem to feel somewhat marginalized among the formalists, and tend to band together. There is, for instance, the list-serve Formalista, started by Robin Kemp, and also the on-line journal *Mezzo Cammin*, for women's formal poetry, edited by Kim Bridgford. It is interesting to me that on a formal-friendly forum, Eratosphere at Able Muse, announcements for women-only form projects, such as an anthology of funny formal poetry by women, have sometimes been greeted by as much anger as encouragement. I myself have mixed feelings about appearing in women-only formal ventures—indeed, about appearing in formal-only ventures (I have certainly never felt excluded from them in any way–quite the opposite)—since I'd like to see more mixing, more of a true Main Stream; but I am surprised at the aggressive antipathy towards such projects.

(It is interesting that women are active participants on list-servs, but not as involved in criticism or blogging, perhaps because these activities are perceived as more antagonistic, whereas list-servs provide something of a community? On the other hand, list-servs have their own problems–group pressures of consensus and assumptions–and it is difficult to openly discuss or review the work of a poet who is, also, a member of the list serv, or who has friends who are.)

I suppose one of the reasons for that feeling of marginality is not so much representation on faculty or publications, as respect for women writers of the past in these venues. There have been panels at West Chester (the conference on Form and Narrative) on neglected women formalists (keep in mind though that most dead women writers would have been, as would most dead poets, by definition, "formalists"), but relatively few panels on a single woman writer (I don't have statistics to hand). The keynote speakers have also tended to be male—only about a quarter have been women. But I think the conference (disclosure: I have taught there many years) is sensitive to these questions and does strive to improve ratios when the issue is brought forward.

Consider a form-friendly (though by no means form exclusive) on-line journal such as *Contemporary Poetry Review* (*CPR*). A year or two back, I noticed some recent issue had been entirely written by men (no longer the case, I should add). I backchanneled the editor about this. The editor was surprised, pointed out other issues with women reviewers, and then said, well, we mostly get queried by men, we'd love to include more women, would you write something for us? And there I was stumped. I was e-mailing with a baby on my knee, occasionally (and unsuccessfully) trying to eke out a poem during his naps. There were books I wanted to review (or read for that matter), but that would have obliterated any of my own writing at the time. Indeed, it was all I could do to finish up a decade-old translation project, years behind deadline, that had almost slowed to absolute zero after the birth of my son. I had to say no—I didn't have time.

And round and round we go.

Originally published at Harriet: a blog from the Poetry Foundation, www. poetryfoundation.org/harriet/2007/11/numbers-trouble, November 3, 2007.

# On Feminism, Women of Color, Poetics, and Reticence: Some Considerations

BARBARA JANE REYES

Subsequent to the *Chicago Review's* publishing of Juliana Spahr's and Stephanie Young's now notorious essay, "Numbers Trouble," on gender disparity in the US experimental poetry scene, these two authors initiated a project entitled "Tell US Poets," and issued a call for information on feminism as it exists for women writers in the world outside of North America. I responded to Spahr and Young, and to my relief, they were both receptive to my criticisms and questions. I asked if they were interested in hearing about American feminisms from the perspective of women writers from communities of color, for I was troubled by what appeared implicit to me in their request for non-North American information: that all women in North America experience and define gender relations, power dynamics, and feminism in the same manner.

This is a dangerous assumption, for Third World conditions exist in North America, in North American countries that are not Canada and the USA, among Native Hawaiians and the First Peoples of Canada, on Native American reservations, in the prison industrial complex, inner cities, rural and agricultural settings. I suspect that women in these communities do not have access to the feminism which exists in white American middle class households and their corresponding professional workplaces and educational institutions.

As well, North America is comprised of many immigrant communities (one of which I am a part), who have different beliefs and practices of gender relations, and who live in varying degrees of integration into and isolation from mainstream institutions and popular culture.

And so I have come to both appreciate and resent this, "Tell us what we need to know about feminism in ____," (fill in blank with a name of a place that isn't in America) coming from white American women who are middle class and professionals.

Perhaps a "Please," and a withholding of any initial assumptions would have made me appreciate the request a little bit more. This "Please," would have made the request sound like a request and not a command. I would have also appreciated an explanation of why the requesters feel they do not know enough or anything at all about the feminism of "other" women, why this information is not something they have found, where they have looked, to whom they have spoken as they have attempted to gather information.

I am critical of the assumption that communities of "others," or those of "other" places deemphasize feminism because of these "other" communities' inherent or essential misogyny.

I am critical of the assumption that "other" communities' misogyny is essential.

I am critical of the assumption that "innovative" poetry coming from these "other" places will abide by the same standards by which "white," "avant garde" American poetry abides; I find this problematic precisely because these standards are determined by this same "avant garde," their cultural values, and their relationships with English.

As well, I would ask that this American "avant garde" reconsider that we of "other" communities may not group ourselves in the groupings set up for us by those who do not live in our communities.

Consider that Filipino American poets may have more historical and linguistic commonalities with Chicano and Latino poets.

Consider that Filipino American poets may have more aesthetic commonalities with African American poets.

Consider that Filipino American poets may have more oral tradition/storytelling commonalities with Native American poets.

In thinking about what is "innovative" poetry for women of color poets, and in thinking about this alleged reticence of women poets to submit their work to journal and anthology editors for publication, here are a couple of my reference points:

(1) Chris Chen, who curated the *Asian American Poetry Now* reading at the Berkeley Art Museum in October 2007, discussed "post identity poetry," for contemporary Asian American poets, as a process of movement and negotiation, between the already used and overused tropes of cultural artifact and sentimentality, and its binary opposite of blanket disavowal of any ethnic identifiers.

Cathy Park Hong's *Dance Dance Revolution* reenvisions the American city and American language. Bruna Mori's *Dérive* witnesses, engages, and participates in American city and its farthest reaches, via public mass transit. Sarah Gambito's *Matadora* persona is full of rage despite her apparent delicacy. Yoko Ono, Mei-mei Berssenbrugge, Shin Yu Pai, and Eileen Tabios write from visual and conceptual art.

(2) On the Harriet blog of the Poetry Foundation, Rigoberto González reminds us that not all poets are published (yet), or seek print publication. This may be interpreted as reticence but let me offer this possibility: Many poets not widely published are perhaps invested in live and recorded performance, which makes sense for communities for whom oral tradition is underscored over written tradition.

Harryette Mullen's *Muse and Drudge* draws from scat's improvisation, verbal games such as playground rhyme, and the dozens. The chanting of Mazatec curandera María Sabina, and of Tibetan Buddhism, Anne Waldman borrows and utilizes in her incantatory long poem, "Fast Speaking Woman." In a similar vein, Genny Lim's incantations draw from her Buddhist traditions and from Jazz.

Cecilia Vicuña draws upon the quipu tradition of the Andean people, elongating her words as she intones, as one spins fibers into thread. She incorporates actual string into her performance, tying herself to the space, and to her audience. She writes threads of words upon the handwritten pages of *Instan.*

In *Storyteller,* Leslie Marmon Silko writes that words set into motion, much like the casting of a spell, cannot simply be taken back. There are consequences to speaking, and so it should not be done lightly or carelessly. Here, word is the thing and the representation of the thing.

Spanning or blending poetry and theatre, Ntozake Shange's choreopoem, *For Colored Girls Who Have Considered Suicide When the Rainbow is Enuf,* is performed by an ensemble of women. Jessica Hagedorn, one of the original Colored Girls, has performed poetic work with her rock band, the West Coast Gangster Choir. We can consider the ensemble poetic performance productions of Aimee Suzara's *Pagbabalik,* and Maiana Minahal's *Before Their Words* as descendants of Shange's *Colored Girls* and Hagedorn's Gangster Choir.

An emphasis on oral tradition in part explains the popularity of Def Poetry, slam poetry, Hip-hop theatre, multidisciplinary performance which is neither "new" nor "innovative" a thing to do, but extensions of oral traditions. Hip-hop generation poets are the descendants of Black Arts and Jazz Poets, Gwendolyn Brooks, Jayne Cortez, Sonia Sanchez, Nikki Giovanni. This Hip-hop generation includes such poets as LaTasha N. Nevada Diggs, Ishle Yi Park, Tara Betts, Kelly Zen-Yie Tsai, Aya De León, Staceyann Chin, and Chinaka Hodge. As well, we see many of these poets actively pursuing publication, literary awards, graduate degrees, writing and teaching fellowships, acceptance and participation in artist in residency programs, and professorships.

Still, another reason for this perceived "reticence" of women writers of color to publish also has to do with a general and justifiable distrust of American letters and Western institutions. I say "justifiable," for the historical exclusion of women of color voices from American letters, but I am also wary of blanket rejections of poetry written by women of color who are products of MFA programs, erroneously thought of as not ethnic enough, not political enough, not invested in nor informed by the communities from which these writers come.

A member of an Asian American writers' listserv some years ago attempted to make the argument that the poetry of Myung Mi Kim did not speak to the Asian American experience because Kim was a "Language Poet." Here, I interpret this listserv member's inaccurate use of the term "Language Poetry" to describe Kim's fractured usage of language, narrative, and expansive use of white space. But it is precisely these fractures and caesurae in *Under Flag* which embody and enact some Korean Americans' experiences of war, American Occupation, and subsequent displacement from their homeland, of struggling to learn new language and culture, and of negotiating between what is native, acquired, and imposed.

Catalina Cariaga's *Cultural Evidence,* in utilizing white space and inventing poetic form; Tsering Wangmo Dhompa's *In the Absent Everyday*, in questioning English words' conventional meanings; and Heather Nagami's *Hostile,* in examining translation and in criticisms of Asian American tropes, are descendants of Kim's works.

What is "innovative" in our communities then includes various permutations of code switching, translating, fracturing language, polyglottism, vernacular; integrating performance and music onto the page presentation; integrating our own cultures' art, oral, and poetic forms into written English and Western poetic forms.

Debra Kang Dean's *Precipitates* synthesizes koan and haiku with American Transcendentalism. Michelle Bautista's *Kali's Blade* integrates the movements of the Filipino martial art, kali, into written free verse. In *Teeth,* Aracelis Girmay pays very close attention to poetics rhythm and meter which mimic those of the African slaves working the American South's sugarcane fields. Evie Shockley writes sonnet ballads in *a half red sea,* in the tradition of Gwendolyn Brooks.

Do editors of American publications recognize these innovations? How do these editors read or deal with the "foreign" elements in this work, and especially "foreign" elements that do not abide by these editors' preconceived notions, assumptions, and prejudices? For example, not all Asian American poets are East Asian. Not all East Asian poets have Buddhist sensibilities. Not all Hip-hop poets are African American. Not all African American poets are Hip-hop. Not all Spanish writing comes from Latino/a and/or Chicano/a poets. Not all ethnic "innovative" poets disavow ethnicity; many enact rather than simply tell.

What happens to the work of "ethnic" poets who do not conform to some American editors' expectations? How is this work received? Where does that work go? Who publishes it? Is this reticence when we do not see this work in print?

One major theme I find in the poetic work of women of color is body politics, and its intersections with war, imperialism, race, and ethnicity. Combine these issues with the above explorations of language, vernacular, bi/multilingualism, oral tradition, and performance. How is this work read and received by predominantly white, maybe predominantly male American editors?

Tara Betts and Patricia Smith write about the racially motivated abduction, torture, and extreme sexual abuse of Megan Williams. On the Harriet blog of the Poetry Foundation, Smith posted mug shots of Williams' assailants, telling us, "This is where poetry comes from."

In *Trimmings* and *S\*PeRM\*\*K\*T*, Harryette Mullen writes of femininity, fashion accessories, advertising, marketing, and reproduction, in ways that verge upon pornography.

Invoking the spirit of Harryette Mullen's *Sleeping with the Dictionary,* Ching-In Chen's "Ku Li," utilizes strategies of sound association and wordplay, and in the process, tests her readers' sensitivities at hearing this racially derogatory term in repetition.

Elizabeth Alexander writes of Saartjie Baartman, popularly known as the Venus Hottentot, whose prominent buttocks and *sinus pudoris* (elongated labia) placed her body in the Western world as a living display piece. Her preserved genitals remained on display in Paris, after her death in 1815 and until 1974.

Evie Shockley writes of the Middle Passage, of rivers in the tradition of Langston Hughes (this talk of rivers which influenced Jean-Michel Basquiat), and women who navigate these rivers: Phyllis Wheatley, Gwendolyn Brooks, Sally Hemmings, Billie Holiday, and Anita Hill, to name a few.

Suheir Hammad writes of the plight of Arab women negotiating tradition and war, surviving tradition and war, and of forming alliances and communities with women across ethnicity.

In the largely imagistic, "Spanglish" and "Chinglish" poems of *Crazy Melon, Chinese Apple*, Frances Chung has written about the inhabitants of New York Chinatown, pushed off the sidewalks and forced to walk in the gutters, Oriental curio objects gazed upon by white tourists.

Maile Arvin writes also of tourism, which continues to push native Hawaiians off their land and away from their depleting natural resources. Arvin also writes of Hawaiian Sovereignty as it permeates every aspect of her poetic speaker's daily life.

Irene Faye Duller, confronting the global perception of Filipino women as sexual commodities and domestics, has written, "I am the maid of the world, and the world has made me dirty."

I write about Third World women in war and military occupation — Filipina brides, the gang rapes of Iraqi women, the Comfort Women of WWII, linking these power dynamics to pornography.

We are American poets and we are American feminists.

I don't think we are reticent.

Originally published in *XCP,* 20 (2008) 107-112.

# Dear CAConrad,

JULIANA SPAHR & STEPHANIE YOUNG

Dear CAConrad,

   We are editing a collection called *A Megaphone*. A draft of it is attached.

   We've had a lot of conversations in the last weeks about how to end this collection. And now we are turning to you for help.

   We want to end this collection with a shout-out to the feminist work that writers are already doing, and to work that they might do in the future, maybe work that they do together, even if they do it at separate desks. We want to shout into alliance with those who are also in their own ways stabbing at the surface of this social space we all share as writers. We want to build a sticky web.

   But we can't figure out how to do it.

   We first thought that we might return to iconic feminist body art of the 1970s and imagine what it might do if enacted in our shared social poetic space. So we wrote something that went:

   What if two poets stood naked in the doorway entrance to a reading so that those who wanted to listen to another poet's reading had to walk between them, touching them?

   What if instead of reading poetry yet again, a poet cleaned the floor of the lecture hall/gallery/living room on her hands and knees with a wet sponge?

What if the audience entered the darkened room of the
   reading in which a single light illuminated her body
   stripped from the waist down, smeared with blood
   and stretched and bound to the table?

What if a poet arrived at readings, readings in our
   community, but also at universities and other
   institutional spaces, with the crotch cut out of her
   jeans and carrying a machine gun?

What if a poet wrote only while inhabiting a glass-fronted,
   white, box-like room, dressed in white, against which
   the menstrual blood was visible?

What if one poet masturbated in the corner while another
   poet read?

What if, while she edited her work, she struggled to remain
   standing in a transparent plastic cubicle filled with
   wet clay, repeatedly slipping and falling?

What if a poet read her work with the foreshortened barrel
   of a gun pointing toward the viewer?

What if poets began each reading by documenting their
   relationship to women's working conditions?

What if a poet invited the audience to use some objects
   on her body and/or cut off her clothes while she was
   reading?

What if a poet cut off the clothes of some audience
   members, and/or did some things to her own body
   with a series of objects?

What if a poet regularly stashed her reading materials in
   her bras/panties/socks/assholes and removed them
   before reading?

What if a poet showed up to readings in stinking clothes
   with balloons attached to her ears, nose, hair, and
   teeth?

But then we thought the only way to make it matter at all was if we put the names of specific writers into it. Then we got stuck figuring out what names to include. We thought we might do a procedure on the names of women included in women-only anthologies that we mention in our article "Numbers Trouble." So we rewrote it using the names of the women still alive in *Moving Borders* so it went like this:

What if Kathleen Fraser and Bernadette Mayer stood naked in the doorway entrance to a reading so that those who wanted to listen to Rosmarie Waldrop reading had to walk between them, touching them?

What if instead of reading poetry yet again, Nicole Brossard cleaned the floor of the lecture hall/gallery/living room on her hands and knees with a wet sponge?

What if the audience entered the darkened room of the reading in which a single light illuminated Anne Waldman's body stripped from the waist down, smeared with blood and stretched and bound to the table?

What if Fanny Howe arrived at readings, readings in our community, but also at universities and other institutional spaces, with the crotch cut out of her jeans and carrying a machine gun?

What if Lyn Hejinian wrote only while inhabiting a glass-fronted, white, box-like room, dressed in white, against which the menstrual blood was visible?

What if Ann Lauterbach masturbated in the corner while Alice Notley read?

What if, while Maureen Owen edited her work, she struggled to remain standing in a transparent plastic cubicle filled with wet clay, repeatedly slipping and falling?

What if Beverly Dahlen read her work with the foreshortened barrel of a gun pointing toward the viewer?

What if Mei-mei Berssenbrugge and Abigail Child began
each reading by documenting their relationship to
women's working conditions?

What if Rae Armantrout invited the audience to use some
objects on her body and/or cut off her clothes while
she was reading?

What if Susan Howe cut off the clothes of some audience
members, and/or did some things to her own body
with a series of objects?

What if Johanna Drucker regularly stashed her reading
materials in her bras/panties/socks/assholes and
removed them before reading?

What if Lynne Dreyer showed up to readings in stinking
clothes with balloons attached to her ears, nose, hair,
and teeth?

And so on . . .

Then when we read the piece, we felt as if we were
suggesting that the work these women had already done was not
adequate which was not our intent at all. And while this body
centered work that felt so moving to us often addressed violence
done to women's bodies or did violence to women's bodies, we
felt that when we used the names of writers that we were doing
something to their bodies without their consent.

So then we thought, what if we used men's names also?
And so we rewrote it like this, using *In the American Tree* as
our source:

What if Robert Grenier and Barrett Watten stood naked in
the doorway entrance to a reading so that those who
wanted to listen to Lyn Hejinian reading had to walk
between them, touching them?

What if instead of reading poetry yet again, Bob Perelman cleaned the floor of the lecture hall/gallery/living room on his hands and knees with a wet sponge?

What if the audience entered the darkened room of the reading in which a single light illuminated Jean Day's body stripped from the waist down, smeared with blood and stretched and bound to the table?

What if David Melnick arrived at readings, readings in our community, but also at universities and other institutional spaces, with the crotch cut out of his jeans and carrying a machine gun?

What if Michael Palmer wrote only while inhabiting a glass-fronted, white, box-like room, dressed in white, against which the menstrual blood was visible?

What if Larry Price masturbated in the corner while Kit Robinson read?

What if, while Ron Silliman edited his work, he struggled to remain standing in a transparent plastic cubicle filled with wet clay, repeatedly slipping and falling?

What if Rae Armantrout read her work with the foreshortened barrel of a gun pointing toward the viewer?

What if Carla Harryman and Alan Bernheimer began each reading by documenting their relationship to women's working conditions?

What if Steve Benson invited the audience to use some objects on his body and/or cut off his clothes while he was reading?

What if Michael Davidson cut off the clothes of some audience members, and/or did some things to his own body with a series of objects?

What if Tom Mandel regularly stashed his reading materials in his bra/panties/socks/asshole and removed them before reading?

What if David Bromige showed up to readings in stinking clothes with balloons attached to his ears, nose, hair, and teeth?

And so on . . .

But then again, as you yourself can see, it isn't really working.

No matter what we did we felt as if we were attacking, when what we really wanted to do was talk as many people as we could into self-declaring as feminist, although we admit here to wanting a specific sort of feminist, not the Hillary Clinton or Sarah Palin sort of feminist, not the consumerist, imperialist feminist. We wanted to suggest an an anti-consumerist, anti-imperialist, anti-nationalist feminism of uneasy alliances, full of recognized difference and unexpected knowledges.

So then we thought what if we ended by doing some procedure of homage on an iconic poem, a poem that we feel helps us negotiate this weird aggression against anything that even suggests the possibility of the need for a contemporary feminism. We liked the idea of including some poetry because *A Megaphone* is all about the social world of poetry and has little to no actual poetry in it.

Many of the descriptions of iconic 1970s body art in our earlier ideas came from a poem Stephanie had written, where she used language from the *WACK!* Catalog and substituted descriptions of feminist body art for the word "farm" every time it appears in Bernadette Mayer's poem "Essay." Mayer's poem seems to be talking partly about property and owners, about who owns the land, and also who owns literary history. The poem begins by saying it's too late for the "I" to start farming, too late to live on a farm, too late to be a farmer. And maybe Mayer's poem is saying it was always too late already, because farming isn't really *for* this I, not for this I's class or identity or gender as situated in social and economic relations of the poem's time. At a certain point Mayer's poem starts talking about poets who did or do own land, poets who were farmers, or at least landed gentry of a sort, and the group is mostly men. At first, Stephanie continued to substitute feminist body art descriptions for the word "farm," even when the men's names started coming up, so that the poem might say: "Faulkner may have wandered through a field of wheat and a forest, wrapped in an armature of bandages, a little." But then Jen Hofer suggested that it might be more interesting, when the men's names came up, to substitute some of the heroic masculine body art of the 1960s and 1970s so that now the poem might say: "Faulkner may have spent three days in a gallery with a coyote, a little." At this point the poem gets a little out of control, it goes like this:

> Very few poets are really going to the library carrying a
> > concealed tape recording of loud belches
> If William Carlos Williams could be a doctor and Charlie
> > Vermont too,
> If Yves Klein could be an artist, and Jackson Pollock too,
> Why not a poet who was also dying of lymphoma and
> > making a series of life size photographs, self-portrait
> > watercolors, medical object-sculptures and collages
> > made with the hair she lost during chemotherapy
> Of course there was Brook Farm
> And Virgil raised bees
> Perhaps some poets of the past were overseers of the
> > meticulous chronicle of the feeding and excretory
> > cycles of her son during the first six months of his
> > life
> I guess poets tend to live more momentarily
> Than life in her body as the object of her own sculpting
> > activity would allow

You could never leave the structures made of wood, rope
and concrete blocks assembled to form stocks and
racks, to give a reading
Or to go to a lecture by Emerson in Concord
I don't want to be continuously scrubbing the flesh off of
cow bones with a cleaning brush but my mother was
right
I should never have tried to rise out of the proletariat
Unless I can convince myself as Satan argues with Eve
That we are among a proletariat of poets of all the classes
Each ill-paid and surviving on nothing
Or on as little as one needs to survive
Steadfast as any person's glottis, photographed with a
laryngoscope, speaking the following words: "The
power of language continues to show its trace for a
long time after silence" and fixed as the stars
Tenants of a vision we rent out endlessly

It seemed like this poem was doing something, but we weren't
exactly sure what. Partly it was making a joke on belatedness,
a joke that Juliana refused to understand. And it managed at
moments to ask some questions that felt useful, such as "Who
are the simultaneously-the-beneficiary-of-our-cultural-heritage-
and-a-victim-of-it-poets," but often it was making some bitter
or cynical jokes, the poem said things like "I guess examining
women's working conditions is just too difficult."

Then we had a long slightly insane conversation about
whether Mayer's "Essay" or her poem "The Way To Keep Going
in Antarctica" was the better iconic source for a procedure that
might end this book. It was an argument about which poem
better represented the possibility of alliance and at the same time
which poem better spoke to our exhaustion. The farm, Stephanie
kept saying, again with some irony or with her tongue in her

cheek; "too much work and still to be poets." Antarctica, Juliana kept saying, again with some hopeless sincerity; "Perhaps this is why you love the presence of other people so much."

That conversation ended with the idea that we should take one of these poems and attribute, with footnotes, each word in the poem to a writer whose work had appeared in one of the women only anthologies of the last twenty years. Then we would take each line that the word appeared in and put these lines together so the poem would make another poem and the singular author would be turned into many authors. When we realized there was no electronic text version of these anthologies available for quick key word searches, we gave up. Plus, we continued to wonder about those who were not in these anthologies, the younger writers and the writers who did not live in North America and the queermos and . . .

Our least sophisticated idea (and we will not confess to the procedure we used to obtain these names other than to say it was uniquely complicated and probably would not make much sense unless described in great detail) was simply a paragraph that called out "we love you get up." And by this we did not mean anyone had fallen, but rather to say get up, get on up, stay on the scene, come back if you left, please don't go if you're going strong, stay if you are just arriving, we see you, the work you are doing, you are amazing, we breathe you, we talk, we smile, we touch your hair, you are the one, you are the one who did this to us, you are our own, we are crying hard, there was blood, no one told us, no one knew, mother knows, there is a world love center inside my ribcage, there is a world hate center inside too, to acquire a political meaning you don't even have to be human, raw materials will do, or protein feed, or crude oil, abuse of power comes as no surprise, the fires have begun, the fires have begun, no dark corner of the poor, no fugue work of hate, no hierarchies of strength, knowledge or love, no impure water spasming from rock, you grew tired of my embrace and my smell, aren't you just as tired of the fear within me? Your oldest fears are your worst ones, it is in your self-interest to find a way to be very tender, after every war someone has to tidy up, things won't pick themselves up, after all, what happens quietly: someone's dropping from exhaustion, what happens loudly: so you're here? Still dizzy from another dodge, close shave, reprieve? One hole in the net and you slipped through?

Hey Aimee Nezhukumatathil. We love you get up. Hey Amber DiPietra. We love you get up. Hey Alli Warren. We love you get up. Hey Amy King. We love you get up. Hey Ange Mlinko. We love you get up. Hey Anne Boyer. We love you get up. Hey Anne Lesley Selcer. We love you get up. Hey Ariana Reines. We love you get up. Hey Barbara Jane Reyes. We love you get up. Hey Bhanu Kapil. We love you get up. Hey Brenda Cárdenas. We love you get up. Hey Brenda Iijima. We love you get up. Hey Bruna Mori. We love you get up. Hey Camille Dungy. We love you get up. Hey Camille Roy. We love you get up. Hey Caroline Bergvall. We love you get up. Hey Caroline Sinaviana. We love you get up. Hey Catalina Cariaga. We love you get up. Hey Cate Marvin. We love you get up. Hey Catherine Daly. We love you get up. Hey Catherine Meng. We love you get up. Hey Catherine Wagner. We love you get up. Hey Cathy Park Hong. We love you get up. Hey Carmen Gimenéz Smith. We love you get up. Hey Cecilia Vicuña. We love you get up. Hey Christine Wertheim. We love you get up. Hey Corina Copp. We love you get up. Hey Cynthia Sailers. We love you get up. Hey Dana Teen Lomax. We love you get up. Hey Dawn Lundy Martin. We love you get up. Hey Deborah Meadows. We love you get up. Hey devorah major. We love you get up. Hey Diane Glancy. We love you get up. Hey Dodie Bellamy. We love you get up. Hey Dolores Dorantes. We love you get up. Hey Dorothea Lasky. We love you get up. Hey E. Tracy Grinnell. We love you get up. Hey Eileen Myles. We love you get up. Hey Eileen Tabios. We love you get up. Hey Eleni Stecopoulos. We love you get up. Hey Elisa Gabbert. We love you get up. Hey Elizabeth Treadwell. We love you get up. Hey Emily Critchley. We love you get up. Hey Emma Bernstein. We love the memory of you get up. Hey Erica Hunt. We love you get up. Hey Erika Staiti. We love you get up. Hey Erin Morrill. We love you get up. Hey Evie Shockley. We love you get up. Hey Genny Lim. We love you get up. Hey Geraldine Monk. We love you get up. Hey giovanni singleton. We love you get up. Hey Harryette Mullen. We love you get up. Hey Hiromi Ito. We love you get up. Hey Hoa Nguyen. We love you get up. Hey Ida Yoshinaga. We love you get up. Hey Jai Arun Ravine. We love you get up. Hey Jane Sprague. We love you get up. Hey Jayne Cortez. We love you get up. Hey Jen Hofer. We love you get up. Hey Jennifer Bartlett. We love you get up. Hey Jessica Smith. We love you get up. Hey Jocelyn Saidenberg. We love you get up. Hey Judith Goldman. We love you get up. Hey Julia Bloch. We love you get up. Hey Julian T. Brolaski. We love you get up. Hey Julie Patton. We love you get up. Hey June Jordan. We love the memory of you get up. Hey K. Lorraine Graham. We love you get up. Hey Kaia Sand. We love you get up. Hey kari edwards. We love the memory of you get up. Hey Kathy Dee Kaleokealoha Kaloloahilani Banggo. We love you get up. Hey Kate Pringle. We love you get up. Hey Kim Hyesoon. We love you get up. Hey Kimiko Hahn. We love you get up. Hey Kristin Palm. We love you get up. Hey Kristin Prevallet. We love you get up. Hey Kuʻualoha Hoʻomanawanui. We love you get up. Hey

LaTasha N. Nevada Diggs. We love you get up. Hey Laura Carter. We love you get up. Hey Laura Elrick. We love you get up. Hey Laura Moriarty. We love you get up. Hey Lauren Levin. We love you get up. Hey Lauren Shufran. We love you get up. Hey Laynie Browne. We love you get up. Hey Lee Ann Brown. We love you get up. Hey Linda Russo. We love you get up. Hey Lindsey Boldt. We love you get up. Hey Lisa Linn Kanae. We love you get up. Hey Lisa Robertson. We love you get up. Hey Lynn Xu. We love you get up. Hey Maggie Zurawski. We love you get up. Hey M. NourbeSe Philip. We love you get up. Hey Mairead Byrne. We love you get up. Hey Margaret Rhee. We love you get up. Hey Mei-mei Berssenbrugge. We love you get up. Hey Michelle Bautista. We love you get up. Hey Michelle Detorie. We love you get up. Hey Michelle Naka Pierce. We love you get up. Hey Monica Hand. We love you get up. Hey Myung Mi Kim. We love you get up. Hey Nada Gordon. We love you get up. Hey Norma Cole. We love you get up. Hey Pamela Lu. We love you get up. Hey Rachel Zolf. We love you get up. Hey Reb Livingston. We love you get up. Hey Renee Gladman. We love you get up. Hey Rita Wong. We love you get up. Hey Samantha Giles. We love you get up. Hey Sara Larsen. We love you get up. Hey Sara Mumolo. We love you get up. Hey Sara Wintz. We love you get up. Hey Sawako Nakayasu. We love you get up. Hey Shanna Compton. We love you get up. Hey Stacy Szymaszek. We love you get up. Hey Staceyann Chin. We love you get up. Hey Stefani Barber. We love you get up. Hey Summi Kaipa. We love you get up. Hey Susan Schultz. We love you get up. Hey Suzanne Stein. We love you get up. Hey Teresa Carmody. We love you get up. Hey Tisa Bryant. We love you get up. Hey Tonya Foster. We love you get up. Hey Trace Peterson. We love you get up. We love you get up. Hey Tsering Wangmo Dhompa. We love you get up. Hey Vanessa Place. We love you get up. Hey Wanda Coleman. We love you get up. Hey Wanda Phipps. We love you get up. Hey Yedda Morrison. We love you get up.

But of course we immediately realized that this listing might not be the best way to make an alliance because there was no way for it not to exclude someone and yet the longer it got the less specific and less meaningful it became.

So here we are, writing to you. We want the impossible really. Could you please make a somatic writing assignment for us that might help us generate the impossible: open and yet still meaningful, alliance?

Juliana's one request is that the exercise keep in mind her child care duties which require her presence on Tuesday all day, Wednesday afternoons and evenings, Thursday evening, Friday afternoon, all day Saturday and Sunday. Stephanie has to be at the office on weekdays for the usual 9-5 and evening events, usually held on Tuesdays, but during the summer she can often come in at 10 and leave at 4.

Hugs. We love you.

Juliana and Stephanie

# Uneasy Riders: A (Soma)tic Poetry Exercise

CACONRAD

*If you are very frank with yourself and don't mind
how ridiculous anything that comes to you may seem,
you will have a chance of capturing the symbol of
your direct reaction. The antique way to live and express life was to say it according to the rules. But the
modern flings herself at life and lets herself feel what
she does feel, then upon the very tick of the second
she snatches the images of life that fly through the
brain.*
—Mina Loy in a 1917 interview

Gather twelve of your favorite books of poetry by living women
poets. Divide your copy of Maria Raha's *Hellions* into twelve
parts ("Uneasy Riders" is the name of chapter 7). *Hellions* is the
perfect book to accompany this exercise. Talk to twelve women
about visiting them. Tell them you will bring a box, and ask
them to place a small object inside the box, something you're
not to know about. It can be anything: a stone, button, shot glass,
comb, lipstick, dildo, chalk, etc., but ask them to not tell you
what it is. Ask them to sleep with it under their pillow the night
before you visit. I told Maria Raha about this (Soma)tic exercise and asked her if twelve was too many, and she said, "If
you don't know twelve women you need to SELF EXAMINE!"
This is why it's good to ask Maria Raha. Twelve women it is!
Take notes through the process of choosing the books of poetry,
and visiting the twelve women to gather the objects. Write write

write notes notes notes. After you have gathered the books by living women poets, and the box of twelve objects, set aside twelve consecutive days.

DAY ONE: As a preliminary, read the Loy quote aloud, then immediately watch Mary Wigman's 1914 dance HEXEN-TANZ on You Tube: youtube.com/watch?v=cJaYuejjdk8 and watch Wigman with the volume as LOUD as possible. Then read the first of the twelve sections you've created out of *Hellions*. Climb into the bathtub, turn on the shower, open an umbrella, and lie down to read the first book of poems, pausing from time to time to YELL the poet's name! Take notes take notes. Reach inside your box and choose an object, but don't look at it. Smell it, rub it against you. Meditate with the object in the middle of your chest while thinking of the twelve women, water beating against the umbrella. SCREAM YOUR NAME with eyes closed in meditation. SCREAM YOUR NAME with eyes open. Harryette Mullen says, "proceed with abandon / finding yourself where you are." Look at the object. Do not put it back in the box, but do take more notes.

Choose a different location for each of the next eleven days. Stand in mud, hunch in the back seat of a car, in the basement with a candle, sit in a graveyard, on the steps of a courthouse, or stand facing the statue of a very dead old man. But be somewhere completely different each day. Before reading from *Hellions*, and the next book of poetry, and fondling an object in your box, read the Loy quote aloud, and watch Wigman's HEX-ENTANZ dance. Let these brilliant grandmothers loosen any knots, and always remember as Laura Riding says, "the words are only part of the poetic formula: the rest is ritual, and the reason in them must contend with the mechanics of magic-making in it—and must not win." Your notes might seem an endless chore of notes once you've completed your twelve days, but carry them around with you, and take more notes while reading them, putting them into a frame. The poem will come to you from those notes, it's in there, no doubt about it. You've infused the (Soma)tic with these others, and now your new poem is waiting.

# CONTRIBUTORS

Demosthenes Agrafiotis is a poet, performer/intermedia artist, series editor, translator, and emeritus Professor of Sociology.

Katerina Anghelaki-Rook is a poet and translator.

Ana Arzoumanian was born in Buenos Aires in 1962. She is a lawyer who works in the academic fields, especially on Holocaust and Genocide. Her publications include *La mujer de ellos* (2001), *El ahogadero* (2002), *La granada* (2003), *Mía* (2004), *Juana I* (2006), *Cuando todo acabe todo acabará* (2008). She translated *The Long and the Short of Holocaust Verse* by Susan Gubar (2007), and *Sade et l'écriture de l'orgie* by Lucienne Frappier Mazur (2006).

Maria Attanasio was born in Caltagirone, Italy, in 1943, where she still lives, writes, and teaches philosophy. She is the author of five collections of poetry and four works of historical fiction. Her latest work, *Il Falsario di Caltagirone*, was the recipient of the prestigious Premio Vittorini. Her most recent books of poetry are *Ludica mente* (*Ludic mind, or Ludically*) (Avagliano, 2000) and *Amnesia del movimento delle nuvole* (*Amnesia of the Movement of Clouds*) (La Vita Felice, 2003), forthcoming in English translation by Carla Billitteri. Her works in prose include *Correva l'anno 1698 e nella citta' avvenne il fatto memorabile* (*It Was the Year 1698 and in the City the Memorable Fact Occurred*) (Sellerio 1994) and *Di Concetta e le sue donne* (*Of Concetta and Her Women*) (Sellerio, 1999).

Aida Bagić was born in Zagreb, Croatia in 1965. Aida has worked as a journalist, dishwasher, shop assistant, model, interpreter for English and German, journal editor and researcher, and has founded several feminist and peace organizations. Her poetry has been translated into German, Polish, and Slovene, and published in literary journals in Croatia (*Quorum, Zarez, Poezija, Erato*) and Serbia (*ProFemina*), on various websites (Knjigomat, Labris, Kontura) and on the walls of a public toilet (FemFest).

Asja Bakić, born in 1982, is a Bosnian poet. Her poetry has been published in several ex-Yugoslav literary magazines (*Profemina, Diwan, Tema, Zarez, Quorum, Poezija*), and on the Internet (Litkon, airBeletrina, Poboscza). Her first book of poems is *Može i kaktus, samo neka bode* (*Cactus Is Okay, As Long As It Stings*). She currently lives in Zagreb (Croatia) with her husband and their deaf cat.

Zsófia Bán was born in Rio de Janeiro in 1957 and grew up in Brazil and Hungary. She is a writer, literary historian, and critic. Her short stories have been widely anthologized, and she is working on a new volume of short stories and a novel. She lives and works in Budapest.

Vesna Biga was born in 1948 in Zagreb, Croatia. She has worked as a research assistant in psychology at the University of Zagreb, as a disability studies researcher, school psychologist and high-school lecturer, editor, translator, and, primarily, an independent artist. During the war in former Yugoslavia, she often traveled between Zagreb and Belgrade; her 1991-1995 travel diaries were published under the title *Bus People* (Durieux, 1998). She is the author of fourteen books of poetry and prose.

Tatjana Bijelić was born in Sisak, Croatia, in 1974. In 2000, she won a prestigious Chevening scholarship to the Oxford Brookes University in the UK. She earned her PhD degree from the University of Banja Luka, where she currently teaches. Her fields of interest are modern and contemporary British, American, Canadian and Ex-Yu literature, especially writing by women. She has published a number of scholarly papers, two poetry collections, and a book of translations.

Jana Bodnárová has published seventeen books of prose and poetry for adults and children. Twelve of her plays have been broadcast on Slovak radio. She has written several plays for theatre, one of them also staged in the Slovak National Theatre in 2005. Her most recent book of prose is entitled *Takmer neviditeľná* (*Insomnia*) (Aspekt, 2005).

Ana Božičević was born in Zagreb, Croatia, in 1977. She emigrated to NYC in 1997. *Stars of the Night Commute* (Tarpaulin Sky Press, November 2009) is her first book of poems. Her fifth chapbook, *Depth Hoar*, will be published by Cinematheque Press in 2010. With Amy King, Ana co-curates The Stain of Poetry reading series in Brooklyn, and is co-editing an anthology, *The Urban Poetic,* forthcoming from Factory School. She works at the Center for the Humanities of The Graduate Center, CUNY.

Julian T. Brolaski is the author of *gowanus atropolis* (Ugly Duckling Presse, 2001). Brolaski's second full length book, *Advice for Lovers*, is forthcoming from City Lights in spring 2012. Brolaski lives in Brooklyn where xe is an editor at Litmus Press, curates vaudeville shows and plays country music as Juan dos Pistolas and with The Invert Family Singers. New work is on the blog hermofwarsaw.

Rocío Cerón, born 1972 in Mexico City, is a poet and editor. Her publications include *Basalto* (ESN-CONACULTA, 2002), which received the Premio Nacional de Literatura Gilberto Owen 2000, *Litoral* (filodecaballos, 2001), *Soma* (Eloísa, Buenos Aires, 2003), and *Imperio* (Monte Carmelo, 2008; 2nd edition: FONCA-CONACULTA-MotínPoeta, 2009, bilingual and interdisciplinary edition). She is the editor of Ediciones El Billar de Lucrecia and co-founder of the collective MotínPoeta. She maintains the blog de enseres verbales: rocioceron. blogspot.com

Choi Youngmi was born in 1961. When the Democratization Struggle of 1980 turned to a bloody massacre in Kwangju, Choi became active in the student pro-democracy struggle. Her first volume of poems, *At Thirty the Party was Over* (1994), has sold over half a million copies. She is the author of a second volume of poems, *Bicycling in Dreamland* (1998) and a book of travel essays, *Melancholy of the Era* (1997).

Laura Cingolani was born in Ancona and lives in Rome. With Fabio Lapiana she is part of the duo Esse Zeta Atona: an experimental laboratory for voice, writing and other media. She founded the sound project called Idrante with Daniele Salvati. She has published poems, short stories and criticism in the journals *Liberatura*, *accattone*, *Catastrophe*, *Aufgabe*, *35mm*, and *Crak!web* and in the anthologies *Letteratura Chimica Italiana*, *Fuori dal Cielo*, *L'esperienza--divenire delle arti*, *Sperimentare il plurale*, and *Slam--antologia europea*.

Olivia Coetzee, poet, artist, and activist. Born in Mariental, Namibia, grew up in Northern Suburbs of Cape Town. Starting her poet's journey in 2009, she has been published in *Sparkling Women 1* and *2*, *Water-Cycles* and *Cyphers* (anthology formed out of a workshop held by Winslow Schalkwyk) and *Ugandan Sexuality Reader* (still to be released). Read more of her work on her blog slamversusflow.blogspot.com.

CAConrad's (Soma)tic exercises are free and available online at CAConrad.blogspot.com.

Aleksandra Čvorović, born 1976 in Banja Luka, is working towards a PhD in library and computer science, and currently works as a librarian. She has published three books of poetry and one short story collection.

She is on the editorial board for several magazines and her work has been translated into German, English, Polish, Slovene and Danish.

Veronika Czapáry is a writer, poet, essayist, critic, and handicraft artist (glass).

Lenka Dańhelová, born in 1973 in Krnow, is a poet, writer, artist, and translator. She works as a journalist, translator, interpreter, and editor. Since 2005, she has been the editor of the international Czech journal *Pobocza*, www.pobocza.pl. In 2004, she published a novel *Cizinci*; her second collection, *Pozdrav ze Sudet*, is in print. She publishes her fiction and poetry in both Czech and international journals. She lives in Beroun close to Prague.

Dubravka Djurić is a feminist poet, critic and translator. She began translating US poetry in 1983. She has published several books of poetry, including *Cosmopolitan Alphabet* (Meow Press). With Vladimir Kopicl she co-edited and translated an anthology of US poetry *Novi pesnicki poredak* (New Poetry Order). With Misko Suvakovic she co-edited *Impossible Histories: Avant-Garde, Neo-Avant-Garde, Post-Avant-Garde in Yugoslavia 1918-1991* (The MIT Press, second printing 2006).

Etela Farkašová, born in 1943, is a writer, essayist and philosopher, and a Lecturer at the Faculty of Arts UK in Bratislava. She has published ten books of fiction, two books of essays, and a book of poetic reflections. She is the author of a scientific monograph on images, characters, and problems in feminist philosophy, *Na ceste k vlastnej izbe* (*On the way to one's own room*), and has edited a book of essays and several anthologies of women writers.

Simone Fattal was born in Damascus, Syria, studied Philosophy at the Sorbonne in Paris, and worked as a painter for ten years. In 1980 she settled in California and, in 1982, founded The Post-Apollo Press. In 1989, she returned to an artistic career and started doing sculpture in ceramics. She was part of the itinerant exhibit of Women Artists from the Arab World in the US, *Forces of Change* (1994) and her new works were recently exhibited in Beirut, Lebanon.

Mária Ferenčuhová works at the Faculty for film and TV studies at the Academy of Fine Arts in Bratislava. She is the editor of the journal for film theory *Kino-Ikon*. She translates essays and fiction from French authors such as Paul Virilio, Philippe Brenot, Amelie Nothomb, Phillipe Solers, and Jean Eschenoz). She has published a collection of poetry *Skryté titulky* (*Hidden Subtitles*, 2003).

Daniela Fischerová, born 1948, is a playwright, screenwriter, and writer. Her theater plays include *Hodina mezi psem a vlkem, Báj,* and *Náhlé neštěstí,* and her radio plays are: *Velká vteřina, Zapřený Albert, Cesta k pólu* and others. She has published several books of short stories and the novel *Happy End.* She also writes screenplays (*Neúplné zatmění, Vlčí bouda*) and children's fiction.

Romina Freschi, born 1974, holds an MA and is a Professor of Literature at The University of Buenos Aires. She has published the poetry books *redondel* (1998, 2003), *estremezcales* (2000), *eL-Pe-Yo* (2003), and the chapbooks *Incrustaciones en confite* (1999), *Villa Ventana* (2003), *3/3/3* (2005), and *Solaris* (2007), among others. She directs the poetry review *Plebella* and many websites dedicated to poetry.

Pavla Frýdlová is a screenwriter, a documentarist, a publicist, the co-founder of the NGO Gender Studies, vice-president of the Czech Society for Oral History, and coordinator of the international project The Memory of Women, for which she has edited several publications, a radio cycle and a documentary movie. Her earlier work is on issues in film, including

*Malý labyrint filmu* (with Jan Bernard, 1988), *Philippe Noiret—Hvězdou proti své vůli* (1995).

Megan M. Garr is the founder and editor of the Amsterdam-based literary journal *Versal*. Recent publications of her poetry and writings on translocality include *RHINO, Tuesday: An Art Journal*, and *St. Petersburg Review*. She lives in Amsterdam, the Netherlands with her partner, artist Shayna Schapp.

Milli Graffi, Milanese, was born in 1940. Beginning her career as part of the neoavantgarde movement "poesia totale," she has produced works of sound poetry (*Salnitro; Farfalla ronzar; tralci*) and four poetry collections, *Mille graffi e venti poesie* (1979); *Fragili film* (1987); *L'amore meccanico* (1994); and *embargo voice* (2006), as well as the novella *Centimetri due* (Edizioni d'If, 2004). She has translated Lewis Carroll and Charles Dickens, and has written criticism on nonsense, futurist words-in-freedom, and the comic function in the early avant-gardes. She is editor-in-chief of the pioneering journal *Il Verri*.

E. Tracy Grinnell is the author of *Helen: A Fugue* (Belladonna Elder Series #1, 2008), *Some Clear Souvenir* (O Books, 2006), and *Music or Forgetting* (O Books, 2001). She is the founding editor of Litmus Press and Aufgabe and currently lives in Brooklyn.

Anna Grusková is the author, co-author and editor of several publications on contemporary theatre and theatre history, especially from the period of Vienna modernism. She currently works as a dramaturg, playwright and translator from German, and occasionally as a publicist, actor and director. She has been a finalist in several drama competitions for her plays, including *Schaulhust* (*Curiosity*, premiered on Czech radio, Prague 2007), and *Nimandi a nymfomani* (*Nymphomaniacs and Nobodies*, co-author, premiered in Czech Centre, Bratislava 2005).

Silvia Guerra was born in Maldonado, Uruguay, in 1961. She has published many books of poetry, most recently *nada de nadie* (2001), and a series of interviews in collaboration with Verónica D'auria: "conversaciones oblicuas/diálogos entre la cultura y el poder: entrevistas a 10 intelectuales uruguayos" (2002). In 2005, with Chilean poet Verónica Zondek, she edited *El ojo atravesado*, a collection of the letters between Gabriela Mistral and Uruguayan writers. In 2007 she published a fictional biography of the Count of Lautremont, *Fuera del relato*.

Nada Harbaš (1974) B.A. in Turkish Language and Literature, Faculty of Philology, Belgrade, and M.A. in Contemporary Political Theory, University of Westminster, London, UK. Translates from Swedish, as well as from and to English. Among her many published translations are articles by Gil Anidjar, Talal Asad, Mary Kaldor, Omer Bartov, Chantal Mouffe, Miško Šuvaković, Dubravka Đurić, Ana Vujanović, etc.

Born in Aleppo, Syria in 1966, Maha Hassan resides in Paris, France. She left Syria looking for more freedom to write and publish. She is a novelist and also writes critical and literary essays. She is on the board of the online magazine *Alef Today* (www.aleftoday.net). Extracts of her books may be found at www.alawan.org, and her articles and manuscripts may be found here: www.maisondesjournalistes.org/archives_coeur_maha.php.

Farideh Hassanzadeh-Mostafavi is a freelance poet, writer and translator from Iran, who specializes in poetry. Her published translations include T. S. Eliot's *The Rock* and a selection of Marina Tsvetayeva's poems. She is currently working on the biography of Federico Garcia Lorca as well as on a collection of Modern African poetry. The success of her latest book, *Poetry of Women Worldwide,* led to the publication of a second edition after only several months.

Liliana Heer was born in Esperanza, Argentina. She is a writer and a psychoanalyst. She has published many books, including the novels *Bloyd* (Boris Vian Award, 1984), *La tercera mitad* (1988), *Ángeles de vidrio* (1998), *Pretexto Mozart* (2004) and *Neón* (2007). Her other writing includes a collection of short stories, several novellas and poetry. More info: www.lilianaheer.com.ar.

Rade Jarak was born in Dubrovnik, Croatia in 1968. He studied painting in Sarajevo, graduating from the Zagreb Arts Academy. He is a poet, critic and fiction writer.

Poet, performer, and teacher Myesha Jenkins' work is featured in *We are . . .* (ed. Natalia Molebatsi, Penguin 2009), *Canopic Jar* (2009), and *Isis X* (Botsotso Publishing, 2005). Her collection *Breaking the Surface* (Timbila, 2005) sold over 1,200 copies. Her ongoing work as a feminist activist has seen her creating showcases for young poets as well as experiential creative writing workshops in venues ranging from universities to township halls. She is a founding member of the spoken word collective Feela Sistah.

Iva Jevtić, born in 1976, is a writer and translator. She writes prose and essays, and in 2005 the publishing house Apokalipsa published her book of short short stories: *Težnost* (Gravity) and in 2009 the monograph *Mistična podoba* (*Mystic image*).

Paul Foster Johnson's first collection of poetry, *Refrains/Unworkings*, was published by Apostrophe Books, and his second, *Study in Pavilions and Safe Rooms*, is forthcoming from Portable Press at Yo-Yo Labs. With E. Tracy Grinnell, he is the author of the g-o-n-g press chapbook *Quadriga*. His poems have appeared in *The Awl, Jacket, Cannot Exist, GAM, EOAGH, Fence*, and *Octopus*. From 2003 to 2006, he curated the Experiments and Disorders reading series at Dixon Place. He is an editor at Litmus Press and lives in New York.

Jakuba Katalpa (pseudonym of Tereza Jandová, born 1979) graduated in linguistics and literature, Bohemian studies and psychology. In 2006 the publishing house Paseka published her work *Je hlina k snědku?* She lives in a small village not far from Plzno and hopes someday to live in an even smaller village far, far away from Plzno.

Emelihter Kihleng has been teaching in Micronesia since completing her MA in English, Creative Writing at the University of Hawai'i at Manoa in 2006. Her first collection of poetry, *My Urohs*, was published by Kahuaomanoa Press in 2008. She is currently co-editing, with Dr. Evelyn Flores, the first anthology of writing by indigenous Micronesians, and, with Ryan Oishi, Aiko Yamashiro and Mark Guillermo, an anthology about riding the bus in Honolulu, titled *Routes*.

Jana Kolarič works as a freelance writer and playwright. She also writes fiction, poetry and drama. She debuted with a children's play, *Salon Expon* (1976), a hit, especially among the amateurs (but also in the Slovene National Theatre). She edited a collection of plays for children's theatre, *Primadona*. She is the author of a collection of riddles, *Ugibanke male, oblečene v šale* (2005), a novel, *Izpred kongresa* (2006), and the co-author of the novel *Draga Alina, draga Brina* (2008).

Barbara Korun, born in 1963, currently works as a dramaturg and lector in the Ljubljana Drama. She received the Book Fair Award for her first collection of poetry *Ostrina miline* (1999), and has also published a book of poetic prose, *Zapiski iz podmizja* (2003), and a second collection of poetry, *Razpoke* (2004). Her writing has recently appeared in *Songs of Earth and Light* (Cork, Ireland, 2005), and *Krilati šum* (Zagreb, Croatia, 2008).

Uršuľa Kovalyk, born in 1969, is a writer and playwright who declares herself a feminist. She is the director of the No Home Theater for homeless men and women. The author of several books including *Neverné ženy neznášajú vajíčka* (*Unfaithful Women Can't Tolerate Eggs*), she is currently in the process of finishing a novel. Her plays include *Vec* (*Thing*), *Maková panna* (*The Poppy Virgin*), *Oktagon,* and *Deň mŕtvych* (*Day of the Dead*).

Meta Kušar, born in 1953, is a Slovene poet, translator, essayist, publicist, and organizer. She works as a freelancer. Her performance combining music and literature, *Prestol poezije* (*The Throne of Poetry*) has been very successful both home and abroad (Slovinsko 1997, USA 1999). She has published four collections of poetry, some of them multilingual, the last two being *Ljubljana* (2004) and *Jaspis* (Jasper, 2008).

Gidi Loza writes: "I live, write and make graphic design in Tijuana (a place where I find a multiple mixture of voices, perceptions, actions to see, learn and transform myself). In the space-time I live, I work and learn with languages of-from my body, to seek an auto-language (autonomous and collective). I write poetry and essays, and am working on a collective novel (a project of four writers from the northwestern side of Mexico)."

Rachida Madani was born in Tangier, Morocco. Her first collection of poems, *Femme je suis,* was published in 1981, and her second, *Contes d'une tête tranchée*, though written between 1981 and 1984, was only published in 2001, and is translated into English by Marilyn Hacker. Her first novel appeared in 2006, as did a new edition of her early poems. She is a co-founder of the NGO Karama for at-risk women, and has been a volunteer director at a school for the deaf.

Eva Maliti, born in 1953, is a playwright, writer, theoretician, and translator. Her first literary work was a book of poetic prose *Krpaty vrch* (*Little Mountain*, 1994). Her academic works include *Symbolizmus ako princíp videnia* (*Symbolism as a Principle of Looking*, 1996), *Tabuizovaná prekladateľka Zora Jesenská* (*Zora Jesenská, a Marginalized Translator*, 2007). Four of her plays were collected in *Hry* (*Games*, 2007). She translated, into Slovak, Andrei Bely's novel *Petersburg* (2001, 2003).

Bojana Maltarić, born in 1973 in Čakovec, Croatia. Graduated at the University in Ljubljana, Faculty of Arts in 1997; currently postgraduate student at the Department of Slovene Language and Literature. Since 1998 she has been employed as Lecturer of Czech language at the

Department of Slavonic Languages and Literature (Faculty of Arts, Ljubljana). She is a freelance translator from Czech and Croatian into Slovene (Jan Balabán, Miroslav Petříček ml., Michal Viewegh, Pavel Barša, Tomáš Halík, among others).

Maram al-Masri was born in Lattaquieh, Syria, and resides in Paris, France. She moved to France because of the difficulty for a divorced woman to be accepted.

Zethu Matebeni is a PhD fellow at WISER (Wits Institute for Social and Economic Research). Her research is broadly interested in forms of representation of black lesbian lives in South Africa. She is actively involved in many of the LGBT organisations in South Africa and is a co-curator of TRACKS: Sexuality in the City, an exhibit celebrating the lives of LGBT people in the city of Johannesburg. Zethu has contributed to various books and academic journals. Her latest work appears in the forthcoming *African Sexualities Reader*, 2010.

Elfrida Matuč-Mahulja was born in 1967 in Rijeka, Croatia. She lives and works on the island of Krk. Trained as a foreign correspondent, she works as an archival and social services officer for Punat County. She is the author of three books of poetry, a book of short stories, a novel titled *Writing on Water* (in collaboration with Dušan Gojkov, and the recipient of the East-West Award in Belgrade, 2006), and, most recently, a book of autobiographical nonfiction.

Hala Mohammad was born in Lattaquieh, Syria, in 1959. She has worked in film as a costume designer, scriptwriter and director, and also as a freelance journalist. She directed three documentary films on prisons and political freedom of expression, which were shown on *Aljazeera* television and at festivals in Europe, Lebanon, and New Delhi. She has published five collections of poetry, and her work has been widely translated.

Zuzana Mojžišová, born in 1965, teaches at the Academy of Fine Arts in Bratislava, in the department of Film Studies. She publishes short fiction, literary and film reviews in newspapers, journals and reviews (*Slovenské pohľady, Romboid, Kino-Ikon, Frame, Film.sk, týždeň, Pravda*). Her first book of short stories, *Afrodithé*, was published in 1997.

Vida Mokrin-Pauer, poet and writer, has published eleven books of poetry, a CD of her poetry accompanied by piano and sound effects, and co-authored two satirical epistolary novels. Two of her poetry collections were nominated for the Veronika Prize and Jenko Prize. Her poems have been published in ten languages, on three continents, and appeared in several anthologies. For years she worked as a librarian, editor and literary critic; she now lives as a free-lance writer.

Born in Chunnam in 1947, Moon Chung-hee published her first award-winning poem in 1969. Her books include *Wild Rose, For Men, When I See A Tall Man*, and *Come, False Love*. She has won the prestigious Sowol Poetry Prize, the Contemporary Literature Award, and, in 1995, she visited the University of Iowa International Writer's Program. She teaches in the Department of Creative Writing at Dongguk University in Seoul.

Jana Pácalová, born in 1979, graduated in Slovak language and literature and holds a PhD in the history of Slovak literature. She works at the Institute for Slovak literature at the Slovak Academy of Sciences. She specialises in fairy tales of the romantic and classic period and is re-writing them for children. In 2003, her first collection of poetry appeared: *Citová výchova (Sentimental Education)*.

Danica Pavlović was born in Belgrade (Serbia) in 1976. Her books include *Vertical Horizon* (Matica srpska, 2002). Her poetry has been published in several anthologies, and journals in Serbia, Croatia, Slovenia, Bosnia, Herzegovina, and Poland. She is an editor for *Pro Femina*.

Mara Pastor's books include *Alabalacera* and *El origen de los párpados*, published as an artist book in Mexico and Puerto Rico. Her writings have appeared in many journals and literary magazines in Puerto Rico, Spain, Mexico, Argentina, Canada and the US Mara works as an editor, translator and photographer. She blogs regularly about US and Puerto Rican literary culture at www.ohdiosarantza.blogspot.com and a selection of her work can be found at www.losnoveles.net/2008/2008iempastor.htm.

Christian Peet is finishing a nonfiction book about his nephew in prison. He is the author of *Big American Trip* and two chapbooks, *Pluto: Never Forget* and *The Nines*. His work appears in magazines such as *Action Yes* and *Denver Quarterly* and in the anthology, *A Best Of Fence: The First Nine Years*. He is the publisher and the founding editor of Tarpaulin Sky Press.

Sanja Pilić, born in 1954 in Split, is a poet, writer, and children's writer. She has worked as a photographer and a cartoonist, as well as collaborating with the Autonomna ženska kuća/Autonomous Women's House in Zagreb and working with abused children. Her texts have been translated into Slovene, English, German, Dutch, Italian and Hungarian. In 2008 she was awarded the IBBY Honour List for the novel *Have I Fallen in Love?* She lives and works in Zagreb.

Eleonora Pinzuti (www.eleonorapinzuti.info) received her PhD in Italian literature, literary theory and gender studies: her research ranges from textual criticism to recent gender and reception theory. Her poems have appeared in various journals and anthologies, including *Nodo Sottile 3*, (Crocetti, 2002); *L'apparecchio di Junior: Poeti contro la guerra* (Zona, 2002); *Pro/testo* (Fara Editore, 2009); and *Logos* (Perrone, 2009). She was chosen for the 9th Biennial of Young Artists from Europe and the Mediterranean.

Barbara Pleić was born in 1985 in Rijeka, Croatia, but spent most of her life in Slavonski Brod. As a junior in high school, she placed second in the Goran's Spring literary awards, high school division. She has published three books of poetry, most recently *Blood Poems*. Her poetry and reviews have appeared in journals including *Ka/Os, Knjigomat* and *Tema*, as well as online at poezija.online, and cunterview.com. In addition to poetry, she is engaged with many kinds of volunteer work.

Dana Podracká, born in 1954, writes poetry, essays, and children's literature. She works in the Literary Information Centre in Bratislava. Her first book *Mesačna Milenka* (*The Moon's Lover*) was published in 1981. She has published more than 20 books, some of them diptychs, double-books that attempt to talk about problems from two different vantage points. Her most recent books include a diptych of essays, and the poetic diptych *Persona / Morfeus* (2007). She lives in Bratislava.

Ágnes Rapai writes: "Although my poems have been published since 1980, I still don't know what poetry is. Rather than preventing me from writing poems, my ignorance gives me self-assurance. I've had five volumes published in Hungary, two in Switzerland, in German. My favorite poet is Allen Ginsberg which—as one of my critics has remarked— shows in my poetry, as instead of the Hungarian lyrical tradition, my poems feed much rather on the American tradition. So what?"

Tatiani G. Rapatzikou is Assistant Professor in the Department of American Literature and Culture at the School of English of the Aristotle University of Thessaloniki, Greece. Her publications include academic monographs and many editorial projects. Most recently, she co-edited the 2008 special issue of *GRAMMA: Journal of Theory and Criticism* entitled *Revisiting Crisis/Reflecting on Conflict: American Literary Interpretations from World War II to Ground Zero* www.enl.auth.gr/gramma. She is currently working as a Fulbright Visiting Scholar at MIT.

Derek Rebro, born in 1979, is a literary critic, theoretician, poet and feminist. He works with the journals *Aspekt* and *Romboid*, and also *Vlna* and *Knihy a spoločnosť*. He is interested in contemporary women's poetry in Slovakia. He is pursuing his doctoral studies at the Faculty of Arts at the University of Komenski in Bratislava.

Stanislava Chrobáková Repar, born in 1960, is a poet, writer, literary critic, theoretician and editor; both a Slovene and Slovak citizen. Since 2001 she has lived in Ljubljana, Slovenia, working as a researcher, translator and project leader; she is the co-founder and co-ordinator of the international project Review within Review, editor of the literary edition *Fraktal*, and edited the GENDER issues of the journal *Apokalipsa*. She has published four collections of poetry, three books of fiction, and two academic monographs.

Barbara Jane Reyes is the author of *Gravities of Center*, *Poeta en San Francisco*, and *Diwata*. Visit her online at www.barbarajanereyes.com.

Tereza Riedlbauchová, born in 1977, works as a lecturer of Czech at the Sorbonne, where she is also a student. She is the founder and organizer of literary salons in Prague and Paris, and publisher and co-organizer of the Czech-French festival of poetry. She has published three books of poetry. She is currently working on another collection, *Don Vítor si hraje a jiné básně*, and a bilingual, Czech and French selection of her poems.

Ivica Ruttkayová, born in 1963, has been working as an editor at Slovak public radio since 1989. She publishes in the fields of culture, literature, and the arts. In 2002, she published a collection of poetry, *Anjeličkárka—Komentáre* (*Quack—Comments*). Her radio play *Callgirl* (2004) received the Award of the Literary Fund for an original work of fiction. In 2007, she published a collection of fiction, *Marylin miluje literatúru* (*Marilyn loves literature*, 2007).

Born in Athens, Greece, in 1956, Liana Sakelliou is Professor in English at the University of Athens. Her poems, scholarly articles, book reviews, and translations have been published in Greece and the US. She is the recipient of many awards including the Fulbright, and has been a visiting fellow at several universities, most recently at Princeton. In 2008, she published a play on the life of the American poet H. D., which she co-authored with a group of students.

Jussara Salazar, Brazil, is a poet and artist. She has written and published several books: *Inscritos Na Casa de Alice* (1999), *Baobá, poemas de Leticia Volpi* (2002), *Natália* (2004) and *Coloraurisonoros* (Buenos Aires, 2008). She has also published her poetry in several Brazilian and international magazines and anthologies. In 2009, she received the Arts National Foundation Scholarship (Brazil) with the book *Cantigas da Árvore Votiva*. She is the editor of the electronic art and literature magazine *Lagioconda7*, www.lagioconda.art.br.

Fawziya Choueich al-Salem is the author of three plays, five novels, and four books of poetry. She writes: I am a novelist who started as a painter. My painting ambitions stopped the moment my marital life started. The shock that followed the death of my husband turned me into a poet. By coincidence, I wrote some plays. And eventually I found my true passion, which is writing novels. I also have a weekly column in *Aljarida* newspaper.

Alenka Šalej (born in 1963) teaches at the Gymnasium in Velenje. She worked as a lector for Slovenian language at the Faculty of Arts in Bratislava and editor of magazines *Mentor* and *Hotenja*. She translated several literary texts for Vilenica Literary Festival and participated in translation of the anthology *Sto let slovaške književnosti* (*One Hundred Years of Slovak Literature*). Translating from Slovak into Slovenian, she cooperates with the monthly and publishing house Apokalipsa, Radio and TV of Slovenia as well (translations of Mila Haugová, Rudolf Sloboda, Dušan Dušek, among others).

Jelena Savić was born in 1981 in Belgrade, Serbia. was born 1981. in Belgrade, Serbia. She is studing Adult Education on Faculty of Philosophy in Belgrade. She is a blogger, a poet, and a writer of short stories. She considers herself feminist and a Roma feminist. She has one book of poetry *Explosive parts* and has published poems in several journals in Serbia.

Rati Saxena is an eminent Hindi poet, translator and Sanskrit scholar. She has authored three collections of poems in Hindi, and one each in English and Malayalam (in translation). She has also written several research articles on Vedic literature and Indology. Her poems have been translated in Malayalam, Punjabi, KonkaNi and Tamil, and she has translated nine books from Malayalam to Hindi. Her awards include the Kendra Sahitya Akademi Award for Translation in 2000, and the Indira Gandhi National Culture and Arts Fellowship.

Jennifer Scappettone, a poet, translator, and scholar, is the author of *From Dame Quickly* (Litmus, 2009), and of several chapbooks. *Exit 43*—an archaeology of Superfund sites interrupted by pop-up choruses—is in progress. Pop-up scores have been adapted for performance in an evolving collaboration with choreographer Kathy Westwater as *PARK*, with initial showings at New York's Dance Theater Workshop and Freshkills Park in 2010. She edited Belladonna Elders Series #5, featuring her poems and prose and new writing by Etel Adnan and Lyn Hejinian (Belladonna, 2009). As a translator, she guest-edited the feature section of *Aufgabe* 7 (2008), devoted to contemporary Italian "poetry of research," and is completing an edition of selected works by the poet/musicologist Amelia Rosselli. More writing can be found at oikost.com. She is an assistant professor at the University of Chicago.

Simona Schneider is a PhD candidate in Comparative Literature at the University of California, Berkeley, a writer, and translator. She lived and worked in Tangier between 2005 and 2009.

Dale Smith is a poet and critic who lives in Austin, Texas, with Hoa Nguyen, his co-editor through ten issues of *Skanky Possum*. Smith's poems, essays, and reviews have appeared in *Chicago Review, Best American Poetry, Jacket*, and elsewhere. *Poets Beyond the Barricade: Rhetoric, Citizenship, and Dissent after 1960* will be published by the University of Alabama Press next year.

Breda Smolnikar, born in 1941, is a textile engineer by profession, and lives and works in Depala vas. She published her first book, *Otročki, življenje teče dalje*, when she was 22; it was awarded the Levstik Prize. During the 80s, while still politically dissident, she wrote under the pseudonym Lady. She published all of her writing independently and continues to do so. She is known because of the court case against her book *Ko se tam gori olistajo breze*; in 2007, after eight years of trial, all charges were dropped, and the book is now freely available. During the years of the trial she printed indecipherable, stammering, hermetic books.

maja solar, born in 1980, is a poet, writer, philosopher, performer and feminist. She graduated with a degree in philosophy from the University of Novi Sad, where she works as a teaching assistant. She is a member of the poetry-political theatre *Poetic holes* and is the literature and theory editor at the journal *Polja*. She received Branko's award for her first book of poetry, *Makulalalalatura*.

Božena Správcová, born in 1969, studied informatics at the School of Economics. Since 1993, she has worked at the literary journal *Tvar*. She has published four collections of poetry: *Guláš z modrý krávy, Výmluva, Večeře,* and *Požární kniha*; a novella: *Spravedlnost*; two interview books (with Ivan O. Štampach and Jan Jeřábek); and a CD of poetry, *Hranice*. She lives in Prague with two children.

A. E. Stallings has lived in Athens, Greece since 1999. She has published two collections, *Archaic Smile* and *Hapax*, as well as a verse translation of Lucretius, *The Nature of Things*.

Nataša Sukić, lost in time and space, is interested in quantum particles, and especially the molecular composition of words. Her first work of fiction, *Desperadosi in nomadi*, published by ŠKUC—Vizibilija, is an experiment of this kind. Her second book, *Otroci nočnih rož* will also appear from ŠKUC—Vizibilija.

Padcha Tuntha-Obas is the author of *Trespasses* (O Books, 2006) and *composite.diplomacy* (Tinfish Press, 2005), and co-author of *Across & Between the Void* (Achiote Press, 2008). She lives in Bangkok, Thailand.

Ainize Txopitea, born in San Sebastián in 1977, holds a Masters in Digital Art from London University. Her creative work includes graphic design, webpage design for artists, and her own artist's shows. She has published her work in books, art catalogs, magazines, and art and cultural websites, has participated in conferences and gatherings of contemporary poetry, and has shown her work in solo shows as well as in group shows in Spain, Argentina, Germany, England and the US. For more information, visit: www.ainizetxopitea.com and www.cyberpoetry.net.

Lourdes Vázquez is the recipient of several awards including the Juan Rulfo de Cuentos (France). Her recent work includes *A Porcelain Doll with Violet Eyes Staring into Space . . .* , published as an e-chapbook by Wheelhouse Magazine in 2009, and *Salmos del cuerpo ardiente*, an artist book with artist Consuelo Gotay (2007). Her work had appeared in numerous anthologies and journals, and has been translated in English, Italian, Swedish, Rumanian, Galician and Portuguese.

Pramila Venkateswaran is the author of three books, most recently *Draw Me Inmost* (High Watermark Salo[o]n, 2009). A finalist for the

Allen Ginsberg Poetry Award, she has published widely in journals and appeared in several international anthologies. Her essays on gender and culture appear in *The Women's Studies Quarterly*, *Language Crossings*, and anthologies of literary criticism. She teaches English and Women's Studies at Nassau Community College, New York.

Brian Whitener's books include a translation of Colectivo Situaciones' *Genocide in the Neighborhood* from ChainLinks, *Como hacemos lo que hacemos* with the artistic collective La Lleca, and *Haciendo tiempo: Arte/politica desde 1999* from la Universidad Autónoma de la Cuidad de México. His writings and translations have appeared in many US journals, and he is involved in an on-going collaborative translation project of contemporary Latin American poetry that is currently appearing in *Aufgabe*. He is also an editor at Displaced Press.

Makhosazana Xaba is the author of two volumes of poetry: *these hands* and *Tongues of their Mothers*. She is the winner of the 2005 Deon Hofmeyr Award for Creative Writing, holds an MA in Writing (cum laude) from the University of the Witwatersrand, and is a former writing fellow at WISER.

Phillippa Yaa de Villiers wrote for television, taught mime, and acted, before publishing *Taller than Buildings* (self-published) and *The Everyday Wife* (Modjadji, 2010). Her one-woman show, *Original Skin*, has toured in South Africa and Germany. She co-edited *No Serenity Here*, an anthology of African poetry, which will be published in Chinese, English, French, Portuguese, Arabic and Amharic in October 2010, in Shanghai.

Clare Chungbin You has been translating Korean poems into English, including the NCBA Award-winning *The Three Way Tavern* (2006) for many years. She has taught Korean at UC Berkeley for over 25 years and served as the Chair of the Center for Korean Studies (2003-2009). She is the recipient of the Order of Cultural Merit award (2003) from the

President of Korea and works to promote appreciation of Korean poetry in the US and English Poetry in Korea.

George Zarkadakis is a novelist, playwright, science communicator, and publisher.

Argentinean poet Lila Zemborain has been living in New York since 1985. She is the author of five poetry collections, most recently *Guardianes del secreto* (2002) / *Guardians of the Secret* (Las Cruces: Noemi Press, 2009), and, in collaboration with artist Martin Reyna, *La couleur de l'eau / El color del agua* (Paris: Virginie Boissiere, 2008). She directs the MFA in Creative Writing in Spanish at New York University. In 2007 she was awarded a Guggenheim Fellowship for poetry.

Darija Žilić was born in 1972 in Zagreb, Croatia. Her reviews, essays and theoretical writings have appeared in a number of anthologies and journals. She curates cultural events at the Zagreb Multimedia Institute (MAMA) and has worked as a critic, translator and editor. She is a collaborator at kulturpunkt.hr, and a jazz chanteuse. Her publications include the poetry collection *Breasts and Strawberries* (AGM, 2005), and critical essays on women poets, *Writing in Milk* (Altagama, 2008). She is a member of the Croatian Writers Society.

# INDEX OF NAMES, PRIZES, JOURNALS, PRESSES, CONFERENCES, ANTHOLOGIES, BLOGS, AND DISCUSSION LISTS

*25 Poets of the New Formalism* 328

Abramovic, Marina 33, 34, 37, 38, 40, 41, 42

Academy of American Poets 56, 84

Acker, Kathy 38, 40, 41, 42, 239

ACT UP 10

Adorno, Theodor 278, 286

African Feminist Forum 196, 199

Agrafiotis, Demosthenes 251, 257, 367

Alexander, Elizabeth 341

Allen, Donald 50, 51, 72

Allen, Paula Gunn 69

*The American Poetry Review* 328

American Academy of Arts & Letters 56

American Association of University Professors 12, 57, 74

*American Poetry Since 1950: Innovators and Outsiders* 52, 74

*American Women Poets of the 21st Century* 45, 74

Amma, Balamani 217

Andrews, Bruce 51, 72

Andrijašević, Marija 259

Anghelaki-Rook, Katerina 251, 257, 367

*Anthology of New York Poets* 50, 74

Antin, Eleanor 34, 37, 38, 40, 41, 42

Anyodoho, Kofi 181

*Apokalipsa* 122

Armantrout, Rae 28, 66, 72, 348, 349

Artaud, Antonin 296

Artnam, Kemo Mujičić 152

*The Art of Practice: 45 Contemporary Poets* 53, 67

Arvin, Maile 342

Arzoumanian, Ana 242, 251, 253, 367

Ashbery, John 60

Ashby, Caroline 293

Ashton, Jennifer 27, 30, 45, 46, 47, 48, 49, 50, 51, 52, 53, 57, 58, 59, 60, 65, 66, 72, 275, 276, 286

Asian American Poetry Now 337

Aspekt 26, 112, 114, 115, 117, 118, 122, 264, 267

Association for Women's Initiative 159, 160, 162, 164

Atarraya Cartonera 81

Atelos 56

Attanasio, Maria 102

Atwood, Margaret 292

Auden, W.H. 327

*Aufgabe* 26, 275, 280, 283, 284, 285

Avvaiyar 220

AŽIN 153

Baartman, Saartjie 341

Bacelo, Nancy 241

Bagić, Aida 24, 140, 142, 144, 367

Bakić, Asja 25, 144, 145, 368

Banggo, Kathy Dee Kaleokealoha Kaloloahilani 355

Bán, Zsófia 5, 75, 368

Barba, Sharon 73

Barber, Stefani 356

Barone, Dennis 53, 72

Bartlett, Jennifer 355

Basinski, Michael 28

Basquiat, Jean-Michel 341

Baudelaire, Charles 86, 88

Bautista, Michelle 340, 356

Beach, Sylvia 133

Belladonna 52, 245

Bellamy, Dodie 72, 295, 355

Benjelloun, Tahar 92
Benn, Gottfried 102
Benson, Steve 349
Benstock, Shari 101
Berenguer, Amanda 241
Berg, Aase 295, 296, 297
Bergvall, Caroline 41, 42, 354
Bernheimer, Alan 349
Bernstein, Alison 199
Bernstein, Charles 51, 72
Bernstein, Emma 355
Berssenbrugge, Mei-mei 348, 356
Betts, Tara 338, 341
*Big Allis* 51
Biga, Vesna 148, 368
Bijelić, Tatjana 147, 368
Biko, Steve 178, 183
Birman, Lisa 295
Bishop, Elizabeth 100, 290
Bloch, Julia 355
Bodnárová, Jana 251, 267, 369
Bök, Christian 15, 29
Boldt, Lindsey 356
Bordercrossing Berlin 96
Bornstein, Kate 280
Boully, Jenny 295
Boyer, Anne 62, 66, 354
Božičević, Ana 5, 75, 140, 148,
    150, 152, 251, 295, 369
Brady, Taylor 28, 33
Brecht, Bertolt 97
Breillat, Catherine 295
Breton, Andre 296
Bridgford, Kim 330
Brolaski, Julian T. 26, 273, 279,
    355
Bromige, David 350
Brooks, Gwendolyn 338, 341
Brossard, Nicole 347
Brotchie, Alastair 30
Brown, Brandon 278
Browne, Laynie 356

Brown, Lee Ann 356
Brown, Rebecca 293, 295
Brown, Sarah 293
Bryant, Tisa 356
Buffalo Poetics List 313, 314, 315
Building Lesbian Feminist Think-
    ers and Leaders for the
    21st Century 195
Burke, Kenneth 315
Butler, Judith 198, 200, 286, 315,
    318, 319, 320
Butterick, George 51, 72
Buuck, David 28, 52, 62, 66, 71,
    73
Byrne, Mairead 356
CAConrad 343, 370
Cage, John 10
Calhoun, Cheshire 199, 200
Cárdenas, Brenda 354
Cariaga, Catalina 339, 354
Carmody, Teresa 16, 28, 356
Carrion, Ulises 236
Carter, Laura 356
Casamanitas Cartonera 81
Castro, Abril 236
Cerón, Rocío 236, 251, 255, 369
*Chain* 52
Charter of Feminist Principles for
    African Feminists 196
Chen, Ching-In 341
Chen, Chris 337
Chester, Laura 73
*Chicago Review* 18, 20, 27, 28,
    73, 286, 313, 316, 325,
    335, 384
Chigiya, Joyce 181
Child, Abigail 348
Chin, Staceyann 338, 356
Choi Seung-ja 228
Choi Youngmi 229, 230
Cho, Margaret 295
Chung, Frances 341

Cingolani, Laura 104
Cixous, Hélène 129, 133
Claudio, Karina 80
Clausen, Jan 295
Clinton, Hillary 350
Cock, Jacklyn 199
Coetzee, Olivia 184, 256
Cole, Barbara 67, 73
Coleman, Wanda 357
Cole, Norma 69, 356
Colman, Robert 180
Compton, Shanna 356
Congress of South African Writers
   187
Connor, Traci O 295
*Contemporary Poetry Review* 331
*A Controversy of Poets* 50, 73
Copp, Corina 354
Cortez, Jayne 338, 355
Cosman, Carol 73
Crane, Hart 286
Crispin, Jessa 29
Critchley, Emily 355
Čudina, Marija 152
Curtis, John W. 74
Curzan, Anne 279, 286
Čvorović, Aleksandra 147
Czapáry, Veronika 24, 134, 371
H.D. [Hilda Dolittle] 55, 69
Dad, Lal 219
Dahlen, Beverly 348
Daly, Catherine 354
Damon, Maria 319
Daňhelová, Lenka 251, 270, 371
Das, Kamala 217
Davidson, Michael 349
Davis, Jordan 52
Davis, Angela 295
Day, Jean 349
Dean, Debra Kang 340
de Beauvoir, Simone 291
de Burgos, Julia 80, 82

DeDeo, Simon 29
Ded, Lal 219
De León, Aya 338
Deleuze, Gilles 277
Delgado, Nicole Cecilia 80
Delirious Hem 276, 283, 286,
   293, 305
Delirious Lapel 26, 309
Dema, Tjawangwa 181
Derksen, Jeff 39
Derrida, Jacques 173, 316
Detela, Andrej 263
Detorie, Michelle 356
Dhompa, Tsering Wangmo 339,
   357
Dick, Jennifer K. 96, 98, 99
DiFranco, Ani 295
Diggs, LaTasha N. Nevada 338,
   356
digital emunction 286
di Giorgio, Marosa 241
DiPietra, Amber 354
*Diskurzivna tela poezije—Poezija
   i autopoetike pesnikinja
   nove generacije (Discur-
   sive Bodies of Poetry—
   Poetry and Poetics of the
   Women Poets of the New
   Generation)* 162
Djurić, Dubravka 75, 141, 144,
   145, 147, 153, 154, 163,
   165, 173, 371
Donahue, Joseph 53, 74
Dorantes, Dolores 355
Dorn, Edward 314
Dreyer, Lynne 348
Drucker, Johanna 41, 348
Duggan, Prue 96
Duller, Irene Faye 342
Duncan, Isadora 215
Dungy, Camille 354
Dunn, Katherine 295

DuPlessis, Rachel Blau 28, 45, 52, 55, 62, 66, 67, 68, 69, 73, 282
Dutton, Danielle 295
Dworkin,Craig 40
Eddine, Kheir 86
Edgar, Chris 52
edwards, kari 72, 278, 280, 295, 355
Eliot, T.S. 101, 263, 325
Elrick, Laura 356
Emerson, Ralph Waldo 352
Ensler, Eve 295, 307
Epprecht, Mark 199
Eratosphere 330
Ernst, Max 296
Étienne, Luc 14
Evans, Steve 28, 56, 67, 73, 317
*Expansive Poetry* 329
Export, Valie 13, 37, 38, 40, 41, 42
Faesler, Carla 236
Fagan, Kate 52
Farkašová, Etela 24, 110, 111, 117, 251, 265, 371
Fattal, Simone 5, 75, 201, 205, 206, 207, 210, 251, 371
Faulkner, William 351
Feela Sistah 188
Feinberg, Leslie 291
Felski, Rita 133
Ferenčuhová, Mária 251, 267, 372
Ferrin-Aguirre, Isabel 181
Finch, Annie 328
Fischerová, Daniela 251, 270, 372
Fitterman, Rob 41
Flores, Evelyn 234
Florian, Sandy 99, 295
*A Formal Feeling Comes* 328, 329
Formalista 330

Foster, Edward 53
Foster, Tonya 356
Foucault, Michel 318
Fraser, Kathleen 45, 51, 69, 347
Frenkel, Ronit 200
Freschi, Romina 243, 251, 253
Friedan, Betty 291
*From the Other Side of the Century* 52, 73
Frost, Elisabeth A 73
Frýdlová, Pavla 251, 271, 372
Gabbert, Elisa 355
Gambito, Sarah 337
Ganick, Peter 53, 72, 152
Garr, Megan M. 96, 373
*The Gay and Lesbian Review* 306
Gelpí, Juan 82
*Genero* 157
Georas, Chloé 80, 83
Georgiou, Elena 293, 295
Gevirtz, Susan 62, 66
Giles, Samantha 356
Ginsberg, Allen 286
Giovanni, Nikki 338
Girmay, Aracelis 340
Gladman, Renee 62, 66, 69, 295, 356
Glancy, Diane 354
Glave, Thomas 199
Golding, Alan 67, 73
Goldman, Judith 355
Goldsmith, Kenneth 40, 41
González, Rigoberto 337
Goran Award 24, 143
Göransson, Johannes 296
Goran's Spring 143, 144
Goran's Wreath 24, 143
Gordon, Nada 41, 42, 356
Graffi, Milli 106
Graham, K. Lorraine 293, 294, 355
Grangaud, Michelle 14, 41

Green Integer 55, 71
Gregorčič, Simon 262
Grenier, Robert 348
Griffin, S.A. 53
Grinnell, E. Tracy 26, 273, 275, 283, 355, 373
Gromača, Tanja 153
Grosfoguel, Ramón 83
Grusková, Anna 114, 251, 266, 374
Gruss, Irene 246
Guerra, Silvia 26, 241, 251, 254, 373
Guerrilla Girls 16, 34, 395
Guest, Barbara 51
Gunn, Josh 29
Hagedorn, Jessica 338
Hahn, Kimiko 355
Hammad, Suheir 341
Hand, Monica 356
Harare International Festival of the Arts 181
Harbaš, Nada 374
Harriet 27, 29, 133, 331, 337, 341
Harris, Lizzie 293
Harryman, Carla 349
Hassan, Maha 205, 251, 255, 374
Hassanzadeh-Mostafavi, Farideh 213
Hass, Bob 28
The Hat 52
Haugová, Mila 264
Heer, Liliana 244, 251, 254
Hejinian, Lyn 45, 315, 347, 348
Hemingway, Ernest 101
Hemmings, Sally 341
Hendrix Formal Poetry Conference 328
Hess, David 71, 73
Hildesheim, Marianna 29
Hill, Anita 341
Hillman, Brenda 28

Hodge, Chinaka 338
Hofer, Jen 15, 21, 351, 355
Holiday, Billie 341
Hong, Cathy Park 337, 354
hooks, bell 199
Ho'omanawanui, Ku'ualoha 355
Hoover, Paul 53, 73
Horn, Rebecca 41, 42
How2 52
Howe, Fanny 52, 347
Howe, Florence 73
Howe, Susan 348
how(ever) 51, 52
Hrubaničová, I. 117
Hughes, Langston 341
Hugo, Richard 290
Huh Su-kyung 229
Hunt, Erica 355
Hwang In-Sook 228
Iijima, Brenda 295, 354
Innovative Women Poets: An Anthology of Contemporary Poetry and Interviews 73
In the American Tree 51, 67, 74, 348
Ito, Hiromi 355
IVY Writers 96
Jabavu, Noni 192
Jackson, Shelly 295, 298
Jagić, Dorta 259
Jahid, Fatima 85
Jandová, Tereza 375
Jarak, Rade 375
Jayashankar, K.P. 223
Jelinek, Elfriede 295
Jenkins, Myesha 187, 375
Jevtić, Iva 111, 114, 116, 119, 125, 128, 131, 251, 262, 375
Johnson, Paul Foster 6, 26, 273, 275, 276, 375
Jones, LeRoi 286

Jordan, June 355
Joyce, James 133
July, Miranda 295
Kaipa, Summi 356
Kanae, Lisa Linn 356
Kang Eun-gyo 228
Kapil, Bhanu 64, 66, 293, 295, 298, 299, 301, 354
Karimatu, Ana 199
Katalpa, Jakuba 251, 270, 375
Katedza, Rumbi 181
Kaufman, Alan 53, 73
Kaufman, Erica 28
Keefe, Joan 73
Kegljen, Kristina 259
Kelly, Robert 50, 73
Kelsey Street 51, 58, 298
Kemp, Robin 330
Kerkez, Jelena 162
Kgositsile, Keorapetse 181
Khatoon, Habba 219
Kihleng, Emelihter 233, 234, 376
Kim, Hyesoon 228, 295
Kim, Jung-ran 228
Kim, Myung Mi 69, 339, 356
Kim, Seung-hee 228
Kim, Sun-u 229
King, Amy 12, 295, 354
Kingston, Maxine Hong 69
KJCC Poetry Series 246
Klein, Yves 351
Ko Jung-hee 228
Kolarič, Jana 123, 251, 261, 376
Kolozova, Katerina 144
Kordeš, Urban 263
Korun, Barbara 251, 262, 376
Kotz, Liz 52, 73
Kovac, Deirdre 28
Kovačič, Lojze 262
Kovalyk, Uršuľa 117, 251, 268, 376
Kroumi, D. Aouni 212

Kubota, Shigeko 33, 34, 37, 38, 40, 41, 42
Kušar, Meta 26, 251, 263, 377
Laâbi, Abdellatif 86, 88
Lacy, Suzanne 19
Ladik, Katalin 144
*L=A=N=G=U=A=G=E Book* 51, 53, 72
*"Language" Poetries* 51, 73
Lannan Literary Award 56
Larkin, Joan 295, 306
Larsen, David 15, 28
Larsen, Sara 356
Lasky, Dorothea 355
Lauterbach, Ann 347
Lazić, Radmila 144
Leary, Paris 50, 73
Lescure, Jean 15
Levin, Lauren 356
Levitsky, Rachel 28, 52
Liceaga, Yara 80
Lim, Genny 338, 355
Lispector, Clarice 240
Livingston, Reb 30, 356
Lomax, Dana Teen 354
Lorde, Audre 199
Loy, Mina 361, 362
Loza, Gidi 238, 377
Lumley, Joanna 295
Lundin, Emily 99
Lu, Pamela 28, 356
Luthuli, Albert 178
MacArthur Foundation 56
*Mačke ne idu u raj (Cats Don't Go to Heaven)* 161
Jackson Mac Low 39
Madani, Rachida 85, 377
Mafe, Majena 27
Mahadevi, Akka 219, 220
Maia, Circe 241
Maitri, Malini 223
major, devorah 354

Maliti, Eva 251, 268, 377
Maltarić, Bojana 251
Mandel, Tom 349
Maputo Institute 196, 197
Marani, Toni 86
Martin, Dawn Lundy 354
Marvin, Cate 354
Mashile, Lebogang 181
Mason, Dave 328, 329
al-Masri, Maram 201, 367
Matebeni, Zethu 195, 377
Matuč-Mahulja, Elfrida 25, 150, 378
Mayer, Bernadette 28, 30, 347, 350, 351, 352
McCarthy, Pattie 55, 68, 69
McDaniel, Wilma Elizabeth 69
McDougall, Brandy Nalani 235
McSweeney, Joyelle 69, 277, 286, 295, 397
Meadows, Deborah 354
Meera 219
Melnick, David 349
Meltzer, David 50, 73
Mendieta, Ana 42
Menendez, Didi 30
Meng, Catherine 354
Messerli, Douglas 51, 52, 67, 70, 73
*Mezzo Cammin* 330
*Mike & Dale's Younger Poets* 314
Mikell, Gwendolyn 200
Miljković, Branko 149
Minahal, Maiana 338
Mirabai 220
*Mirage* 51, 65, 66
Mizani, Fiona 96, 98
Mlinko, Ange 29, 54, 327, 354
Mohammad, Hala 26, 207, 251, 256, 378
Mohammad, K. Silem 59, 63, 66
Mojžišová, Zuzana 251, 268, 379

Mokrin-Pauer, Vida 251, 263, 379
Monk, Geraldine 355
Monteiro, Anjali 223
Moon Chung-hee 227, 228, 379
Moore, Marianne 325
Moriarty, Laura 356
Mori, Bruna 337, 354
Morrill, Erin 355
Morrison, Toni 292
Morrison, Yedda 52, 357
Moscona, Myriam 236
MotínPoeta 236
*Moving Borders* 45, 47, 48, 51, 52, 65, 74, 283, 347
Muddupallani 220
Mullen, Harryette 41, 295, 337, 341, 355, 362
Mumolo, Sara 356
Musariri, Blessing 181
Myles, Eileen 52, 60, 63, 66, 73, 355
Nagami, Heather 339
Nagy, Ágnes Nemes 138
Nakayasu, Sawako 69, 356
Naoot, Fatima 181
Nealand, Eireene 293
Negrón-Muntaner, Frances 83
*The New American Poetry* 50, 51, 68, 70, 72, 73
*New Drama* 114
*The New Fuck You* 52, 73
*New York Times Book Review* 306
Nezhukumatathil, Aimee 354
Ngai, Sianne 38
Nguyen, Hoa 317, 355, 384
Nico 296
Niedecker, Lorine 51, 325
Nissabouri, Mostafa 86
Nobel Prize 137, 267
*No More Masks!: An Anthology of Twentieth-Century American Women Poets* 50, 73

Noon, Alistair  97, 100
*No Tell Motel*  30
Notley, Alice  69, 347
Noulipo  14, 15, 28, 65, 398
Obrovac, Tamara  140, 144
O'Hara, Frank  286
Olivér, Láng  (Oliver Flame)  138
Olson, Charles  55, 69
Ono, Yoko  337
Oppenheim, Meret  106
Orbán, Eszter  134, 137
*Ország-Világ (World and Country)*
    137
Osman, Jena  4, 29, 41, 52, 69
O'Sullivan, Maggie  45, 52, 73,
    286
*The Other Half of the Avant-
    Garde,* 1910-1940  106
*Oulipo Compendium*  14, 15, 30,
    38
*The Outlaw Bible*  53, 73
*Out of Everywhere*  45, 52, 73, 283
Owen, Maureen  347
Oyèrónké, Oyewùmí  200
Pácalová, Jana  251, 269, 379
Padgett, Ron  50, 74
Pafunda, Danielle  26, 309
Pagemothers Conference  52
Pai, Shin Yu  337
Palin, Sarah  350
Palmer, Michael  349
Palm, Kristin  355
Paniker, Ayyappa  217
Park, Ishle Yi  338
Parton, Dolly  295
Parun, Vesna  152
Pastor, Mara  9, 77, 380
Patel, Shailja  181
Paterson, Don  327
Patton, Julie  355
Pavlovic, Danica  163, 379
Peet, Christian  26, 380

*Penguin Book of Women Poets*
    50, 73
Perelman, Bob  349
Perloff, Marjorie  67, 74
Peterson, Trace  356
Pfanova, Dora  152
Philip, M. NourbeSe  356
Phipps, Wanda  357
Pierce, Michelle Naka  356
Pilić, Sanja  251, 258, 381
Pinzuti, Eleonora  108
Piper, Adrien  40
Pitt Poetry Series  56
Place, Vanessa  357
Plath, Sylvia  100, 259, 290
Pleić, Barbara  251, 259, 380
Podracká, Dana  251, 269, 380
Poetas de Megafono  9, 77, 81, 82
*Poetics Journal*  51, 65
Poetry Foundation  56, 74, 337,
    341
Poetry International Festival  100
Poetry Society of America  84
*The Poker*  56, 73, 317
Pollock, Jackson  351
Possum Ego  286
*Postmodern American Poetry*  53,
    73
*The Postmoderns: The New
    American Poetry Revisited*
    51, 72
Pound, Ezra  55, 69, 101, 327
Power, Nina  19, 30
Prešern Prize  24, 120
Prevallet, Kristin  355
Price, Larry  349
*Primary Trouble: An Anthology of
    Contemporary American
    Poetry*  53, 74
Pringle, Kate  355
*ProFemina*  141, 157, 159, 161
*Psyche: The Feminine Poetic*

Consciousness 50, 74
Pulitzer Prize 267
Pussipo 58
Queer Festival 141
Queneau, Raymond 15
Ra Hee-duk 228
Raddle Moon 51
Raha, Maria 361
Rainey, Carol 74
Rain Taxi 69
Raíz y tumba 82
Ramphele, Mamphele 183
Rancourt, Mike 282
Rankine, Claudia 45, 74
Rapai, Ágnes 137, 381
Rapatzikou, Tatiani G. 5, 75, 176,
    177, 251, 382
Ravine, Jai Arun 355
Rebeck, Theresa 180, 181
Rebel Angels 328, 329
Rebel Road 246
Rebro, Derek 116, 251, 266, 381
Reddy, Vasu 200
Reilly, Evelyn 278
Reines, Ariana 354
Repar, Stanislava Chrobáková 5,
    24, 26, 75, 111, 114, 116,
    117, 119, 125, 128, 131,
    251, 264, 382
Retallack, Joan 41, 63, 66, 74
Revathi, Kutti 220, 221, 223, 224
Rewords 96
Reyes, Barbara Jane 20, 54, 333,
    354
Reynosa, Minerva 236
Rhee, Margaret 356
Rhine, Dont 10
Rich, Adrianne 290
Riding, Laura 362
Riedlbauchová, Tereza 251, 271,
    382
Rimay, Tea Benčić 152

Rising Tides: 20th Century Ameri-
    can Women Poets 50,
    51, 73
Rivera, Elena 281
Robbe-Grillet, Alain 286
Robertson, Lisa 63, 66, 356
Robinson, Kit 349
Robles, Irizelma 80
Roemer, Astrid 199
Roof Books 55
Rooney, Kathleen 27
Rosenfield, Kim 294
Roy, Camille 354
Rumi 279
Ruocco, Joanna 295
Russo, Linda 63, 66, 74, 356
Ruth Lilly Prize 56
Ruttyaková, Ivica 251, 269, 382
Sabina, María 337
Sadoff, Ira 327
Sagan, Françoise 202
Saidenberg, Jocelyn 355
Sailers, Cynthia 281, 354
Sakelliou, Liana 75, 176, 177,
    251, 258, 382
Salazar, Jussara 240, 251, 254,
    383
Šalej, Alenka 114, 116, 251
al-Salem, Fawziya Choueich 209,
    210, 251, 255, 383
al-Samman, Ghada 202
Sanchez, Sonia 338
Sand, Kaia 355
The San Francisco Poets 50, 73
Sankavva, Sule 220
Sartre, Jean-Paul 258
Saterstrom, Selah 293, 295, 302,
    307
Savić, Jelena 25, 165, 383
Saxena, Rati 25, 213, 383
Scalapino, Leslie 65, 66, 69, 283
Scappettone, Jennifer 5, 27, 28,

48, 60, 63, 66, 74, 75, 102,
104, 106, 108, 284
Schneeman, Carolee 33, 34, 37,
38, 40, 41, 42
Schneider, Simona 75, 85, 384
Schultz, Susan 356
Schwartz, Leonard 53, 74
Segnitz, Barbara 74
Selcer, Anne Lesley 354
Shange, Ntozake 338
Shapiro, David 50, 74
Shaw, G. B. 137
Sherry, James 28
Shin Sa-im-dang 229
Shockley, Evie 340, 341, 355
Short, Kim Gek Lin 295
Shufran, Lauren 356
Silko, Leslie Marmon 338
Silliman, Ron 16, 47, 48, 51, 54,
55, 65, 67, 68, 69, 70, 71,
74, 349
Simonds, Sandra 12
Sinaviana, Caroline 354
singleton, giovanni 69, 355
Sjölin, Daniel 298
*Skanky Possum* 317, 384
ŠKUC publishing 128
Slapšak, Svetlana 144
Sloan, Mary Margaret 28, 45, 47,
52, 66, 74, 286
Slovene Comparative Literature
Association 125
Slovene Writers' Association 260
Smith, Carmen Gimenéz 354
Smith, Dale 26, 30, 70, 277, 286,
311, 345, 367, 370, 371,
372, 373, 374, 378, 381,
384, 385, 387
Smith, Jessica 71, 355
Smith, Patricia 341
Smolnikar, Breda 25, 125, 251,
261, 384

solar, maja 173, 385
Sotomayor, Aurea Maria 83
*Souffle* 86
Soyinka, Wole 181
Spallholz, Julianna 293
Sparks, Donita 292
Sprague, Jane 15, 28, 355
Správcová, Božena 251, 271, 384
Sprinkle, Annie 292, 295, 305
Staiti, Erika 19, 355
Stallings, A. E. 27, 29, 30
Staples, Heidi Lynn 295
Staunton, Irene 181
Stecopoulos, Eleni 355
Steiner, Konrad 15, 28
Stein, Suzanne 356
Stevens, Wallace 56
St Marks Poetry Project 84
Stonecipher, Donna 99
Subpress 55, 72
Sukić, Nataša 128, 251, 262
Sukirtharini 224
Sullivan, Gary 30
Sullivan, Robert 234
Suzara, Aimee 338
Szymaszek, Stacy 356
Tabios, Eileen 337, 355
Tadjo, Veronique 181
Taggart, John 68
Tamás, Gáspár Miklós 138
Tarpaulin Sky Press 293
Tatarka Prize 24, 26, 120, 264
Taylor, Shelly 295
Tayson, Richard 306
Telles, Lygia Fagundes 240
*Tema* 152
Terrill, Mark 99
Theater Institute of the Slovak
Academy of Sciences 114
Toscano, Rodrigo 15
*Tragom roda, smisao
angažovanja—Antologija*

savremene poezije (*Tracing Gender, Sense of Engagement—Anthology of Contemporary Poetry*) 162

Tratnik, Suzana 128

Treadwell, Elizabeth 28, 54, 55, 63, 66, 68, 276, 286, 355

*Tripwire* 52, 73

Tsai, Kelly Zen-Yie 338

Tuntha-Obas, Padcha 225, 386

Turnbull, Gael 96

Txopitea, Ainize 94, 251, 253, 386

Ukeles, Mierle Laderman 34, 37, 38, 40, 41, 42

Ultra-red 9, 10, 11, 19

Ungaro, Fabrizio 108

University of California Press 56

University of Iowa Press 56

Upstairs at Duroc 96

Vadanjel, Radenko 153

Várady, Szabolcs 138

Vázquez, Lourdes 83, 84, 386

Velikonja, Nataša 128

Venkateswaran, Pramila 5, 75, 213, 220, 386

Vergine, Lea 106

Vermont, Charlie 351

*Versal* 96

Vicuña, Cecilia 246, 338, 354

VIDA 27

Viegener, Matias 14, 16, 28

Vilariño, Idea 241

Virgil 351

Vitale, Ida 241

*WACK! Art and the Feminist Revolution* 16, 350

Wagner, Catherine 354

Waldman, Anne 51, 337, 347

Waldrop, Rosmarie 295, 347

Wallace, Mark 26, 309

Walters, Wendy S. 295

Ward, Diane 38

Warren, Alli 354

Watten, Barrett 348

Wave Books 56

Weaver, Kathleen 73

Weinberger, Eliot 52, 74

Weiner, Rachel 28

Wekker, Gloria 199

Wendt, Albert 234

Weöres, Sándor 138

Wershler-Henry, Darren 41

Wertheim, Christine 14, 16, 28, 354

Wesleyan University Press 56

West Chester conference 328, 330

West, Martha 28, 74

Whaitiri, Reina 234

Wheatley, Phyllis 341

Whitener, Brian 5, 9, 75, 77, 386

Whitman, Walt 286

Wigman, Mary 362

Wilding, Faith 19

Wilke, Hannah 42

Williams, Amanda Jo 295

Williams, Megan 341

Williams, William Carlos 286, 351

Winters, Anne 290

Wintz, Sara 28, 356

Wits Institute for Social and Economic Research 192, 378

Wong, Rita 356

Woolf, Virginia 137, 292

Xaba, Makhosazana 181, 191, 251, 257, 387

Xiao, Kaiyu 181

X, Malcolm 180

Xu, Lynn 356

Yaa de Villiers, Phillippa 26, 75, 178, 187, 191, 195, 251, 387

yesandno  29
Yoshinaga, Ida  355
You, Clare  227, 230
Zarkadakis, George  177, 387
Zemborain, Lila  75, 84, 94, 236,
        240, 241, 242, 243, 244,
        245, 251, 387
*Ženske studije*  157
Žilić, Darija  152, 388
Zolf, Rachel  356
Zukofsky, Louis  325
Zurawski, Maggie  356